Born in 1933, Jeff Nuttall is a poet, painter, and ex-jazz trumpeter, who was for some years a pivotal force in the London Underground. A selection of his poems has appeared in the Penguin Modern Poets series. He was writer/publisher of *My Own Mag* and is a regular contributor to, and one-time cartoonist for, *International Times*; is writer/producer of the *People Show*, which has performed all over the country during the last three years.

Jeff Nuttall

Bomb Culture

Paladin

Granada Publishing Limited
Published in 1970 by Paladin
3 Upper James Street, London W1R 4BP
Reprinted 1971, 1972

First published by MacGibbon & Kee Ltd. 1968
Copyright © Jeff Nuttall 1968
Made and printed in Great Britain by
Richard Clay (The Chaucer Press), Ltd.,
Bungay, Suffolk
Set in Monotype Fournier

Contents

Preface: 7

Pop: 11

Protest: 37

Art: 67

Sick: 105

The Underground: 137

Index: 247

PREFACE

It is an encouraging fact that the established press in England are perpetually invalidating their own contentions by assuming that whatever has not been articulated does not exist. They are, in any case, anxious to reduce the international student revolt to the meager proportions normally encompassed by their discussion, and to assess the revolt on the basis of its declared *political* intentions is a ready instrument of reduction, a telescope through which the monster can be viewed from the wrong end, picked up with the eyebrow tweezers of cod-sociology and clapped, safely they hope, in the matchbox of some journalistic category.

Actually the plain and obvious fact is that between the autumn of '67 when I completed this manuscript, and the summer of '68 when I am writing this preface, young people, under various pretexts, made war on their elders, and their elders made war on them. The war continues.

The details are common knowledge but it is worth reconstructing them here perhaps, to establish the broad pattern of their development. Through the summer and autumn of '67, like lightning crackling behind the sunshine of the psychedelic movement, a series of violent episodes signalled the storm. A bullet shattered the window of the American Embassy in London. The Pentagon was mobbed. Dr Spock and Norman Mailer were arrested amongst others. A bomb exploded in the American Officers' Club in London. Simultaneously explosions occurred in the premises of right-wing powers all over Europe. Benno Ohnesorg was butchered by the West Berlin police. As winter drew on Columbia University students took over their University. Japanese students waged war in the streets in support of the Viet Cong. Students in Czechoslovakia, Poland and Moscow demonstrated, often violently.

In March '68 the American Embassy in London was mobbed, again in support of the Viet Cong. At the same time somebody shot Rudi Dutschke and the Berlin students went to war against the Springer newspaper group. In May Paris erupted following demonstrations organised by Dany Cohn-Bendit. Students everywhere took over the temporary running of their colleges, notably at Essex University and Hornsey School of Art.

And all these revolts took place for different reasons according to the students' own accounts. The only common element seems to have been a strong displeasure with the Vietnam war. Left-wing attitudes were significantly at variance with all established socialist organisations, more metaphysical than Mao Tse-tung would permit (How did the predicament of Tibet rest in the psychedelic thinking of the Trafalgar Square combatants?), more permissive than Castro (How many revolutionaries would be barred from Cuba for their homosexual propensities?). It was indeed the French Communist Party that emasculated the French revolt by appropriating the spontaneous general strike, condemning the ideas of the Sorbonne students, and splitting the left-wing vote right down the middle. An anonymous poster on the doors of the Sorbonne said, 'The revolution which is beginning will call into question not only capitalist society but industrial society. The consumer society must perish of a violent death. The society of alienation must disappear from history. We are inventing a new and original world. Imagination has seized power.'

The observer who said 'These *enragés* seem to live in a sort of collective dream' stated the case even more clearly but he was largely ignored. The political effectiveness of contagious culture is a subject abhorrent to orthodox thinking for various reasons, not least among which is the threat embodied in the emergent fact that the root of political development is creative and irrational.

Culture, being the broad effect of art, is rootedly irrational and as such is perpetually operating against the economic workaday structure of society. The economic structure works towards stasis centred around the static needs of man. It is centripetal. Culture forces change centred around the changing appetites of man. It is centrifugal.

The effect of culture has never been so direct and widespread as it is amongst the international class of disaffiliated young people, the provotariat. Consequently art itself has seldom been closer to its violent and orgiastic roots. What has happened is that the pressure of restriction preceding nuclear suicide has precipitated a biological reflex compelling the leftist element in the young middle class to join with the delinquent element in the young working class for the re-affirmation of life by orgy and violence. What is happening is an evolutionary convulsion rather than a reformation. Young people are not correcting society. They are regurgitating it. It is the violence of Che Guevara, his life, his rapacious good looks, his fabulous death, which constitute his appeal. Nobody decorates their bed-sitter with posters of Bolivian miners. Similarly it is the violence advocated by Herbert Marcuse and Regis Debray which has promoted their popularity, rather than the utopian socialism towards which they are aimed.

Even in the year that has passed in production of this book the keynote of violence has become predominant in the international subculture, invigorating tired and sentimental forms of popular music and overshadowing the pseudo-mysticism of the John Michel Glastonbury/Flying saucer cult. To stand in a pop club in any of the world's larger cities in these days is to experience a sensation rather like that of being suspended over a vat of boiling oil. The battery of curdling colours projected round the room, the brutal stroboscopes, the aggressive gobbling of the lead guitars, the belligerent animal wails of the singers, the threat and howling hunger always present in the lyrics—'Why can't we reach the sun'—'I want the world and I want it now'—the throbbing danger of the abused amplifiers, the stunned trance of the crowd and total bleak despair of the registered junkies always hovering around the door like predatory crows, all contribute to a ritual that can be nothing if not profoundly disruptive of most things that life has been about up till now.

As always with the subculture, the American negroes were

the initiators of the mood. It was in the free jazz of Charlie Mingus, Ornette Coleman, Albert Ayler and Archie Shepp that the authentic pulse of violence was first felt. 'Two four six eight', sang Mingus, 'I want to teach you hate.' The croaks, angry squeals and aggressive lyrical runs even became translated into a concept of pure metaphysical enlightenment in the last records of John Coltrane. Here, of course, the violence was the expression of direct and simple anger in the face of racial discrimination. That this creative mood should have provided the language for the wider anger of the provotariat is entirely according to the pattern which has predominated since the first rebellious college boy—Bix Beiderbecke?—looked towards the underworld of jazz and hip. Translated into the popular idiom through the music of groups like John Mayall's, Arthur Brown's, the Cream, the Moody Blues, the Jimi Hendrix Experience, and the Pink Floyd, this mood provides the clearest information about the force behind the generation war. It is obviously not verbal information. Irrational in its nature, it can only be irrationally understood. What can be said in words about how the vat was brought to the boil I hope to have put down in the following pages.

JEFF NUTTALL
July, 1968

I
Pop

With the post-Hiroshima teenagers disaffiliation was always automatic rather than deliberate. Being essentially passive, not decisive, in their way of life, the mass of young people would probably not have registered their insecurity so thoroughly, would not have divided themselves off so completely as a cultural group, had they been conscious of the origins and content of their unease.

I

'Hello Central, give me Doctor Jazz.
He's got what I need, I'll say he has.
When this world goes wrong,
And skies turn blue,
He's the guy that makes you get out
Both your dancin' shoes.
Well the more I git the more I want it seems.
I'm pagin' Doctor Jazz now in my dreams.
Got troubles, bound and mixed,
He's the guy that's got you fixed.
Hello Central, give me Doctor Jazz.'

JELLY ROLL MORTON, 1926.

Western society, which the world, for its sins, seeks to follow, is troubled by anxiety over indefinable guilt, bound by outdated taboos, mixed by the double standards of our maintaining these taboos because we can't play any other games. Jazz is exactly the appropriate remedy because it destroys the double standard and the artificial anxiety through being, as it is, the eloquent articulation of the inadmissible. It achieves this from two points of its definition. It is an improvised art. As such it speaks direct from the whole metabolism like any other involuntary expression. It is, indeed, the high skill of the involuntary. As such it could not take place if a censor, outer-official or inner-psychological, were present.

Secondly it is the music of the American, Negro, criminal proletariat, who are comparatively untroubled by such censors in any case, a far cry from the middle-class Viennese Jewry of Freud.

Underground, in the brothel and the speakeasy, jazz incubated for forty years. The established society knew about it as it knew about sex. It confined mention of sex to the curtained room and the lavatory wall and there imprisoned it as a secret. It left jazz in the underworld where it occasionally went slumming to collect a little seasoning for the music of commerce. In the underworld jazz produced an ethos and a pattern of behaviour that the world's young were to grasp like drowning creatures, rushing towards hip as their parents were rushing towards the merciful oblivion of death.

Mezz Mezzrow, the veteran Chicago clarinettist, gives a vivid picture of jazz in function in its secret years: 'I kept on blowing with my eyes glued shut, and then a strange thing happened. All of a sudden somebody was screaming in a choked, high-pitched voice, like she was being strangled, "Stop it, you're killing me! Stop! I can't stand it!" When I opened my eyes it seemed like all the people on the dance floor were melted down into one solid, mesmerized mass; it was an overstuffed sardine-can of an audience, packed in an olive-oil trance. The people were all pasted together, looking up at the band with hypnotic eyes and swaying—at first I saw just a lot of shining eyes bobbing lazily on top of a rolling sea of flesh. But off to one side there was discord, breaking the spell. An entertainer, one of the girls who did a couple of vocals and specialized in suggestive dance routines, was having a ball all to herself. She had cut loose from her partner and was throwing herself around like a snake with the hives. The rhythm really had this queen; her eyes almost jumped out their sockets and the cords on her neck stood out stiff and hard like ropes. What she was doing with the rest of her anatomy isn't discussed in mixed company.

' "Don't do that!" she yelled. "Don't do that to me!" When she wasn't shouting her head off she just moaned way down in her sound box, like an owl gargling.

'Then with one flying leap she sailed up on the bandstand, pulled her dress up to her neck, and began to dance. I don't know if dance is the right word for what she did—she didn't move her feet hardly at all, although she moved practically everything else. She went through her whole routine, bumps and grinds and shakes and breaks, making up new twists as she went along, and I mean twists. A bandstand was sure the wrong place to do what she was trying to do that night. All the time she kept screaming, "Cut it out! It's murder!" but her body wasn't saying no.

'It was a frantic scene, like a nightmare walking, and it got wilder because all the excitement made us come on like gangbusters to accompany this palsy-bug routine. Patrick and his gang of vipers were getting their kicks—the gauge they picked upon was really in there, and it had them treetop tall, mellow as a cello. Monkey Pollack stood in the back, moving a little less than a petrified tree, only his big lips shaking like meatballs with the chills, and the Ragtime Cowboy Jew was staring through the clouds of smoke as though he was watching a coyote do a toe dance. That girl must have been powered with Diesel engines, the way she kept on going. The sweat was rolling down her screwed up face like her pores were faucets, leaving streaks of mascara in the thick rouge. She would have made a scarecrow do a nip up and flip.[1]'

For the word 'jazz' was and is an American slang expression meaning 'fuck'. Jazz music is therefore fuck music—'Jazz Me Blues', 'Jazzin' Babies Blues'—but it is the music of a particular kind of fucking, no gracious domestic coupling of dam and sire, but the hot, intense act of desperate moments, of necessity, of loneliness, of self-affirmation for people who go alone, whose selves seem often to be wandering some way off.

The hipster, or hep-cat, was the first exemplary citizen of the alternative society. He was the big-city twentieth century descendant of the post-emancipation big-talkin' gambler. The mythical Stackolee, Spo'tin' Life and indeed Jelly Roll Morton himself, were prototypes of the Negro sophisticate who achieved, through exquisite co-ordination, detached alertness and very often literal liaison with the Devil (Stackolee was a witch—Muddy Waters' hoochie-coochie man says, 'I got a black cat bone. I got a mojo tooth. I got John the Conqueroo. I'm gonna mess wit' you. I'm gonna make you pretty womens lead me by the han'. Then the worl' is gonna know I'm a hoochie-coochie man'—and Jelly Roll has his whore sing 'I think my man got a black cat bone, 'cos when I leave I gotta run back home')—who achieved *success in action*, who danced,

[1] MEZZ MEZZROW, *Really the Blues*, Secker & Warburg.

blew, fought, gambled and fucked with relentless success, never a bad orgasm, never a fluffed note.

Hipsters became the gourmets of the moment, the athletes of the opportunity. Mezzrow describes the state of mind:

'I was all jammed up full of energy, restless as a Mexican jumping bean. Something was all puffed up in me, but I couldn't dig what it was or give it a name. All the sights and sounds of the Northwest Side, the balalaika chords my father used to strum, the tunes we blew on our mouth organs, the gang fights and the pool rooms, the gats we packed in our hip pockets and aimed at each other for fun, Bow Gistensohn and Murph Steinberg and Emil Burbacher and the coloured boy Sullivan, the squealing girls—they were all jumbled up in my head. I went around humming and whistling all the time, trying to straighten out this jumble. When we hung out at The Corner, I'd keep working my fingers like I was playing the piano or the balalaika or maybe a sax, anything that would make the right patterns of sound when you worked over it hard with plenty of feeling. Sometimes I patted the pavement with my foot, or beat the top of a garbage can with a couple of sticks, making time the way I'd seen Sullivan do when the spirit hit him. It got me so bad most of the time I couldn't sit still, I felt like I wanted to jump out of my skin, hop off into space on a C & A locomotive, anything but stay put.'[1]

They wore the ultra-fashionable in clothes, but developed quickly a uniform which was a highly sophisticated *alternative* to the dictated trends of haute couture. Sophistication was, for them, a close point of pride, the delicate weapon of defence against subservience. Their underworld would be elaborate and highly demanding in its own skills (jazz quickly became a virtuoso music), distinctive and audacious in its own clothes (pork-pie sombreros, zoot-suits, candystripe shirts, two-tone shoes, later the goatee and beret), and would formulate a language close to cockney rhyming slang in its verbal side-stepping and code-signalling, a language which the established respectable world could not understand, firstly because they lacked the vocabulary which was, in any case, perpetually changing, and secondly, because the rhythm of wit, thought

[1] MEZZ MEZZROW, *Really the Blues*, Secker & Warburg.

and syntax was different and much, much faster than their own. In a civilization of science, steel, concrete and moral paradox, the hipster was constructing an alternative civilization of movement, speed, grace and intuitive response. Two of his code-words have stayed constant, the adjectives 'hip' and 'square'. Wherever they have been in use over the last thirty years has always been, mysteriously, the place where the truly significant socio-cultural developments were taking place. Norman Mailer defines the terms well: 'In short, whether the life is criminal or not, the decision is to encourage the psychopath in oneself, to explore the domain of experience where security is boredom and therefore sickness, and one exists in the present, in that enormous present which is without past or future, memory or planned intention, the life where a man must go until he is beat, where he must gamble with his energies through all those small or large crises of courage and unforeseen situations which beset his day, where he must be with it or doomed not to swing. The unstated essence of hip, its psychopathic brilliance, quivers with the knowledge that new kinds of victories increase one's power for new kinds of perception; and defeats, the wrong kinds of defeats, attack the body and imprison one's energy until one is jailed in the prison air of other people's habits, other people's defeats, boredom, quiet desperation, and muted icy self-destroying rage. One is hip or one is square (the alternative which each new generation coming into American life is beginning to feel), one is a rebel or one conforms, one is a frontiersman in the Wild West of American night life, or else a square cell, trapped in the totalitarian issues of American society, doomed willy-nilly to conform if one is to succeed'.[1]

The language, the terminology, the culture, the hep-cat himself, only became clearly discernible in the mid-thirties. Jazz itself, at that time, was split between semi-dance music for the squares and the desperate competitive sound orgies of the free-for-all jam session where truly incredible virtuosity was not only developing, but was indeed stringently necessary. The humour, the unspoken understanding reinforcing the allusions and understatements, the zeitgeist of the culture

[1] NORMAN MAILER, *The White Negro*, City Lights.

itself, was called, then, 'jive'. The musicians who typify jive are probably Fats Waller, Louis Jordan and the wildly inventive surrealistic scat singer Leo Watson. Drugs, particularly marihuana, were beginning to become important. Mezz Mezzrow remembers pushing in Harlem in those years:

'I'm standing under the Tree of Hope, pushing my gauge. The vipers come up, one by one.

FIRST CAT: Hey there Poppa Mezz, is you anywhere?

ME: Man I'm down with it, stickin' like a honky.

FIRST CAT: Lay a trey on me, ole man.

ME: Got to do it, slot. (Pointing to a man standing in front of Big John's Ginmill.) Gun the snatcher on your left raise— the head mixer laid a bundle his ways, he's posin' back like crime sure pays.

FIRST CAT: Father grab him, I ain't payin' him no rabbit. Jim, this jive you got is a gasser, I'm goin' up to my dommy and dig that new mess Pops laid down for Okeh. I hear he riffed back on 'Zackly.' Pick you up at The Track when the kitten mechanics romp.

SECOND CAT: Hey Mezzie, lay some of that hard-cuttin' mess on me. I'm short a deuce of blips but I'll straighten you later.

ME: Righteous, gizz, you're a poor boy but a good boy— now don't come up crummy.

SECOND CAT: Never no crummy, chummy. I'm gonna lay a drape under the trey of knockers for Tenth Street and I'll be on the scene wearin' the green.'[1]

By 1939 a musician was working in Harlem who was not only the man who most thoroughly exemplifies the character and merits of the hipster, but who was later to be the most considerable creative artist to emerge in any field in the post-war years; a man who presented himself at the opportune moment as a folk-hero, an incarnate god for the subculture, which has endowed him, since the first whispers of his reputation in Harlem to the stentorian acclaim following his death, with supernatural significance; like Jelly Roll and the hoochie-coochie man, he was the Devil's agent.

[1] MEZZ MEZZROW, *Really the Blues*, Secker & Warburg.

In truth, if Charlie Parker was not possessed by supernatural forces, then there's nothing supernatural about genius. The complete brilliant lout, Charlie Parker ate up his life and his own system in an utter commitment to sensation and the articulation of that sensation. Drugs, liquor, women, action, humour, violence, passed through his metabolism and the music poured out. When he died, of the most rewarding life-long debauch in the history of art, he was a magical presence whose music was the wordless bible of the antiworld. There almost seems something in common with the sacrificial deaths of ancient kings about the way in which the word of his death spread in Harlem so that, before twenty-four hours had elapsed, the inscription BIRD LIVES appeared scrawled in the Harlem subways. There seems, also, a supernatural lack of coincidence about the fact that, in private jam sessions, under-ground, away from the spotlights, Parker had been perfecting his revolution in the way jazz was to be played, perfected be-bop so that he could release it on the world at exactly the right time, when it and he and his whole sub-culture were so desperately needed, in 1945.

Norman Mailer again puts it neatly:

'…on this bleak scene…a phenomenon…appeared: the American existentialist—the hipster, the man who knows that if our collective condition is to live with instant death by atomic war, relatively quick death by the State as *l'univers concentra-tionnaire*, or by a slow death by conformity with every rebel-lious and creative instinct stifled (at what damage to the mind and the heart and the liver and the nerves no research founda-tion for cancer will discover in a hurry), if the fate of twentieth century man is to live with death from adolescence to pre-mature senescence, why then the only life-giving answer is to accept the terms of death, to live with death as immediate danger, to divorce oneself from society, to exist without roots, to set out on that uncharted journey into the rebellious im-peratives of the self.'

[1] NORMAN MAILER, *The White Negro*, City Lights.

II

VE Night took place in one world and VJ Night in another. The world of the European victory was a brown, smelly, fallible, lovable place, an old-fashioned, earthy, stable place, a place in which there was considerable sure and common ground between men on issues of morality, where good was good and bad was bad, where loyalty to country, class, family and friends could be taken for granted, where no one felt the responsibility for public evils resting on their own shoulders, where people felt that if things were wrong then history had ample time remaining in which they could be rectified, where evolution took place in the benevolent house of nature, where society took place in the benevolent house of evolution, where man lived his short life in the benevolent house of society. We had survived the war, exorcized the Bavarian poltergeist, struck a positive at the end of the long, hideous negative. We had found each other in our collective suffering and triumph. We had reconfirmed the ancient merits of honour, self-sacrifice, courage, will and companionship. The destruction was over. We knew the Devil and had killed him. The future yawned ahead for illimitable construction and if there was another war, we could survive again.

The world of the Japanese victory was a world in which an evil had been precipitated whose scope was immeasurable, the act being, in itself, not an event, but a continuum, not an occasion but the beginning of a condition. We knocked out the second enemy (by no means such a discernible villain as Hitler whom we could easily condemn through the sensational shock of the concentration camps and the obvious poisonous violence of his rhetoric) by alienating all those values we had confirmed in the first victory. We had espoused a continuum that negated (running parallel to) the continuum of society.

We had espoused an evil as great as the Nazi genocide, we had espoused the instrument for the termination of our benevolent institution, society, and our certain identity, human. We had espoused a monstrous uncertainty both of future and of morality. If, besides the 'narzi gangsters', we were also wrong, who was ever right? If no one was right, what was right, and was right anyway relevant, and what could guide us through the terrifying freedom such a concept offered? Whatever the answer it had best be a good one for we could not rely on ourselves any more than the little yellow man or the evil hun. We had driven honour away a few short months after finding it. Neither could we survive the next war, for the next wasn't going to be remotely like the one we had 'shown we could take'. The next war would certainly be more terrible than anything we had known, was probably more terrible than we could calculate, was possibly going to terminate the entire species.

The first victory was a victory confirming our merits and security. The second victory destroyed them irrevocably.

In the new world the light was harsh, a perpetual noon of decisions, every action crucial being possibly final. No man was certain any more of anything but his own volition so the only value was pragmatic. Moral values, thought absolute, were now seen to be comparative, for all social entities around which morality had revolved were now called into doubt and nothing of morality remained. The society for which we had more or less cheerfully fought and (some of us) more or less cheerfully died had dropped its mask and in doing so had robbed all its institutions of church, political party, social class, happy family, of moral authority. No longer could teacher, magistrate, politician, don, or even loving parent, guide the young. Their membership of the H-bomb society automatically cancelled anything they might have to say on questions of right and wrong. Even Nature had come to mean poisoned stratosphere, contaminated rain, vegetables and milk that made men breed monsters, instincts that threw creatures compulsively into patterns that had little meaning but their own intrinsic intensities, and those intensities only assessed privately by the individual for the individual. It was difficult to share. We, in

England, knew the hipster only remotely. For a while we made our own way.

What way we made in 1945 and in the following years depended largely on our age, for right at that point, at the point of the dropping of the bombs on Hiroshima and Nagasaki, the generations became divided in a very crucial way.

The people who had passed puberty at the time of the bomb found that they were incapable of conceiving of life *without* a future. Their patterns of habit had formed, the steady job, the pension, the mortgage, the insurance policy, personal savings, support and respect for the protection of the law, all the paraphernalia of constructive, secure family life. They had learned their game and it was the only game they knew. To acknowledge the truth of their predicament would be to abandon the whole pattern of their lives. They would therefore have to pretend, much as they had pretended about ecstasy not being there, and they proceeded to pretend as cheerfully as ever. In any case, to look the danger in the eye might wreck the chances of that ultimate total security their deepest selves had contrived, death by H-bomb.

The people who had not yet reached puberty at the time of the bomb were incapable of conceiving of life *with* a future. They might not have had any direct preoccupation with the bomb. This depended largely on their sophistication. But they never knew a sense of future. The hipster was there. Charlie Parker's records began to be distributed. The hipster became increasingly present in popular music and young people moved in his direction. They pretended too, but they did not enter the pretence at all cheerfully. In fact they entered the pretence reluctantly, in pain and confusion, in hostility which they increasingly showed. Dad was a liar. He lied about the war and he lied about sex. He lied about the bomb and he lied about the future. He lived his life on an elaborate system of pretence that had been going on for hundreds of years. The so-called 'generation gap' started then and has been increasing ever since.

Our first reaction, as I remember, was one of formalized stoicism which we borrowed from the spivs, from demobbed soldiers, and from Hollywood movies, which we took and transmuted into a romanticism of toughness and aggression and subsequently wore like a suit of armour.

Popular culture was, at that time, not ours. It was the province of the young adult, contrived and modified by the promoters and impresarios and aimed at the mid-twenties age group. In particular it was aimed at the working-class, for this was the heyday of the vast popular dance-halls, the Mecca and the Locarno; popular culture was utterly separate from highbrow culture; the avant-garde was part of highbrow culture and both were posh.

Popular culture, then, was the culture of the jitterbug, of the snap-brim trilby and the double-breasted, wasp-waisted, wide-trousered pinstripe suit, of the hand-painted silk tie and the Boston haircut, of camiknickers and bright red lipstick, of the bombshell blonde and the streamlined bustline, of gilded pin-tables and lime-green ice-cream, of two-inch crepe soles and black-market nylons, of Betty Grable and Veronica Lake; of Humphrey Bogart and Alan Ladd, of Peter Cheyney and James Hadley Chase, a culture of brashness, raw colours, hard gloss, discord, cold eyes and cruel rouged lips, a culture of the original comic-book super-heroes, of SPLAT and BAM and ZOWIE, of spotlit trumpet sections standing up in rows, of exhibitionist, gum-chewing drum solos and bull-voiced tenor saxes, for somewhere in the middle of it all, this was the culture of swing, and somewhere in the middle of swing was jazz.

We flew to this culture not our own because at that time it provided for two of our needs; it protected and disguised our vulnerability and it provided a formalized mode of behaviour to compensate for our own directional poverty. The face was the flat-eyed half-sneer; the voice was belligerent and thrusting; the syntax was monosyllabic and summary. 'Oh yeah', 'So what', and 'Go to hell' were ritual catchphrases. Girls were 'dames', impersonalized as far as possible, called 'it', worn on the arm, treated with a modish brutality. There was a whole row of popular heroes at that time who depicted the bruised and whimpering child-individual, machine-gunning desperately through a character armour of shellac. Richard Attenborough played Pinky in *Brighton Rock*. Griffith Jones hammered his dame around the screen in an epic of the black market, Stewart Granger did likewise in *Waterloo Road*. Lemmy Caution, Peter Cheyney's hardmouth detective, specialized in the casual third-degree, bourbon in one hand, rubber-truncheon in the other; Slim Callaghan, Cheyney's other hero, was given to weeks of alcoholic oblivion while women grieved over his exemplary impotence. The example, the sanction and the prototype was there for us. The Allies were using their popular culture to exorcize their envy of the mythical Gestapo and we all joined in.

I am talking to a friend in a pub. My friend is sixteen. His cigarette and pint are insignia. The trilby on the back of his head is distorted into a curious silhouette. The hat is a shadow of the SS cheesecutter. He is pale to the point of looking ill. His eyes are calculatedly veiled—a contrived expression so formalized it almost suggests make-up.

    'Hiya.'

    'Hiya, son.'

    ''Cha bin doin'?'

    'Bin around.'

    He exhales, admiring his fine jet of smoke in the bar mirror.

    'Getcher finger away las' night?'

    'Nah. Don' bother with dames.'

    I recall the other boy who kissed girls with the cigarette stub in his mouth—another who beat up his girl each time she had him, for betraying the distorted purity for which she was supposed to stand—and the common practice of walking away from girls on discovering that they were menstruating, just getting up and walking away—the paradoxical idealization and objectification of the female…

    ''Cha do las' night then?'

    'T'riffic laugh. Got pissed, me an' Ginger. Got this R.A.F. bloke, so pissed 'e couldn't move, took 'im up an alley an' beat 'im up.'

    'Yeah?'

    'Yeah. Face one mass o' blood. Should 'a' been with us Saturday though. Got three then. One of 'em tried to report us to the cops. We'll get 'im again. Great.'

A group of us come together in a youth club. We signal with cold eyes, each one of us, in his own mind, a cinema close-up. We imagine the youth club to be a pool-hall. We drift towards the door. We are going to get Bobby. Bobby is a mongol with wealthy parents. They own the Palm Beach Milk Bar. Sometimes Bobby hides in the alley outside the youth club and flashes his cock at the girls. We are going to find him and punish him. The terrible fine point of drama in the situation derives from the irony that we are flagellating ourselves, or a scapegoat for ourselves, attempting to cauterize the dependence springing from our own desires. Our brutality towards Bobby is a brutality towards our own cringing, yearning hopelessness.

We cruise around milk bars, pubs, alleyways. We find him up the alley behind a cinema. The big booming voices are coming through the projection room window. We beat him up with dead monosyllables and hard, flat little sounds. He crouches on the ground at our feet, head huddled between his knees, greasy hair hanging, flash double-breasted overcoat hanging in the slime. He is making funny noises like a frightened puppy and he is drooling blood down between his orange suede shoes. We file past him formally. Each of us spits on his head and one of us kicks him. He yelps. Then we go away. We feel cleansed and hard and impregnable.

But it would be false to dismiss the culture and the role as being merely a mask. It was a mask whose quality was particularly appropriate, being neither the image of our inward terror nor the image of the outward lie, but being, rather, the image of the sour, dynamic discomfort it was to contain such hypersensitive solitude. The raw 'pastel' shades, the discordant glitter, the metallic breasts, the military shoulders, the screeching tenor saxophones were the very aesthetic of the severed nerve, for our nerves were severed, severed from certainty, severed from social and family warmth, and above all severed from future. We were stranded with our sensations, our sensations screamed and we recognized the aesthetic of the scream.

Swing music was the art of this sensibility with its frantic tempo, powerhouse volume, stratospheric brass, explosive discords and brilliant dynamics. Woody Herman's 'Apple Honey' or Dizzy Gillespie's 'Things To Come' are records which epitomize all these qualities. For swing was that derivation of jazz that had come out of the underground during the war and proved to be the right music for the night before the final op. Briefly it also proved to be the music for the night after. In front of every shimmering orchestra there was one man, the soloist, writhing and grimacing towards his aural climax and that man was a hipster. His voice sounded like one from which we could learn a method of living. It was and we started to learn.

The liars, the willing pretenders who put the bomb next to sex in the locked closet, could not hear jazz. They said it was cacophony and they meant it. They were rectangular, conformist, rigid, strictured. They were square.

So we knew where we stood. We knew how it felt to stand there but we also stuck to our masks and our artificialities. We knew how to keep our noses clean, for not one of us, no solitary one, had any serious political preoccupation or any belief in the changeability of society and events. No single solitary one amongst us had the slightest spark of hope or gave a damn about a thing except the crackling certainty of Now.

III

The fashionable female torso of the forties was not flesh but metal, a *cuirasse*. It was armour. The whole popular mode was armour. We used it to conceal our distress and confusion but our distress and confusion arose from our hatred of lies so the shield, the mask, had to drop. It took a long time and the process involved a running fight with the squares insofar as each time a group of young people created their own culture the squares bought it up, streamlined it and sold it back on a large scale, invalidating it and making it necessary for young people to side-step again. Thus, in current fashion, as soon as a style is in the shop windows it's virtually dead unless the shop window is that of a boutique which is, in the genuine sense, hip, run and owned by people of the right and recognizable climate of mind.

The first peep over the top of the shield was the teenage response to the earthy which began in the early fifties. In those years certain records appeared on the hit parade which reflected a certain folksiness, an awareness of American country music, hoe-down and blues. Tennessee Ernie's 'Shotgun Boogie' had an explosive singing style and a hard, rim-shot off-beat, a big-sounding hillbilly electric guitar and even a 'protest' lyric on the reverse side, 'Sixteen Ton'. It signalled the way things were going. Frankie Laine and Johnny Ray lifted their styles from gospel singing. Ray, particularly, introduced to popular music that mode of histrionic self-exposure that had always been natural to country blues singers and circuit preachers. The vocalists with the highly mechanized swing bands had always been curiously reserved in their spotlights. The self exposure was left to the instrumental soloists whose orgies Ray now put into words and actions. This, then, was the style of an act which sanctified the outsider. As far as the squares knew Parker had been a man making silly noises on a saxophone. But there was no escaping Ray. There he was, deaf, neurotic, crying, camp, crucifying himself twice nightly to everybody's delight, driving himself to public orgasm in 'Oh What A Night It Was', beginning the disintegration of that micrometer precision control that had put the opaque chrome finish on swing music.

Also in the early fifties, Savile Row attempted a revival in Edwardian men's fashions. In Savile Row it failed but quickly succeeded in Hammersmith Palais. Like the hipsters' zoot suit, it became, for English teenagers, the first uniform which distinguished the group from their floppy-trousered fathers. The shield dropped a little further. Teddy suits with their frock-coats, fancy waistcoats, moleskin collars and drainpipe trousers, and, for the girls, hobble skirts, black-seam nylons and coolie hats, were the first public showing, in England at any rate, of radical social divergence on the part of young people. No teddy boy, at that time, was sufficiently clear in his own mind to know, or sufficiently articulate to say, what his deepest responses knew, that the established world was the emanation of gigantic falsehood and he wanted out. He also wanted to stop using the shield of the official pokerface popular culture. One swift generation after my own this culture was seen and rejected for its artificiality. The peroxide glitter and the mile-wide shoulders were all of a piece with Dunkirk jingoism, hopes and promises of peace, nudging pornographic sex, the never-emergent nipple and the never-mentioned fuck.

Teenage culture had not then started to formulate its own fashions but it is extremely significant that the style chosen was one designed for a completely different social group. There was, in fact, no small element of deliberate irony about the way in which the style was lifted from under the very noses of the adult, upper class world, the world of Anthony Eden and Duncan Sandys. The patronizing dungaree-and-tartan fashions aimed at the teenage market were disdained. The fashion designer had not exactly been spotted, but he had been scented on the night air. From then on he was due for an increasing amount of sullen suspicion.

The violence and stoicism remained but formalized itself into tribal routines, rituals. Vast gangs formed in South London and began to hold pitched battles, armed with bicycle chains and flick-knives. Some dance-halls banned teddy suits but it made no difference. The separation had merely been acknowledged by the squares. Certain police witnesses seemed, in court, to grow more conscious of the dress than the deeds of their young defendants. Their instinct was true. The new dress heralded a new kind of crime and a new kind of social problem for anybody who was anxious for the stability of society. The young people permitted open show of emotion only to the public performer. Emotion was only acknowledged in terms of hard action, dance, fight or copulation. Excitement was set in the place where emotion had formerly been. The group rituals were conducted not in the interest of self-punishment, of power-competition, but in the interest of excitement. We, immediately after the war, had been senselessly brutal but we had not been insensitive. Rather had our brutalities perversely wrung our overwrought sensitivities. We needed the mask. But many of the teddy boys seemed to need no mask. The stoicism for them was not a mask but a blank. A new affectlessness was becoming commonplace at an un-nerving rate.

In 1953 a boy was stabbed to death on Clapham Common. He was no slum boy, nor was his killer. He came from a seemingly happy family in a seemingly comfortable home. The murder was not done for gain or revenge or the hand of a girl. It was the first fatal casualty in the excitement game, the first of an unending series of teenage killings. Similar crimes in Europe could have been put down to the occupation. Similar crimes in America could be put down to Puerto Rican immigration. But in London the older people were as bewildered as they were by jazz. The excitement game was unrelated to 'constructive' living. Theft was understandable. Revenge was understandable but the principle of excitement was not. That only made sense in terms of the moment, to the people who were trapped within it.

'I was standing by the bus-stop. Just standing there waiting for a 34 and this kid comes up and joins the queue. There's me and this woman and this kid and 'e's a bit breathless as though 'e's been playin' tag an' then this other kid comes round the corner and stops runnin' an' walks towards the bus-stop an' 'e's gigglin'

27

an' they're both gigglin' an' gettin' ready to dodge one another as though they was playin' tag an' then they comes real close together an' they're still gigglin' an' the second one's got 'is 'and be'ind 'is back an' 'e whips out 'is 'and and stabs the first one in the guts an' then runs away laughin' 'is 'ead off. And we didn't know what 'ad 'appened until we noticed the blood...'

'...Well we was in this club sir, all playin' ping-pong an' dancin' sir an' some of us was chattin' up birds like, and this door comes open an' it's about a dozen blokes from Muswell 'ill. Well they was always about like, after the birds, so we don't take no notice and next thing I noticed they was goin' out an' I thought "Well that's them, then" and then I noticed about twenty blokes about the club was all doubled over groanin'. Twenty they got, clean as a whistle, ahtside in the motors an' off to go, back to Muswell 'ill.'

''Ey sir, killin' up the Rock-a-Cha las' night. They gorrim though. It was only my fella, the bloke wot done it. Well, murder's gear, innit...'

The teds were sparked into violence by any and every occasion. It became a means of celebration and signature. The smashed lamp standard or the lacerated train compartment was no gesture of anger against local government or society at large. They were simply a means of saying 'Tom, Dick or Harry *was here.*'

Early British performances of the Bill Haley band and the first showings of Elvis Presley films were celebrated by rows of razored seats in the theatres concerned. These again did not indicate dissatisfaction with the performance or anger with the management. They were signatures. They said, if anything, 'Thank you Bill, Elvis, for making your violence for us. Now we'll make ours for you...' Tribal gestures of tribal significance. Society, far from being an enemy, was not even a consideration, outside the magic...

Ray Gosling: 'That was the very first time I come to Liverpool. Must have been '57. I remember coming from Crosby by train. There was some meeting at a club. I'd got a message for a bloke. Got my trains all mixed up, that's why I was coming in from Crosby. Don't know how I got to Crosby. Got no idea. I can't remember much, but then I was on this train and there was blood all over, and a gash on my face, and there was blood in my mouth and there was an old lady sitting opposite, and the train rocked, and she kept saying—dreadful, dreadful. I stood up and there was blood all over, and all over my suit, and I looked in the mirror; it was just like my face had been used as a bit of cheese in a cheese scraper—there was skin and flesh and blood and grit and cuts and bruises and a great big black eye, a real shiner. I looked at this old lady, and I said I was sorry but I thought someone must have done me over, though I couldn't remember a thing like—and she just sat there with her little gloved hands all folded over her handbag muttering away—dreadful, dreadful—and I went out to the w.c. and I was sick. And when I got back we were coming through Widnes and Runcorn over the river like…'[1]

The teddy boys were waiting for Elvis Presley. Everybody under twenty all over the world was waiting. He was the super-salesman of mass-distribution hip. Unfortunately he had to be white. Otherwise one of the Chicago blues singers, Muddy Waters, Buddy Guy, Howlin' Wolf, would have done. He had to play to large audiences in the south. He had to have the cowboy/Spanish element. He had to have the Adonis profile. He had to have the overtones of the queer-boy's pin-up, the packed jeans, the sullen long-lashed eyes, the rosebud mouth, the lavish greasy hair and gilded drag.

Like Brando, he was a point at which separate attitudes could merge. He had all the flash and glitter of showbiz but most of his repertoire was slightly modified country blues. He was smooth and greasy and sexy and young but he played with the rhythms of boogie pianists and mountain bands. He was, like Tennessee Williams' 'Orpheus Descending', a public butch god with the insolence of a Genet murderer. Most of all he was unvarnished sex taken and set way out in the open. From the first quavering orgastic stutter to the final bull scream, from the first beads of sweat on his upper lip to the final frantic blows of his loins against the curved fetish of his guitar he was the incarnate spirit of the fast lay and his audience of adolescents responded, not only sexually but also with some gratitude, for here was someone who was acting out in

[1] RAY GOSLING, *Sum Total*, Faber & Faber.

the open something that was still a secret from the adults. He broke the secret and made himself a god all over the world.

'God' is not too strong a word here. The Presley riots were a revengeful rediscovery of the Dionysian ceremony. He was the idol in a literal sense, a deity incarnate on the old primitive pattern, the catalyst of a rediscovered appetite for community in its fundamental form, orgastic ritual. Presley's success had implications far beyond the hopes or intentions of his managers and promoters. He was awarded an identity far greater than the one he intended for himself, an identity that invalidated the brash commercialism of his promotion. The Presley riots were the first big spontaneous gatherings of the community of the new sensibilities. Riots over previous idols had been sentimental rather than sexual. The Presley riots were temple ceremonials of the futureless.

It was partly through such ceremonials that the disaffiliated teenager began to identify himself and his aims. Ray Gosling launched a teenage club in Leicester that aimed at considerably more than 'keeping them off the streets': 'I remember coming back one night from Oxford, and it was around four in the morning, and as we came in over the bridge to the Central Station I could see the lights and the open door. Walking down the street from the station and in through the door, and the juke-box was playing and there were two dancing couples, beautifully and slowly soft, and one behind the bar. There had been a good take-in from the till, and the coffee was still good and hot and fresh. There was blood on the floor, and the dirt from a fast night. It had a wonderful used look about it. It was an oasis in a city of the dead. The only place open. That was the way I liked it. That was the way it could have been. It became that night, both open and exclusive; the sort of place where I could feel proud at being a customer…I saw something happen. I saw in fact what I'd only been able to dream about. It won't die. Things like that, they don't die…Nice and nasty, nice and naughty—and I sided with the nasty and the naughty, painting a seedy picture of tin pot skiffle groups, grubby lads and louts, a club no decent person would want to belong to, romancing on the seamy side…'[1]

[1] RAY GOSLING, *Sum Total*, Faber & Faber.

IV

It's worth noting that the brute-heroes, the hipster-heroes, the *pain*-heroes, Johnny Ray, Marlon Brando, James Dean (whose death sparked off a fantastic orgy of identificatory reaction), Elvis Presley (whose softening image did not), were the product and, in turn, the catalysts of a particular section of the teenage group—the motorcycle cowboys, the 'Wild Ones'. Their uniform, the second to emerge in England, possibly the first in America, consisted, still consists, of skin-tight jeans and black leather jacket. Accessories could include peaked cap (further shades of the ss), calf-length boots, neck bandanas, Nazi war relics, big brash colour transfers and later, in England, where the 'ton-up boys' became the 'rockers' (indicating a defensive adherence to the simple early forms of rock 'n' roll) ornate patterns of brass studs, tiger-tails, fringes, chains and bells.

Very little has come out of the whole teenage development that has more beauty than decorated rocker-jackets. They showed the creative impulse at its purest and most inventive. Without any sentimentality it's possible to say that they constitute tribal art of a high degree, symmetrical, ritualistic, with a bizarre metallic brilliance and a high fetishistic power.

Thom Gunn, a conscious existentialist, Cambridge graduate, poet of action, found in the American midwestern black-leather cowboy a naïve whose method of living provided a way out of the spiritual cul-de-sac in which intellectual life seemed caught, a way in which it was possible to avoid the contemptible business of squatting 'irresolute all day at stool/ Inside the heart'. His most well-known poem on the subject, however, amplifies the pragmatic merits of the earlier hipster with an additional dynamism, the hard edge of will applied to the crucial moment, an aggressive masculinity of principle

expressed in the barbaric decorations and the atmosphere of oil
and petrol.

A minute holds them, who have come to go:
The self-defined astride the created will
They burst away; the towns they travel through
Are home for neither bird nor holiness,
For birds and saints complete their purposes.
At worst, one is in motion; and at best,
Reaching no absolute, in which to rest,
One is always nearer by not keeping still.[1]

There had been something of the fop about the hep-cat,
with his loose clothes and his elliptical speech. Lester Young
brought hip to a fine point in his last years by wearing ribbons
in his hair and camping crazily about the bandstand. The
leather-jackets indicated a reversion, in many of their tribal
conventions, to the stoical mask (goggles, cultivated toughness) and the metallic severity (the motor-bikes, the fierce
array of buckles and studs) of the 1945 generation. Even the
transfers on their shoulders were ten-year-old images adopted
for their very brashness and crudity from what remained of the
post-war pop culture in the highway cafés and gas stations.

The American pattern, the original of this particular mode,
was older and more brutal than its English counterpart. They
were veritable hoods, anxious to demonstrate their power over
respectable road-users by more than speed. The twist, poker-
faced, untouching, violently erotic, was their dance. Their way
of life is hilariously depicted in Steve Wilson's complex
cartoons.

In England the pivotal skill was not brutality or dancing
but simply fast and dangerous riding. In the early sixties every
London hospital was crowded to overflowing with motorcycle casualties. The main rendezvous were the Ace and the
Busy Bee, two sprawling seedy petrol-station cafés near the
London terminus of the M1. In the tangled mess of the road
systems, the jungle of glittering signs, the endless hypnotic
cat's eyes, the monotonous lanes of traffic, the desolate motorway cafeterias, the rockers were a strange and heartening

[1] THOM GUNN, *The Sense of Movement*, Faber & Faber.

breath of wildness and preserved integrity. They would come roaring down to London at the week-end in tribes, studs glittering, tangled greasy hair flying out behind them. There was something satisfying about the way in which a traffic stream on a hot Saturday, stalled, crammed with sweaty pink families trapped with one another as the Mini-Minor was trapped in the queue, could be utterly negated, cancelled, by a column of gleaming rockers hurtling past them to the round-about.

Rockers were not the direct descendants of the teddy boys. They were a younger generation who imitated the American pattern of rebellion. With their tribal dance, two rows facing one another and chopping their torsos twice to this side twice to that, with their extrovert swagger, they overshadowed the more sophisticated group who professed the cool demeanour, who were thus the true followers of the fly, elliptical attitude, who adopted the muted stripes, short collarless jackets, pointed shoes, narrow ties, cropped hair, mock-collegiate mood of Italian fashion. This group, the real inheritors of the teddy boys' fussy vanity, far too fastidious for the motorway caff, stuck to modern jazz clubs, particularly the Marquee and the Flamingo, and to pubs. Rockers, if they drank, drank at the roadside outside the 'offo' (off-licence).

In the late fifties the rockers began to call the others mods. The mods called the others rockers. 'Mod' meant effeminate, stuck-up, emulating the middle classes, aspiring to a competitive sophistication, snobbish, phony. 'Rocker' meant hopelessly naïve, loutish, scruffy, and, above all, betraying; for the mods, like the hep-cats, wanted a good image for the rebel group, the polished sharp image that would offset the adult patronization by which this increasingly self-aware world of the adolescent might be disarmed. Rockers were so clearly 'going through a phase'. Mods, in whom alienation had become something of a deliberate stance, were embarrassed and angered by this. Ray Gosling wrote: 'The teddy suit has gone, and given way to the Italian thing. The aggression has moved into an arrogance. This hip, this reaction from an all-pervading niceness, it's got in place. The dignity has come back, and the anarchy and aggression, the tin pot, seedy, grubby and screaming selections have gone and the vision is that much clearer. The fight against all them has moved into an arrogance, this sure knowledge that we're going to come through, oil or no oil. We're going through the rubble and tin cans and we're picking out the ones that will be of use, and clearing the site and digging the foundations and then build, build…'[1]

It was the beginning of a short war. Before the huge pitched battles of 1964, however, the mods and popular music changed still further. Small group rhythm-and-blues, a belligerent American Negro folk form from which rock 'n' roll had taken a good deal, began to be popular. Alexis Korner and Cyril Davies, who had, for years, run a very dedicated scene called the Blues and Barrelhouse Club, now opened in the Moist Hoist, a notoriously evil cellar opposite Ealing Tube Station. They opened with amplifiers full on and Dick Heckstall-Smith on tenor. Something was happening to the sincerity and authenticity cult. The group moved to the Marquee fairly quickly where they attracted not only mods but also an even more sophisticated crowd from the art schools. Art students and popular music had, until this point, been separate, except for an odd overlapping in the world of trad and skiffle. But R & B was that bit less commercial than rock had been. It appealed to the authenticity cult *and* the rock 'n' roll cult. The students and the mods cross-fertilized, particularly in Liverpool. Purple hearts appeared in strange profusion. Bell-bottoms blossomed into wild colours. Shoes were painted with Woolworths lacquer. Both sexes wore make-up and dyed their hair. The art students brought their acid colour combinations, their lilacs, tangerines and lime greens from abstract painting. The air in the streets and clubs was tingling with a new delirium. The handful of art-student pop groups appeared, with their louder, more violent music, their cultivated hysteria, their painful amplifiers, the Rolling Stones, the Pretty Things, the Kinks, the Beatles. 'Kinky' was a word very much in the air. Everywhere there were zippers, leathers, boots, PVC, see-through plastics, male make-up, a thousand overtones of sexual deviation, particularly sadism, and everywhere, mixed in with amphetamines, was the birth pill. The established

[1] RAY GOSLING, *Sum Total*, Faber & Faber.

business world, the square commercial world, the promoters, the deathwishers, were completely out-distanced. All they could do was run to keep up, for unless they could keep up an appetite for living might emerge from all this parrot-coloured chaos and the suicide plan might be wrecked.

In 1964 the rival groups, the mods, amoral, hysterical, and the rockers, who by this time seemed almost endearingly butch, clashed on August bank-holiday at Margate. The small seaside town was suddenly full of warring kids, up to their skulls in amphetamine, wrecking the cafés, hunting one another in great bloodthirsty packs across the beach. They didn't even turn off the transistors as they put the boot in. Affectlessness was complete. It was impossible to live with the bomb and the cold war and retain the sympathetic faculties. The situation remained, so sensitivity had to go. The mods and rockers riots were not only the next step in the excitement game, they were the extended, tawdry funeral of compassion. It was the only way the growing mind could deal with the constant probability of unprecedented pain and horror which the squares took such trouble to preserve.

By the mid-sixties defensive brutality had formed its first completely formalized society. Since Elvis first presented himself as the shaman of psychopathic sex, violence and anti-domestic narcissism, the whole subculture had been increasingly tribal in its customs and hierarchies. It was inevitable that ultimately it would form at least one really vast and organized local tribe. In California the tribe clarified itself in the official ranks, chapters, membership rituals and savagery of Hell's Angels.

Eulogized by poets Ginsberg, Kesey and McClure, the Angels, under their president Sonny Barger, terrorized Cali-fornian society by their arrogant mindless brutality, the extravagant splendour of their filthy array, and their custom of multiple rape.

Hell's Angels are by no means a teenage gang however. All the post-Hiroshima generations are represented in their ranks. The adulating West Coast liberals, who saw in Hell's Angels a virile rebellion to reinforce their own intellectual's impotence, were left bewildered when a contingent of Angels, complete in

35

cut-down denims and swastikas, sided with Reagan, Rockwell and the police and attacked a Berkeley peace march.

What sociologists, liberals, Beats, and even the Angels themselves didn't realize was finally that they had been provoked by the twittering hypocrisy of a middle-class movement—an hypocrisy which merely masked with fragile good intentions the viciousness of the social psyche it had fallen to the Angels to demonstrate. "The world is Hell and we are Hell's Angels" What ultimately terrifies the Californian squares is surely not the total lack of affect on the Angels' part. Rather are they terrified by the total lack of hypocrisy whereby their own profound destructiveness is reflected with such devastating clarity.

II
Protest

Disaffiliation was deliberate and conscious, even self-conscious, among the demonstrators who appeared in the fifties—unavoidably; disaffiliation is a prerequisite of protest.

I

Paris, after the war, has been the traditional home of bohemianism. The particular brand it offered to the rubbernecking middle-class students who flooded over the channel at vacation, to the first American expatriates, the demobbed GIs, was called existentialist. It was a popular way of life among young people, based, fairly remotely, on existentialist philosophy, particularly that of Camus and Sartre. Its popular idols were Juliette Greco, Anouk and Edith Piaf, whose 'Je ne regrette rien' was yet another statement of the required attitude, gallic and wistful this time, but in essence the same as the attitude of the hipster and Gunn's leather-jacket, a philosophy of the moment. The pale face of Juliette, without make-up except around the eyes, with whited lips, has been the mask for female middle-class rebels ever since. The style, with its necrophiliac overtones, constitutes another device for living with the possibility of death. Boredom was a mode. The crumbling cellars in Saint-Germain were unsmiling. The sex was casual. There wasn't any violence.

For all the modish fed-upness it was in this group that the post-war optimism began to make itself felt. Cut off from the spivs and the teddy boys by class, scorning the popular culture of the day as being phony and over-commercialized, the post-war pop-bohemianism launched itself with a cult of the primitive, of ceramic beads and dirndl skirts, of ankle-thong sandals and curtain-hoop ear-rings, of shaggy corduroys and ten-day beards, of seamen's sweaters and home-dyed battle-dress. Swing music, with its drilled, precision section work, was despised. The hipster was misunderstood. The small-band collective improvization of twenties New Orleans jazz, propagated by critics like Hugues Panassié and Rudi Blesh, was held up as the exemplary art form. Naïvety was equated with honesty, ineptitude was equated with sincerity, and merit was gauged in terms of proximity to the animal and the vegetable. It was a natural reaction after the harsh metal of war. It was a hungering for the green and intuitive life, almost for the pastoral, and held, in its reverence for intuition, something in common with the hipster; but finally intuition, to this group, was a sentimental thing, more to do with Ethel Waters than the Harlem Globetrotters.

Nevertheless, the clubs which set themselves up in London and Paris and promoted New Orleans jazz like a religion were totally outside of commerce, running at the start of things on a non-profit-making basis, employing amateur bands, collections of students, particularly art students, who imitated the great recordings by King Oliver, Louis Armstrong and Jelly Roll Morton with varying skill and complete self-deception. Claude Luter in France, Humphrey Lyttleton in England and Lu Watters in America were about the best. France imported the brilliant jazz pioneer Sydney Bechet and appointed him to the head of the priesthood. There had always been something gallic about his vibrato anyway. The following was a minority following, self-conscious and partisan, opinionated and crusading. The world was evil, governed by Mammon and Moloch. New Orleans jazz was a music straight from the heart and the swamp, unclouded by the corrupting touch of civilization. It would refertilize the world.

The adherence to traditional jazz led to an adherence to country blues singing and folk music. Alan Lomax was still making his illuminating field recordings for the Library of Congress. They had the quality of sincerity which was thought to supersede all other creative merits; they were sociologically authentic and somehow authenticity was held to be a creative merit. Alan Lomax came to England and showed us what was left of our own folk music. Alan Lomax had a theory about folk music which contradicted the people at Cecil Sharp House. They said not 'who' but 'what', so Owen Brannigan singing 'The Foggy Dew' was folk music. Lomax said not 'what' but 'who' and 'how', so 'Irene Goodnight' sung by Leadbelly was folk music. The trad jazz following picked up on this quickly, made a fetish of the unaccompanied, cracked voice, failed to see the pragmatic contradiction when they imitated the dialects and quaverings in order to be as authentic and sincere as they could possibly contrive. Later it started to pay. Uncle John Renshaw, a band-leader of the time, used to say with some irony 'I'm in the sincerity racket, meself.' Not everybody saw the joke.

Among the people who didn't see the joke were left-wing intellectuals like Ewan MacColl and Pete and Peggy Seeger, who had worked up a cute little line in authenticity and sincerity. They didn't see the joke because, for them, merit lay in the political ideals to which they were being faithful, and here, right here in the early stages, lay the pathetic fallacy undermining the whole movement. Art, creativity, mind and passion were signed over to an exterior morality, a cart-before-the-horse process, lamentably and typically middle-class in its nature, whereby art, creativity, mind and passion were robbed of any real authenticity and morality was consequently devitalized, a matter of policy rather than conviction, the exact reverse of hip.

It was this gross sentimentality that ultimately led British revivalist musicians to copy the music of primitive New Orleans septuagenarians resurrected by intellectual critics, rather than continuing to copy the robust and virile records of the twenties. George Lewis was too musically illiterate to attempt even rudimentary arrangements. He was too feeble to encompass the violent lyrical power of a Dodds or a Bechet. He was therefore more sincere and authentic. In London the Crane River Jazz Band led this tendency. It ultimately transmuted itself into the Ken Colyer Jazz Band.

By the mid-fifties the Colyer band had found a cult following of considerable size. A small group within the band, encouraged by guitarist Alexis Korner, played the more danceable Negro folk tunes and called their music skiffle. The original skiffle had been the music of Chicago jug bands. London skiffle didn't sound much like it. The Colyer Club was perpetually packed. So were the halls up and down the country where the band played one-night stands. The Chris Barber Band, an offshoot of the Colyer band, was getting into the Top Twenty, providing possibly the first bridge between the separate worlds of the middle-class students and the working-class rock 'n' roll fans, the teds. Skiffle provided an even wider bridge. With its three-chord guitars and its tea-chest basses, it was, like trad, a do-it-yourself music quickly adopted by the teenage group at large. Singers like Tommy Steele were singing 'John Henry' and 'Jailhouse Rock' in the same programme. Some groups were beginning to write their own numbers. The later flowering of British pop music was clearly foreshadowed. Lonnie Donnegan, Barber's banjo player, was making big money with his nasal imitations of Leadbelly. Skiffle was a major breakthrough in that, briefly, it was the first popular music that disdained the adult-commercial completely. The squares moved fast however. After Donnegan the idiom had been bought off and emasculated.

Soho was alive with cellar coffee-bars, where skiffle and jazz could be played and heard informally and where the rich odour of marihuana became, for the first time, a familiar part of the London atmosphere. Sam Widges was the most popular. Also there was the Nucleus, the Gyre and Gimble, the Farm. They were open most of the night and often the management would leave you to sleep where you sat. It was a place to stay in the dry if you didn't want to go home. It became obvious that parental control was going to stop at about the age of fifteen for a large number of young people. Teenage wages were going up and so were student grants. It was becoming possible to push the leaky boat of adult delusions a little further away. The Soho Fair, which ran annually for three years, was a festival of the ravers. Bands and guitars and cossack hats and sheepskin waistcoats flooded out of the cellars and into the streets. It was so good that it had to be stopped, so good that it was in the first Soho Fair that the real spirit of Aldermaston was born.

All the attached commercialism was despised by the hard-core Colyer fans. Solemnly dedicated, grimly puritan, with their black jeans, shoulder-length hair, donkey jackets, the sexes only distinguishable by breasts and beards, they constructed a left-wing romanticism based on that patronizing idolization of the lumpen proletariat that only the repressed children of the middle class could have contrived. Over the years they developed into an extensive nomadic group, haunting the beaches of the coastal resorts during the summer, flooding back to London when the cold weather started, and ultimately returning to home and job for good. A number drifted into the Young Communist League.

How much such egalitarian dreams have to do with the hard facts of Communism is perhaps best illustrated by Doris Lessing's character Harry—'He used to dress in a sort of bush shirt, or tunic, and sandals, with a military haircut. He never smiled. A portrait of Lenin on the wall—well that certainly goes without saying. A smaller one of Trotsky.' Harry eventually fulfils his life-long dream of going to Russia—'The delegation proceeds on its flowery way of visits to factories, schools, Palaces of Culture, and the University, not to mention speeches and banquets. And there is Harry, in his tunic, with his gammy leg, and his revolutionary sternness, the living incarnation of Lenin only these foolish Russians never recognized him. They adored him of course for his high seriousness, but more than once they inquired why Harry wore such bizarre clothes, and even, as I recall, if he had a secret sorrow...'[1]

The real benefit of this left-wing zeal was finally not felt in the society but in the practitioners themselves. They had developed in their own minds an idealism which acted as an antidote to the sickness attendant on living with the bomb. Barefoot and cross-legged on the floor of the Colyer club, they avoided the sado-masochistic symptoms of their working-class counterparts. Their greater literacy had enabled them to construct their own myth of a future. For a while longer they could avoid the yawning facts. It is ultimately to their credit that when harsh reality came in 1956 they were willing to test the truth of their beliefs and accept the subsequent failure as disproof.

[1] DORIS LESSING, *The Golden Notebook*, Michael Joseph.

I have just hitch-hiked back from London. A lorry driver has told me the news. My wife is curled in the armchair in the front room of our cottage sobbing helplessly. The radio is giving the latest casualty figures from Budapest. On Sunday we go to church, the only time we ever have or ever will. It just conceivably might have helped. I put up a collecting box at the school where I'm working. I send my ten pounds savings and put ten shillings in the box. At the end of two days it contains ten shillings, and sevenpence ha'penny. The other teachers are irritated by the news flashes which interrupt reports of the Olympic Games. Sunday night we invite some friends round to try and snap out of it. They file in, sit round for an hour or so, saying nothing. My wife cries a little. Then, one by one, they make their excuses and go. I pass my days waiting for my reserve papers to call me out to Suez, wondering what the hell I'm going to do if they arrive...

It's difficult to analyse or describe what it was to young people, living through the autumn of 1956. As Presley had put sex out in the open while the teenagers applauded, so the square world had now made utterly clear its suicidal intentions. Our reluctant pretences could drop. Every young person was forced to admit to himself: 'The bastards are going to do it and they're going to do it soon'.

The teds were ready with a sneer. The young middle class, softer and more starry-eyed, had to meet the emergency with their ideals if their ideals were to amount to anything at all.

Earlier that year an important play had appeared on the London stage. Jimmy Porter, the carping, egocentric, trad trumpeter hero of John Osborne's *Look Back In Anger* was by no means a sacred figure like Parker, Bechet, Elvis or James

Dean, but he was the voice of the rebel middle class for all his plebeian pretensions. His self-abusive bitterness was the right note to spark off the chorus of mass protest that started on the night of Eden's announcements about the invasion of Suez—
'Halleluyah! I'm alive! I've an idea. Why don't we have a little game? Let's pretend we're human beings, and that we're actually alive, just for a while. What do you say? Let's pretend we're human. Oh brother, it's such a long time since I was with anyone who got enthusiastic about anything... I suppose people of our generation aren't able to die for good causes any more. We had all that done for us, in the thirties and forties, when we were still kids. There aren't any good brave causes left. If the big bang does come, and we all get killed off, it won't be in aid of the old fashioned grand design. It'll just be for the Brave New-nothing-very-much-thank-you. About as pointless and inglorious as stepping in front of a bus'.[1]

So the hunger for the cause was there. The trad clubs were full of kids with their anxieties and their half-formed Trotskyism. The politicians were stepping up the suicide programme. The Left hoiked up its capacious knickers and got mobile. There was, in England, a small established nucleus of pacifists centred around George Lansbury's old Peace Pledge Union and their newspaper *Peace News*. Heretofore this group had shown little particularization in the direction of nuclear war. There had also been a parliamentary movement called the Hydrogen Bomb National Campaign whereby the Methodist minister Donald Soper and the socialist Anglican Canon Collins together with six Labour MPs drummed up 1,000,000 signatures for a petition against the bomb. This organization was distrusted by veteran pacifists, however, as being mere political window-dressing. More consequential things were happening in North London where Gertrude Fishwick, a member of Finchley Labour Party who was ill with anxiety about the bomb, organized Golders Green Committee for the Abolition of Nuclear Weapons. With the strenuous support of Peggy Duff, another energetic Labour Party member, this changed to a National Organization for the Abolition of Nuclear Weapons Tests. These were days when the fall-out

[1] JOHN OSBORNE, *Look Back in Anger*, Faber & Faber.

level was climbing steeply. Nobody knew how many were dying as a result but everybody knew somebody was dying. Peggy Duff organized a London March of Women. Werner Pelz, a Lancashire parson and a German refugee, had precipitated a good deal of local concern in the north of England. The sharper and more authentic terror of annihilation was, however, more clearly discernible in the tiny Operation Gandhi which had formed in 1951 with eighteen-year-old Mike Randle and thirteen-year-old April Carter affiliated. Operation Gandhi had held a War Office sit-down as early as 1952 and had followed this up with early demonstrations at Aldermaston and Mildenhall. Tom Driberg, the Labour MP, suggested, on the commencement of British bomb tests, that a boat load of people go and place themselves deliberately in the danger zone. Two Malvern Quakers, Harold and Sheila Steele, volunteered. Harold went but was prevented from embarking in his solitary little boat. On his return he attended a meeting at the YMCA, Great Russell St. Present were Hugh Brock, Bertrand Russell and Spike Milligan, amongst others. They decided on a march and co-opted Pat Arrowsmith from Peggy Duff's organization to arrange it.

The social nucleus of these activities was increasingly the Partisan Coffee House. Set under the library and office of the *Universities and Left Review*, it had a puritan atmosphere that you could cut with a knife. Upstairs were 'good' food, coffee and paintings; downstairs brute furniture, folk sessions, trad jam sessions and political harangues. The notice board was perpetually covered with petitions on an array of subjects that became monotonous, the bomb, the hungry, the death sentence.

The march committee expanded itself. John Berger, Wolf Mankowitz, Michael Tippet, Philip Toynbee, John Braine, George Melly, John Osborne, Linus Pauling, Sydney Silverman were included in its widening ranks. It became called the Direct Action Committee. Its energy and organizing nucleus came from the old Operation Gandhi, Mike Randle, April Carter, Reverend Michael Scott, Pat Arrowsmith. On Good Friday 1958 they gathered in Trafalgar Square for their march to Aldermaston. Bayard Rustin of the NAACP made a speech and a few others made speeches and they set off. The weather was grim. Trad jazz floated out over the sodden Berkshire fields. When they got to the austere secretive place of barbed wire, concrete and little civic lavatories they didn't walk in and smash it up, as some more realistic marchers had hoped, but they did discover that they were not alone. The march had gathered numbers impressively. After all the snarling and planning in shuttered rooms the public response was deliriously encouraging. Denis Knight recalls 'The approach and entry into Reading were the gayest parts of the whole walk. It was a succession of

> 'Oh when the saints, Oh when the saints
> Oh when the saints go marching in!
> Oh Lord, I want to be in that number
> When the saints go marching in!'

and

> 'It's a long way to Aldermaston
> It's a long way to go!'

and

> 'Men and women, stand together
> Do not heed the men of war
> Make your minds up now or never
> Ban the bomb for evermore.'

'All these songs, the variations on old songs and new, the invention of new slogans, and the fun of trying to make them catch on all up and down the column, together with the thought of the approaching town and the knowledge that it was our last night on the march, all helped to quicken the pace and increase the feeling of gaiety and expectancy. In the centre of Reading is a wide and long market street, St Mary's Butts, and this was now packed with people who had turned out to see the fun. It was about half-past five as we entered this square at a very fast pace, with every instrument that could play playing, all mixed up with groups shouting or singing. Above our heads the bells of St Mary's were clanging wildly (we heard later the vicar was giving his bell ringers an extra practice) and the marchers, accompanied by occasional police on foot or in cars, were cheering and counter cheering in turn as they filed past one another until gradually the centre of the square was packed tight, though the column of marchers still entering seemed never to be coming to an end…Shortly after leaving Burghfield, the fields began to wear an aspect less green and pleasant, as we entered a tract of sandy heath that grew nothing but gorse and fir. "Radioactive country" said Christopher…Between the regiments of sour and drab fir, planted up to the very edges of the road, there was moving forward a great mass of men, women and children, four or five or six abreast, in a procession that was probably the longest that English roads have seen these centuries on foot, and was certainly the most purposeful. Its purpose was significant not only for England, but for every other country East and West, because it became clearer with every yard walked that this was more than an old-fashioned peace demonstration, more than a spiritual hunger march. It was felt, as we walked almost in silence through those menacing and monotonous woods, that this was above all a civilizing mission, a march away from fear towards normality, towards human standards, towards the real people in the nursery rhyme whose houses are over the hill but not so far away that we cannot get there by candlelight, whose hands are set to the plough and the making of things…'[1]

Next year the Campaign for Nuclear Disarmament, which had grown out of Peggy Duff's organization as the Direct Action Committee had grown out of Operation Gandhi, joined forces with DAC for the second march and for the next four years the Aldermaston March, reversing its direction from Aldermaston to London, served as a gathering point for the population who wanted to express their disturbance, to comfort themselves that there were perhaps enough people of like mind to be politically effective, to test the potency of their anxieties and ideals in the democracy, and above all to re-instate common decency as the condition of man. No politician in power so much as showed his dribbling nose outside his door or bothered to acknowledge the communications pinned there. So common decency continued to go begging. The teds knew anyway.

The Aldermaston March numbers were vast, by far the

[1] Quoted by CHRISTOPHER DRIVER in *The Disarmers*.

largest ever assembled for political/humanitarian aims. 10,000 at the end of the first march, 20,000 at the end of the second, 100,000 at the end of the third. Furthermore, although teenagers made up by no means the bulk of the marchers, as the square press consistently claimed they did, they nevertheless made each march into a carnival of optimism. The Colyer fans, by now dubbed beatniks, although they differed from the Venice West originals in many important ways, appeared from nowhere in their grime and tatters, with their slogan-daubed crazy hats and streaming filthy hair, hammering their banjos, strumming aggressively on their guitars, blowing their antiquated cornets and sousaphones, capering out in front of the march, destroying the wooden dignity of Canon Collins, Jacquetta Hawkes, Sydney Silverman and other celebrities who were the official leaders of the cavalcade. It was this wild public festival spirit that spread the CND symbol through all the jazz clubs and secondary schools in an incredibly short time. Protest was associated with festivity. There was a new feeling of licence granted by the obvious humanitarian attitude of the ravers themselves…

We thumb a lift ahead of the march. We file into the cheap cafe and we park the instruments and we order egg and chips and sit round the gas fire trying to dry out. I take off a shoe and a sock. Before I can take off the other a marshal comes in and says the march is approaching and they need some music in weather like this. So Dave Aspinwall picks up his trombone and I get my cornet and Mick Wright gets his banjo and we go and stand at the curb in the pissing rain. The column comes near, grey through the grey London rain. We play Didn't He Ramble and we play it again and again and the blood is trickling down Dave's lip and the girls bring out the egg and chips on plates and put them on the pavement by my one bare foot and the rain makes bubble patterns in the grease and we play Didn't He Ramble and the column disappears and what with the rain on the chips and one shoe off and one shoe on and the beautiful girls carrying food and Dave and Mick and me playing Didn't He Ramble, well, that was one of the good times, one of the really good moments if you know what I mean…

A BBC programme at the time, written and produced by René Cutforth, finished with the pertinent observation that perhaps the Aldermaston Marchers were already the only people left alive. They were certainly people who were making a genuine and desperate attempt to rediscover and reinstate the traditional moral virtues of honour and selflessness that had been obliterated at Hiroshima and the young people among them were attempting to make of their leftish romanticism some respectable reality. If it is living to extend an optimistic attitude towards the moralities, then Cutforth was right, for the head-in-the-sand course followed by the rest of the world was a signing-off of decency as it had been understood, was in fact a subconscious contrivance for the only final total peace. CND, with their banjos and banners and good intentions, stood little chance against such a wide-spread and deep-seated death-wish.

The committee at the head of CND, who eventually set up the London office and organized the local branches throughout the country (even throughout the world, for many nations were represented on the Aldermaston marches) so that a secretary and minimal staff could be paid from contributions, were moderate liberals in their approach. Growing to some extent out of the Hydrogen Bomb Campaign and the Labour Party-motivated National Organization for the Abolition of Nuclear Weapons Tests, pivoted around the cautious humanism of Canon Collins and the Labour Party efficiency of secretary Peggy Duff, they were ultimately embarrassed by the very different approach of the Direct Action Committee and their own following of unwashed extremists. If CND grew by the infectious enthusiasm of the beatnik group, it grew under the auspices of comparatively cosy-minded people who had *not* come to maturity with the certainty of uncertainty twisting in their guts, who had not acknowledged the vacuum where the future used to be. They were squares, hardworking well-meaning squares, whose particular refuge was in the lie of socialist progress. The campaign, for them, far from being a cry of emergency, was just the next step in the developing pattern of socialism. When committee-member Michael Foot was asked if he would vote for an anti-bomb conservative rather than a pro-bomb labourite, he replied 'Certainly not!'

Thus they aimed at having their views aired effectively in parliament by the time-honoured, bourgeois methods of keeping your nose and collar clean. It was at the height of CND's colossal numerical power that the CND committee gently edged the whole organization towards protest not only against the bomb, but against hunger, old age pensions and the whole gamut of socialist grievances. Thus they destroyed the universality of the organization in which Conservatives had marched with Communists, Roman Catholics with Anarchists, *Crossbow* with the *Universities and Left Review*, by that gross crudity of the perceptions which made them unable to distinguish between humanity which is a biological species, evolutionarily threatened, and socialism which is a point of view, politically engaged. With that same desolate puritanism carried to an even further degree they banned funny hats on the march and hired official bands to play instead of the old anarchic assemblies of banjos and punctured euphoniums. When a kid was nabbed pinching a beer mug along the Aldermaston route his mother received a letter from the secretary complaining of her son soiling the CND image and exacting a contribution in recompense. The Irish clergy could scarcely have done better. The division between the political standpoint and the creative impulse couldn't have been more graphically displayed, nor the poverty of the former and the necessity of the latter more clearly illustrated than in the consequent long, slow death of CND. So devitalized was it, even six short months after its biggest Trafalgar Square turnout, that when Frank Cousins and his Transport and General Workers Union turned in a block unilateralist vote at the Labour Party Conference in Scarborough in 1960, that should and could have decided the Labour Party's defence policy, they permitted the twittering Gaitskell to overrule the vote by evoking an antiquated clause from the rules of conference procedure and even, in some cases, shed a tremulous tear at Gaitskell's 'fight, fight and fight again to save the Party we love'. They even mourned his death.

The Committee of 100 centred around Bertrand Russell and was, finally, the facelift bestowed on the Direct Action Committee by American Ralph Schoenman. DAC had already followed up the first Aldermaston march with demonstrations at the nuclear rocket bases at Swaffham and Pickenham. Their method and attitude was markedly different from that of CND. They were young and ran on a screaming moral hunger. To hear Mike Randle, Pat Arrowsmith or George Clarke speak to a crowd was not to hear socialist platitudes in an anti-nuclear disguise but to hear young human beings speaking from their own anguish and necessity, from themselves and not from the book. Furthermore the Committee was intelligent about politicians having realized that politics is, by now, not a persuasion but a profession and is therefore not susceptible to argument, merely to power.

Taking the example of Gandhi and the ideas of Thoreau, with a long nominal roll of celebrities, they carried out a wide and successful programme of civil disobedience. This, like CND, gathered numbers and momentum. The first demonstration was a mass sit-down outside the Ministry of Defence. No one was arrested. There was a good moment when Bertrand Russell, like some diminutive elfin emperor, walked away from the Ministry door where he had pinned his message. His face was grim and gothic. A tousled youth in jeans and combat jacket careened down the pavement to the kerb and roared in hoarse cockney 'Good ol' Bertie' and Russell's face swathed itself in beatific glee like a child with a very special present. For me the whole thing meant the sensation of openly stepping outside the law. No secretive thieving, this. No back-alley punch-ups. An open and formal gesture to indicate just where I stood with regard to the good old kindly British bobby.

There were further sit-downs but fines remained low and the occasional prison sentences lighter than they might have been. The establishment hoped that its old weapons of patronization ('They're really very touching') and ridicule ('Hope they all get wet bottoms') would work. The real test, not only of the Committee, CND, the trad-fan idealism, but of traditional morality itself and its continued virility under post-Hiroshima conditions, came on September 17, 1961, Battle of Britain Day, when the Metropolitan Police forbade the use of Trafalgar

Square for a meeting and cordoned it off. This measure was, in itself, a sign that the Committee was drawing blood. The blood ran free when the police cordon proved ineffective and, long hours after the demonstrations had been planned to end, police officers, violent and frightened by this time, were still tumbling demonstrators into the vans and driving them off to be booked. Randle and Clarke were imprisoned.

The government was shaken. The police had been shown to be ineffectual, ridiculous and brutal. There was one thing that saved the squares and their death-wish in the months following the September sit-down and that was the squareness and death-wish of the demonstrators themselves. Rather than carry the awful weight of reorganizing the defence and appropriating power, rather than face themselves in the realization of their own minds and bodies, for better or worse, the Committee immediately avoided the issue by dissipating its force over the same wide area as CND to encompass world health, wild life preservation, care of ancient monuments and so on. The next demonstration emasculated itself by dividing its only real strength, its numbers, between Ruislip and Weathersfield. Despite the almost impossible grit of Pat Arrowsmith, with her attempt to get Liverpool dockers to black war goods, a grit which carried her through jail and jail and jail again, through forced feeding and God knows what other vileness, despite the sheer guts of Randle and Clarke and Terry Chandler and Pat Pottle and all the others who did prison sentences, despite the RSG exposure (RSGs are bomb shelters for the privileged), the Spies for Peace programme and Pat Pottle's short-lived outlawry, despite Shoenman's fanaticism and Russell's continuing clarity of definition, the Committee of 100 went into decline.

They said from the plinth it had been the biggest of the marches. We marched on from Trafalgar Square to Grosvenor Square and sat in the road. There were some noisy exchanges with the police. Now we are sitting in a pub sharing two half-pints between five. All but me are teenagers. They are cynical teenagers. It wasn't easy to climb out of despair and try the old moralities. They are cynical, sophisticated kids. It hasn't come

51

easy, addressing banal brown envelopes, systematically door-to-dooring throughout the previous year. We sit in the pub and the dusk light falls across their faces. They have sacrificed a lot, have come out of vital protective shells of isolation. They have walked three days and risked arrest again and again. They have been ignored again, snubbed. In the half-lit pub I can see profound hatred for the organized world instill itself in their very flesh like poison.

What remains of the anti-bomb movement? The Committee still exists and is still active but activities cling to traditional patterns, march, banner, sit-down, which are known to be safe and ineffective. Occasional excursions into Provo-type activities like those at Brighton where a church service at which the Prime Minister was present was interrupted, have fallen comparatively flat. The Bertrand Russell Peace Foundation has done little but organize an art show that lost money and a top-name jury on Vietnam. CND has tried to enliven the Easter picnic with Mike Kustow's Chinese-inspired satirical puppet plays. The Anarchists, a professedly violent group, including young extremists and older veterans of the twenties and thirties when Rocker was more than a myth have been promisingly troublesome.

Nevertheless, the eyes of the demonstrators no longer look at the public with defiance and hurt but at one another in a slimy masochism of mutual congratulation. And the eyes of the public smile fondly, the danger over from this quarter, the suicide programme still uninterrupted and well under way. The ideals and the morals proved false. They are perceptible now in the voices and manners of the pacifists, as a memory, wistful, despicably fatalistic.[1]

[1] Since the time of writing, the violent demonstrations of German students, Polish students and English Viet Cong sympathisers have done much to dispel the fond smile of the public, who now are inclined to use CND marches as an example of the kind of demonstration they find tolerable.

III

A glance through the list of the early Committee of 100 (a list that changed as various members withdrew to prison or pessimism) shows more writers than politicians. John Braine, Arnold Wesker, John Osborne, Doris Lessing, were among many who served their brief time on the nominal roll. In fact one of the techniques of the anti-bomb movement, sheer name-dropping, could have served as an early warning to young activists that these people were fatally and unalterably square.

The protesting writers were all, more or less, representative of the direction English writing had taken as a result of the climate of opinion in the fifties. Earth-yearning and prole-petting did little harm to jazz. Modernists, aware of Parker and of the necessity for total pragmatism, continued to develop jazz as a vital practice. But the self-conscious arts, what might be called the Cultured Arts, reflected the trend to the exclusion of art itself. It was the dark night of the kitchen sink.

Not that there's anything wrong with plays, novels, poems and paintings about working class life. Art can use any subject matter it chooses, one is as good as another. The danger, indeed the sickness, was the subjection of art to morality, the concept that a certain demonstrable moral attitude unambiguously expressed in the content of art was the paramount aim, at whatever cost to the intrinsic vitality and aesthetic validity of the work itself as a fetishistic object. Even this can be obliquely productive of exciting work. Swift, Mayakovsky, Brecht are obvious examples. So it was in the fifties. Osborne's plays, Hinde's and Sillitoe's novels, some of the poetry of Larkin, Gunn and Hughes, and subsequently Porter, MacBeth, Lucie-Smith and a number of others, have produced writing which is, to say the least, not negligible. Porter, Brock and

MacBeth particularly have reached certain points of penetrating vision which are only possible in provincial literature.

What was totally damaging about the trend was the dictatorial criticism which propagated and accompanied it. This criticism was a piece of opportunism on the part of left-wing academics, often of working class origin, whose access to the middle class and intellectual life of any sort had been through the universities. Until the mid-fifties such minds, confronted with creative writing of the kind that had become internationally prevalent in the twentieth century, were in a cul-de-sac. Their much-revered university training, so highly esteemed in their working-class homes ('Ee, Mrs 'Oggart, I 'ear yower Dick's goin' t' university') had given them certain much-revered skills in political ethics and semantic analysis. These skills were as useless in coming to terms with Joyce, Faulkner, Pound, Lorca, Breton, Benn, as they were in coming to terms with Picasso or Webern. All the new academic could do when confronted with art was hide behind a salon-platitude ('My God, how tactile!') or frankly bleat 'I don't know what it means'.

Many such minds, however, were well positioned in the press, the universities and publishing, to construct a criticism which might discard literature, or at least the thing literature had become; which could reconstruct literature according to a pattern in which there was a secure and easily fulfilled function for the new academic, a seemly literature which contained its emotions and subjugated itself to the more trustworthy principles of philosophy and ethics. The fifties morality test provided the opportunity and they took it.

Prime-movers in this gigantic confidence trick were Robert Conquest, Donald Davie, John Wain, Kingsley Amis and Kenneth Tynan. More original thinkers, like Colin Wilson, Stuart Holroyd, and Bill Hopkins were picked up for their working class origins and then dropped like hot pennies for their right-wing sympathies. They were no great loss. Their actual performance was scarcely preferable to that of the Left—not just pedestrian, club-footed.

It's perhaps in the theatre that the concept rose to gigantic proportions. With Tynan, who threw Wilson, Amis, Osborne and Wain together and called them the 'Angry Young Men', with Tynan as wonder boy theatre critic of the *Observer*, that newspaper gained remarkable propagandist power. The anti-bomb youngsters devoured the liberal press with an almost indecent appetite. The *Observer* responded, pushing its gimmicks remorselessly. At one time it seemed impossible to read the *Observer*, *Guardian* or *Statesman* without the subject of the column, from cooking to foreign affairs, being related, by some devious perambulation, to Amis' philistine hero Lucky Jim.

Osborne, being an artist, went on to other things. Behan and Delaney made their brief curtsies at Stratford East, both of them upstaging the real talent of Joan Littlewood. Arnold Wesker took up the flaming torch of romantic socialism. His spaniel-eyed trilogy was surely the clearest case possible of 'I want you all to be free—my way', with nasty overtones of 'All men are equal and anybody who disagrees is inferior'.

That Wesker, more than any other, was putting the moral cart before the creative horse became clearer than ever when he abandoned his potential as a playwright to concentrate on his Centre 42 project. No sooner had he publicized his idea of bringing art to the workers than it was put to the test when he was invited to produce a chain of arts festivals throughout the Midlands. That the festivals happened, and on remarkably short notice, is very much to Wesker's credit. Also to his credit is his truly fantastic altruism. Very little else is to his credit.

In a room in Birmingham Art Gallery adjacent to the gallery where Epstein's Lucifer stands, his majestic wings and penis casting a fine irony on the proceedings, a number of actors are miming to music. The mime is anti-war. The music is modern, not serial but angular and discordant. The music is played by a section from a symphony orchestra. They play it very well. They wear evening dress. The mime is mimed by dedicated young men. They mime it very nicely. They wear black leotards. The whole is witnessed by a handful of local labour-party members with their wives, who stay throughout in order to prove that they are equal. They look a little worn, as if a whole week of sitting for hours nursing a secret longing for 'Lilac Time' has begun to take its toll.

In the ballroom of Ansell's Brewery, down the road, a swing band comprising most of the top London session-men is running smoothly through a series of ultra-competent Basie pastiches by Tommy Watts. Dancing is sparse. Shop stewards steer their sequinned wives proudly and cautiously across the disinfected floor. The bar is crowded. There is that atmosphere of brilliantine and beer that identifies a real working class dance. The young people, however, are mostly in the bar adjacent to the dance floor. They are trying to look as though they are enjoying themselves. The music is not theirs however, and only the assurance of their union official that it is better than theirs prevents them pushing off down the road to the Bijou. Wesker and a group of his friends are drinking in one corner. A shrill Central European accent and a self-regarding ULR blah ride prettily above the singsong of Midland voices. The olive complexions stand out among the beer-flushed pinks of the locals. An anti-semitist sneer flickers subtly around the faces of a group of teds. Elsewhere in the city Bob Davenport and a crowd of fellow folk singers are clearing the public bars at a brisk rate.

Since the last of the festivals Wesker addressed himself to setting up an art centre in London. After a great deal of further dedication he acquired a vast railway shed in Chalk Farm, called it Centre 42 and proceeded to drum up funds for its decoration and appointment. This took a long time and for years the gaunt majestic premises, with its smoky wood and gothic cast-iron, stayed unused. Wesker felt very broken up about it.

Gradually, however, the artists broke in. Starting with the *International Times* birthday party in September 1966 it became the scene of a series of light-and-sound raves which gave the place a very healthy notoriety, the very antidote needed for that air of preciosity that the festivals had acquired for Wesker and his projects. But it was no good. Wesker was embarrassed. Like Peggy Duff he didn't want anybody snotting up his image with the Labour Party. A recent report in the anarchist newspaper *Freedom* shows what happened: 'On

July 20, Mrs Wilson gave a tea party at No. 10 Downing Street, to raise the money for Centre 42 to buy the freehold of the Roundhouse at Chalk Farm. When the party was over, the money was there. So it seems that at last Arnold Wesker's plans for purveying culture to the masses will go ahead. The first phase of development will be to convert the building for use as a rehearsal hall for three London symphony orchestras. The cost—£8,000—is to be paid by the Arts Council. The Centre hopes to open in two years' time with its own theatre company, ballet rehearsal rooms, opera, writers' workshops etc. For me, the whole scheme makes a grim and sad contrast to the use the Roundhouse was put to during the last two weeks of July.

'The building is Victorian, functional, magnificent and extremely shabby. The roof leaks in several places, the floor is covered in dust, the yard is full of junk. There, for two weeks, we heard lectures by some of the most revolutionary thinkers in the western world, we sang mantras with Allen Ginsberg, we rebelled, we organized, we talked, we learned how to get high on oxygen, how to get stoned on human communication. Several people brought sleeping bags and actually lived there. The local kids, too, wandered in and made themselves at home. A huge swing had been hung from the gallery, and kids and grown-ups swung and climbed. One afternoon, when a large audience was sitting waiting for Herbert Marcuse to arrive for a lecture, the kids settled themselves on the platform; one urchin took the microphone and announced that he would now recite some of his own verses. He did so, to enthusiastic applause.

'On the last day a gang of kids appeared with some hollyhocks each about six foot tall: goodness knows where they'd nicked them from but they made a splendid parade around the hall, and gave a hollyhock away to anyone who wanted one, saying they could easily get more.

'Meanwhile, the grown-ups also played. A pedal organ in one corner was in constant use. Impromptu poetry recitals were held. Poems were pinned up on the wall, and were joined by a set of charcoal drawings. Someone discovered an old piano frame in the yard and began playing it with two sticks:

others joined in with metal pipes, milk crates, tin cans and produced a mind-blowing sound. At odd moments people played flutes, banjos, recorders. Another time a middle-aged Dane announced that he felt like dancing: he danced, someone played a tambourine, others clapped or beat a rhythm on the hollow iron pillars.

'I doubt if Centre 42 will see as much real creativity in ten years as we saw in these two weeks of the "Dialectics of Liberation" congress. And I doubt if, when the roundhouse has become Arnold Wesker's People's Palace of Culture, the local Chalk Farm kids will come within spitting distance of it. Or if they do, it will probably be to break a window or chalk rude words on the newly smart walls, not to recite poems and hand out flowers.'[1]

Wesker is a microcosm of the pathetic errors of the Left. Art terrifies him as it terrifies the establishment. It terrifies him because it takes place outside any containing anticipatable mores. It is defined by its acknowledgement of the unforseeable. If values are complete art dies. Art lives when values melt and present a situation of opportunity instead of certainty. As future, particularly since Hiroshima, is an uncertainty, art is that human practice best defined to cope with it, being the most thoroughly addressed to it. A practice which has the limitlessness of opportunity so centrally placed in its functioning is guaranteed to give Wesker and any other leftist agoraphobia. So Wesker makes use of exactly the same gelding iron as the establishment, the museum. He uses only that art which is accepted or acceptable. He uses only the respectable, or that which can be rendered acceptable by scholastic objectification, the museum routine (thus Picasso, the most violent of artists, has somehow been rendered acceptable; thus also Stravinsky).

The festivals were remarkable for their air of nothing taking place *initially*, nothing being presented that hadn't been tested and double tested, nothing being dared in the arts themselves and therefore no art, only Art, no culture, only Culture. And you don't have to be a drunken navvy to throw up in the face of that lot.

[1] A. M. FEARON in *Freedom*, 25 August 1967.

IV

Anti-nuclear protest was one thing that passed across the Atlantic the other way, East to West. It took root and grew fairly easily in the memory of the New Deal, the Depression, the Wobblies and the McCarthy Committee, which last probably did more than any other single body to reawaken left-wing feeling in America. The Peacemakers, using the same march-and-banner techniques as CND, organized themselves and began to be active. There were sit-down demonstrations and some people, including the poet Ed Sanders, swam out into New York harbour to try and board Polaris-carrying submarines. Some were arrested and some jailed.

Bob Dylan, following Jack Elliot and the openly Communist Pete Seeger, popularized protest songs to such a degree that it was forgotten fairly quickly that his style, like Seeger's and Elliot's, was lifted directly from the Oakie singer of the thirties, Woody Guthrie. Dylan had an effectively glamorous image. He was a sort of bad-tempered pixie. He became the early model for the English singer, Donovan, whose sharp lyrics fall short of the wit and vitality of Dylan's writing. The creative brilliance of Dylan's writing and his profound sourness of delivery was the first sign that popular music was transcending its commercial situation. Joan Baez and Julie Felix became the prima donnas of protest.

Although the same symbol was adopted the American movement was, from the start, broader in its aims than CND. The bomb became just one item amidst the violent actualities of the Negro civil rights programme. Martin Luther King and his followers demonstrated with dogged courage all over the South. Bayard Rustin, an original Direct Action Committee member, organized his massive but ineffective march on Washington. When Kennedy ordered integration in education Mississippi University and the schools of Little Rock, Arkansas, became focal points of the dispute. Demonstrators were murdered. Little children burned. After events like this, coupled with the way in which the Vietnam war has been conducted, Johnson's overseas bodyguard is no paranoiac gesture. Norman Morrison soaked himself with petrol and burned himself on the steps of the Pentagon in protest against the Vietnam war. After the stunned humiliation following this event, the question nevertheless arose—Would it perhaps have taken greater courage to set fire to the President? A body of men who sleep soundly on a daily programme of sanctioned mass-murder are surely only disturbed by personal danger.

The American movement also addressed itself to lifting the crushing weight of American sexual hypocrisy. Here it directly varied with the English movement. It would be ludicrous to see Ed Sanders' Gobble Poems printed in *Peace News*—'and the monster cock/made consuela's/mouth/taut//& round/ as a peace-button'.

The university at Berkeley, California, became the fermenting core of the protest movement. Peter Beagle describes how much more closely the American kids lived to the uncountenanceable facts: 'sometime after dinner, sam got to talking about people we have both known in berkeley four or five years ago. I must have started him off by asking about this one or that one; the summer of 1961, spent in berkeley, was a strange, wandery one, during which I floated down waterfalls reading a book and drifted round and round the edges of the whirlpools thinking that only my writer/s eye detected a certain uneasiness in the water. I made two or three good friends that summer, in spite of myself, and brushed against more odd souls than ever before or since. I wonder about them still, and ask for news of them, listening as sam talks for news of myself, then and now.

'much of what he told me was old stuff to sam—this happened a year ago, this guy hasn/t been by since last winter—but I live eighty miles from berkeley and don/t mind my tidings mouldy. he spoke of ray fisher, once the unanointed king of the folk guitarists along the hippie axis, which runs from berkeley to the village by way of denver, madison, ann arbor, and cambridge. when I met ray he couldn't have been over eighteen:

a skinny kid with the bob dylan look before it had the name—depending on the shadow and the moment, he looked like an avenging angel, a bull dyke, and harpo marx. run away from home in newark at the age of fourteen or so and on the road ever since, "playing on the corners for gay gas money and looking for songs in the scary backwoods", as an israel young blurb about him in *sing out* once ran. there was a brief stopover at the university of michigan, and I think that/s where he really learned to play the guitar; most of ray/s teachers were probably the same dazzling kids I saw in berkeley—pale teenagers, expressionlessly picking their new york martins with unbelievable skill and sureness. the bass driving, the treble strings singing and stinging. in time I understood that most of it was technique and most of that nothing but motor reflexes. there were only a few real musicians. ray was one of them...

'when I was first in berkeley pot was so common I forgot it wasn/t legal, and I don/t think I was the only one. not everybody turned on regularly, but the stuff was always around seemingly no more in need of a pusher than love in eden. I remember sweet young hostesses passing butts out after dinner, like dessert...in a world of beautiful toys that demanded nothing from you, getting hooked was considered pretty square...

'but that was almost five years ago, and either the scene/s changed or I just didn/t know. ray/s been shooting up for some time, sam told me, the real stuff, the killers. they had him in jail for a while..when he got out it was the same as before, and there is still the trial to face, and his wife is divorcing him.

(I wonder what she was like, that pretty little ghost I saw in a photograph once. who would marry ray? someone told me she was a female ray with an MA in philosophy—but what does that mean? I wish I had known her.)

'sam had seen ray a few days before, for about ten minutes. "I think he was high. I asked him about the trial, and he said, man, I ain/t going to jail, cause I feel too good, and he floated on out again."

'and the girls! the girls of the class of '61, the lovely young girls who came out to berkeley looking for trouble. most of them were far above the average for intelligence and looks, and for that wary wit which is sometimes called hipness. they seemed assured of real lives, wanting to spend a little time luxuriating in their own potential before they started walking one way or the other. I grew dizzy sometimes, savoring them in carload lots—they were all so pretty, and so well-equipped.

'but what happened to them?...there is a bit that girls do, a pattern that I have almost come to expect of the brightest and most aware of them. it varies a great deal, but it nearly always includes these two constants: a complete lack of center of control (which must be why there are so many of them forever sort of going to school); and a strange search for degradation, for the grubbiest kinds of mess and misery. the wrong man always always; the drinking, the abortions, and now the drugs, the bit.'[1]

Nevertheless, protest constituted the same test of ideals as in Britain, and being idealist, even regarding Negro emancipation, created a direct difficulty for the hipster, whose already developed resistance was essentially elliptical, subversive, dependent on the chameleon fluctuations of a nerve whose sensitivity would be shattered by the frontal techniques of mass demonstration. Mailer puts the dilemma in the words of his character Shago Martin: 'Contemplate this. I did the Freedom Rider bit. Like I was running for President of the blackass U.S.A. That's the Dick Gregory bit, not mine, but I did it. I did it. And I mean I got nothing but elegance to sell, plus a big beat. And that big beat comes from up High, it don't come from me, I'm a lily-white devil in a black ass. I'm just the future, in love with myself, that's the future. I got twenty faces, I talk the tongues, I'm a devil, what's the devil doing on a Freedom Ride? Why, you seen my act, I remember you, you brought your wife back to me, that battleship with the pearls around her neck, you think I forget, I got elegance, man, and elegance is nothing but memory. I mean I got elegance when I do my act...'[2]

James Baldwin, writing *The Fire Next Time* saved his elegance with threats. That his threats have been carried out in the bonfires of Watts, Detroit and Newark, may or may not

[1] PETER BEAGLE in *Klactoveedsedsteen*, no. 3, May 1966.
[2] NORMAN MAILER, *An American Dream*, André Deutsch, 1965.

make a point about the prophetic potency of elegance. In any case potency is very much at stake, beyond equality, in the Negro struggle. The acceleration from claims for human rights to claims of black supremacy is a heroic attempt on the part of the American Negro to disinherit Uncle Sam's pathetic impotence.

The American Anarchist movement, centred around Bernard Marzalek and his Chicago bookstore and the New York Black Mask group has, for some time, been drumming the hard and hip fact that liberal idealism and beat mysticism will not save the sinking boat in time, that violence is the only realistic measure in political protest, politics being a power structure and force being the pivot on which power rests. Thus they champion the Black Power movement of Stokeley Carmichael and his predecessor Malcolm X. They also keep a clear head about the nature of art. Their manifesto reads: 'Rejecting, totally, the political, theological, literary, philosophical and academic assumptions which hinge our society to the withered refrigerator of civilization (and which are in any case, rooted in the stupidity of class interest) and insisting, moreover, on our own irresistible emotional autonomy, we find it essential to *affirm*, here and now, without reservation and at any price, the marvellous red and black validity of *absolute revolt*, the only attitude worthy of survival in the present millenium of streets and dreams.

'More than ever, with everything continuously at stake, we find it necessary to affirm the impassioned use of the most dangerous weapons in the arsenal of freedom:

'MAD LOVE: totally subversive, the absolute enemy of bourgeois culture;

'POETRY: (as opposed to literature) breathing like a machine gun, exterminating the blind flags of immediate reality;

'HUMOUR: the dynamite and guerrilla warfare of the mind, as effective in its own domain as material dynamite and guerrilla warfare in the streets (when necessary, however, rest assured: we shall use every means at our disposal);

'SABOTAGE: ruthless and relentless destruction of the bureaucratic and cultural machinery of oppression.

'It is necessary, at times (and this is one of them) to speak bluntly: we affirm deliriously and simply TOTAL LIBERATION OF MAN. Long live the Negros of Watts, the Puerto Ricans of Chicago, the Provos of Amsterdam, the Zengakuren of Japan and the youth of all countries who burn cop cars in the streets and demonstrate by these exemplary manifestations that the struggle for freedom cannot be guided by the rulebooks of priests and politicians!!

'Long live the New Guinea tribe who, aware of the stupidity of technological civilization, massacred the managers of a washing-machine factory, took over the building and converted it into a temple for the marvellous but elusive Rabbit-god!!

'Long live the youth of Fairbanks, Alaska, who, after being forbidden by law to drop out of school, retaliated by burning down the school-house!!

'Long live the lunatic who escaped from an asylum and calmly robbed a downtown bank only to have his "sane" brother tell the man!! Long live Barry Bondhus of Big Lake, Minnesota, who dumped two buckets of shit into the file drawers of his draft board!!! Long live the twelve Fort Lauderdale, Florida, teens who prevented by their schools from meaningful experimentation, independently began manufacturing LSD, two sizes of plastic bombs, smoke bombs and a varied and catalytic assortment of revolutionary hardware!! Long live the Incredible Hulk, wildcat strikers, the Nat Turner Insurrection, high-school drop-outs, draft-dodgers, deserters, delinquents, saboteurs and all those soul-brothers, wild-eyed dreamers, real and imaginary heroes of defiance and rebellion who pool their collective resources in the exquisite, material transformation of the world according to desire!!!

'The lucidity of alley apples and broken bottles have replaced autumn leaves—the crushing subservience to authority scorched by molotov cocktails of fantastic destruction, and, far from finally, the expressionless caress has been deliciously transcended by the touch that stimulates to unheard of heights the sensuous pores of the only dynamism that matters. As liberated souls (and we are, for our quest cannot be stopped now) we have necessarily an historically enviable role as cosmic architects armed with hammers, electric guitars, and apocalyptic visions, but more significantly, armed with the exhilarating knowledge that we are able to crush systematically all obstacles placed in the way of our desires and build a new EVERYTHING.

> 'Signed, Surrealist Group.
> The Rebel Worker Group, Chicago.
> Anarchist Horde.'[1]

The London Anarchist magazines *Cuddon's* and *Heatwave* echo this admiration for the Negro rioters, the only demonstrators whose protest has proved more than masochistic, as their admiration is indeed reflected in the recently bullet-shattered windows of the American Embassy. Just what the Revolutionary Solidarity Movement is, or who the precise members of the May I Group are, is unknown, but besides gunning the American Embassy in London they also planted a couple of well-placed bombs in the Greek and Bolivian Embassies in Bonn. Issue 7 of *Black Mask* has some subtle points to make about the Negro riots. It quotes Governor Hughes from an interview with *Time*: 'The thing that repelled me most was the holiday atmosphere...it's like laughing at a funeral' he had said, after touring the ravaged streets; and it quotes the *New York Times* for 16.7.67: 'At times, amidst the scenes of riot and destruction that made parts of the city look like a battlefield, there was an almost carnival atmosphere'.

That carnival atmosphere in the midst of social metamorphosis is the very living breath of culture. With such a breath the internationally organized Vietnam demonstrations in the autumn of 1967 with their commendable violence and their astute organization (CND beginning to look her lovely self again perhaps) may have been the beginning of a revitalized protest movement. As it was they achieved little more constructive than the arrest of Norman Mailer and Doctor Spock.[2]

---

[1] Manifesto published in *Heatwave*, no. 2, October 1966.

[2] Since the time of writing protest has, of course, revitalized itself in a wave of international riots, all of which have been informed by a certain air of gaiety, beginning with the Pentagon march.

III
Art

Disaffiliation is the celibacy of the artist whereby he becomes the oracle to whom society can always and only turn.

I

The future is a void. In these days this seems particularly apparent. The only way to deal with void is by a game of chance, some absurd pattern of behaviour. The complete void of the future reveals the fallacy of logic and rationality. The void is infinite and thus absurd. Consequently the only human activities which can be of any use in one's progress into infinite void are absurd practices.

The games are called magic, original ceremonial, more recently are called art. From the silly dances and arbitrary patterns, from the gesture, which by special definition has no reference whatsoever to values previously maintained, by the shot in the dark, the step into the void, from those routes which scorn all reference points, there come objects and experiences which themselves in turn serve as reference points and values for society. Thus Giotto, painting Christ's halo in three-quarter-view perspective, ignoring the allegorical laws of Byzantine art, made patterns which inadvertently brought God down to earth again and led to a vast number of consequent axioms, reference points, values attached to the humanist persuasion. Giotto drew the halo in perspective not because he believed in humanism but because it looked good, it worked, and it was new.

With humanism developed into a civilization of crude technology, however, a rediscovered Giotto could serve as a touchstone to the Deist persuasion. His work would serve equally well in the opposite direction. A well-constructed fetish co-ordinated perfectly in all subliminal terms, a step into the void danced well, a cat's cradle sharply slung, it would serve, like any other tool, to spin man's thought and self-organization into whatsoever course it next must follow. The destination, as far as art is concerned, is the journey itself. Art keeps the thing moving. The only true disaster is the end of the journey, the end of man and his development. This is what we are currently threatened with. It is not the first time we have been threatened with extinction but it is the first time extinction has been probable. If we get out and on, it will be by art, as always.

Art divided from society more radically than previously at the end of the eighteenth century, sensing, as it inevitably must, the enormity of the consequences of an exclusively techno-logical civilization, preparing the attitudes and standards of the young people one hundred and fifty years thence. Art is knit to society by religion. If religion becomes non-religion, corrupt, then art, in order to remain art, must divide itself off from society.

At the end of the eighteenth century religion got found out. It was systematically revealed that organized bodies of worship had ossified into authoritarian hierarchies which defended exploitation and oppression in terms of the divinity of the social order. For man to be free God, King, and the Pope had to be dethroned. The main impact of Romanticism was that the carpet-slippered dreamers, the contemplators of sublime landscape, of desolate streams, Alpine blizzards and Arabic blood-orgies, had shifted the onus of wonderment and vitality from the state and the church to the direct communion between man and Nature. The derogation of the Spanish court in Goya's portraits increased in direct ratio to the intensification of his manic visions of the organic darkness. The sweet harmony of Natural man depicted in the works of the Ancients, Palmer, Calvert and Richmond, was obstructed by Rintrah, Blake's symbol of Tory High Church authority. The means back to Eden was the obliteration of that moral restriction imposed by church, army and police, in the name of God—the murder of the priest who 'bound with briars the joys and desires'. And the destructive power necessary was Orc, Blake's spirit of revolutionary energy; Orc, who would 'sooner murder an infant in its cradle than nurse unacted desires'. Morality was the province of church and hierarchy the prime weapon of control and power. The only true mean-ing of the Sublime was the sublimity of man and the only rightful province of man was the Sublime. Morality preached humble contentment and submission. Thus it stabilized the power of the privileged and emasculated the power of mankind.

But when Orc triumphed, seemingly, and the heads of the French divine authorities dropped into the basket, what resulted was not a conjoining with the organic Sublime but a new subjugation of the individual to a shifting bureaucracy whose principles of imposed equality and justice proved just as obstructing. Politics, pure politics, lost no time in showing its faults. It may have been what the power-movers and political thinkers of the French Revolution had meant but it was not what the artists, the Romantics, Rousseau, Sand, Hugo, Lamartine, Delacroix, Chopin, Liszt, Shelley had meant at all.

The end of the eighteenth century, when God was dethroned, was followed, for the artist, by the early nineteenth century when politics were discredited. Both royalty and republic subjected man to society, the one in the name of divinity, the other in the name of justice. The artist found himself alienated from society by something more fundamental than his traditional eccentricity.

The Romantics were in something of a dilemma as regards terms and fidelities. Their rebellious spirit, their concept of men equal under the face of Nature rather than appointed under the divine rights of kings, their flamboyant advocation of liberty and their love of the wild vitality of the proletariat, had provided the zeitgeist that carried the revolution through and put Europe in a turmoil of political discontent. But their motivating appetite was for the Sublimity of Nature. With God dethroned any pursuit of sublimity was vaguely directed. Their aggressive amorality threw their indignation in the face of the oppressors into mazes of paradox. Their advocacy of the Rights of Man was offset by the Romantic Bohemian temperament to which all the bureaucratic controls through which alone the Rights of Man could be ensured were unacceptable.

Such political vagueness was ultimately, however, the means to the preservation of their integrity. Without it they might have become, like the painter David frequently was, mere propagandists of the State. As it was their vagueness gave them leeway to step aside into their Bohemian ghettoes and continue to practise art. Throughout the nineteenth century artists subverted the State and oscillated between prostration before and sovereignty over Nature. Man being defined not by king and church, much less, as it evolved, by republic, but by the forces of organic energy, both internal and external, then his precise relationship with that energy had to be if not established then neurotically titillated. At the time of the French Revolution a certain deposed fop was writing his curious works. In style they were mannered, naïve and clumsy. Philosophically they constituted a burlesque of relativism. Their author wrote many of them, however, under immense stress during long terms of imprisonment which made his sensibility the very crucible of the conflicting principles of free will and organic energy. The works became obscene tragedies of formidable intensity. The man's name was de Sade.

Battened down in jails and madhouses for much of his life, the tentative deviatory appetites of this man, who was already so imprisoned by the restraints of an aristocratic upbringing that he could only reach orgasm in bellowing discomfort, developed to the demonic force that produced *120 Days of Sodom*. The affectation of the prose and fallacy of the philosophy was transcended in a powerful monument formed from the wrestling elements of energy and pain.

De Sade can readily be seen to be in support of the idea of the state as a mechanism infinitely adaptable to the individual and the idea of the individual as being infinitely free. He believed, for instance, in the right of the individual to murder but not in the right of the state to execute. His repeated creed amounts more or less to this: 'If it exists it's Nature and if it's Nature it should be accommodated in the state'. This initial position differs little from that of the Romantics. Turner stood in such awe of his oceanic sunset that he didn't hesitate to mix with it the blood of jettisoned slaves in *Slave Ship Casting Off The Dead and Dying*. The wild flames which destroyed the Houses of Parliament in his other great painting were the liberating destructive force that would lead the proletariat, banked gawping in the mud across the Thames, into the celestial palaces of truly spiritual government. The Romantic position was largely a masochistic one; salvation lay in being enveloped by the organic. Equality was thus a loss of individual and human identity not in the state but in the Cosmos. As the *120 Days* twist to their abominable peak it becomes clear that de Sade had found that power over Nature, transcendence of the organic, lay in the *un*natural. If the means to conjoining Nature was through the passions freed of church and state, then the means to surmounting Nature was through those passions practised in a way that negated the organic functioning that Nature followed. De Sade's position with regard to Nature was sadistic. Turner, later Rimbaud and Lautréamont, hurled themselves into the grandiloquent storm and hoped there to be absorbed into the Sublime Force. De Sade, and later Nietzsche, Jarry, Jacob, Apollinaire, Picasso, hurled themselves into the Sublime Force and took over.

II

For Baudelaire, de Sade was the 'complete natural man'. By this he meant the man most thoroughly possessed by the amoral forces of Nature. The artists of the irrational tradition submitted so thoroughly to Nature, in the late nineteenth century, that they begat the aesthetics of fragmentation. In the final book of *Maldoror*, in Rimbaud's *Illuminations*, narrative becomes disconnected incident, argument becomes verbal arabesque, description becomes image, image dissolves into the berserk juxtapositions of schizophrenia. De Sade, on the contrary, had moved towards a relentlessly logical pyramidal form. His very perversion, far from being evidence of possession by Nature, indicated his appropriation of the organic flow.

The Impressionists drowned in organic flow. They broke form into juxtaposed colour. The broken brush strokes surged like maggots under Van Gogh's hand into concentric patterns of the organic. Under Monet's hand they blurred and drifted into edgeless dreams of the oceanic. Monet's liquid tides and blots struck echoes on Debussy's de-systemized keyboard, and the echoes died in the silence of total self-immolation. Mallarmé made the pictures for Debussy's silences. It became clear that the dissolution of form as volume was merely the discovery of form as movement, space, colour and time. Thus, in all subsequent developments, the debris of a destroyed tradition proved to be the secure foundation stone of the new. Meanwhile the process of disintegration continued.

'Be drunken, always,' sang Baudelaire. 'That is the point; nothing else matters. If you would not feel the horrible burden of Time weigh you down and crush you to the earth, be drunken continually,'[1] And, as he sang, the organic force of

[1] CHARLES BAUDELAIRE, from *Baudelaire: Rimbaud: Verlaine*, trans. Arthur Symons, Citadel, 1962.

the clap ate him gradually away. 'We are aboard the drunken boat' cried Rimbaud, 'Free, smoking, touched with mists of violet above,/I, who the lurid heavens breached like some rare wall/Which boasts—confection that the goodly poets love—/ Lichens of sunlight on a mucoid azure pall...'[1] But Rimbaud saw the rocks ahead, leapt off at eighteen, and struck out for dry land. 'I would have gone mad', he said. Lautréamont gave himself to his amorous shark and finally did go mad. Huysmans, Wilde, Beardsley and Swinburne toyed perilously and exquisitely with the artificial.

Simultaneously Cézanne painted the images which embodied Nietzsche's ideas. That is, his dictum of 'redoing Poussin from Nature' meant precisely that he wanted to put himself in the same position as Constable or Monet, out there in the weather, grappling face to face with the tangled, oozing, tempestuous monster, not drunk to dissolution despite the Baudelairian lasciviousness of his early work, but appropriating the unbearable sun for the noon dance of Zarathustra— 'Praised be this spirit of all free spirits, the laughing storm which bloweth dust into the eyes of all back-sighted suppurative ones! Ye higher men, what is worst in you is, that none of you hath learnt to dance, as one must dance—to dance beyond yourselves! Raise your hearts, ye good dancers, high! higher! And forget not the good laughter! This crown of rose wreaths—unto you, my brethren, I throw this crown! The laughter I have proclaimed holy. Ye higher men, *learn* how to laugh!'[2]—executing that dance in a violent geometric choreography with the energy of the sun and the strength of the rocks, appropriating the energy by perverting the organic tangle of cypress and mountainside into a riveted structural machine of dynamic rhythm.

Through the rest of the nineteenth and twentieth centuries the aspirants to join nature suffered their traumatic, melancholic disappointments. Valéry comes to the tree in the park, approaches its frantic orgasm of movement, but finishes separate, isolated from Nature as from society—'I have chosen

[1] ARTHUR RIMBAUD, from *Baudelaire: Rimbaud: Verlaine*, trans. Louise Varèse, Citadel, 1962.
[2] FRIEDRICH NIETZSCHE, *Thus Spake Zarathustra*, Penguin.

you, powerful dweller in a park, drunk with your pitching, since the sky exercises you and urges you, O great bow, to give it back language! O, lovingly rivalling the Dryads, may the poet alone caress your polished body as he does the ambitious thigh of the horse!...–No, says the tree, It says: *No*! by the sparkling of its proud head, which the storm universally treats as it does a blade of grass.'[1]

The disappointed poet wandered disconsolate in the park. Verlaine–'In the old, solitary, frosty park two shapes passed by just now. Their eyes are dead and their lips are slack, and their words can hardly be heard. In the old solitary park two ghosts recalled the past. 'Do you remember our old ecstasy?' 'Why will you have me remember it?' 'Does your heart still beat at my mere name? Do you see my soul in dreams?' 'No.' 'Ah! The sweet days of unspeakable happiness when we joined our lips together!' 'It is possible.' 'How blue the sky was and how great our hope!' 'Hope has fled towards the dark sky.' So they walked in the oat grass, and night alone heard their words.'[2] Laforgue–'I am only a lunar reveller making circles in ponds...But where are the moons of yesteryear? And why is God not to be remade?'[2] Stefan George–'Come into the park they say is dead and look...and with this autumnal vision before you gently entwine all that is left of verdant life.'[3] Rilke–'Though the reflection in the pond may often dissolve as we watch it; know the image. Only in the dual realm will the voices be eternal and gentle.'[3]–ultimately Schoenberg, whose Pierrot Lunaire finds in the melancholic moon a scimitar to decapitate his despair. This despair, this unattainability of the organic and eternal, ultimately developed into the twentieth century malaise, the *angst*, Eliot's *Wasteland*–'I sat upon the shore/Fishing, with the arid plain behind me/Shall I set my lands in order?/London Bridge is falling down falling down falling down'[4]–'We are the hollow men/ We are stuffed men...Our dried voices, when/We whisper

[1] PAUL VALERY, from *The Penguin Book of Nineteenth Century French Verse* ed. Anthony Hartley, Penguin.

[2] PAUL VERLAINE and JULES LAFORGUE, from *The Penguin Book of Nineteenth Century French Verse*, ed. Anthony Hartley, Penguin.

[3] STEFAN GEORGE and RAINER MARIA RILKE, from *The Penguin Book of Twentieth Century German Verse*, ed. Patric Bridgwater, Penguin.

[4] T. S. ELIOT, *Collected Poems*, Faber & Faber.

together/Are as quiet and meaningless/As wind in dry grass/ Or rats' feet over broken glass/In our dry cellar'—'This is the way the world ends/This is the way the world ends/This is the way the world ends/Not with a bang but a whimper'[1]—into Kafka's interminable labyrinths, to Becket's desolate beaches, to Gruber's pumiced nudes, to Bacon's ejaculations of disgust. By the year of Hiroshima Sartre had said, with characteristic grit, that he was only interested in what lay beyond despair.

The composer Berg and his friends, painters Kokoschka, Kirchner, Heckel, poets Stadler, Heym and Trakl made the anguish of isolation into a regenerative dynamic. Van Gogh, Munch and Strindberg had done it before them. They created Expressionism.

In Italy the Futurists, Marinetti, Severini, under the Baudelairian guidance of the poet-politician D'Annunzio, attempted a strenuous pantheism of technology, seeing the machine not as the assassin of sublime Nature, as William Morris and D. H. Lawrence saw it, but seeing it as the very emanation of Sublime Energy. Theirs was probably the most aggressive and naive attempt to establish an aesthetic on the preaching of de Sade and Nietzsche. They painted kinetic movement, held concerts using machine sound-patterns, heaped contempt on Italy's cult of the past, and corresponded internationally. Their ideas were adopted fairly directly by Wyndham Lewis, William Roberts, Ezra Pound and Gaudier-Brzeska who called them Vorticism.

The Italian Futurists, under Marinetti, aligned themselves with the Fascists, ultimately. The Russian Futurists, under Mayakovsky, aligned themselves with the Bolsheviks. They heralded the revolution with their wild, disruptive behaviour: 'The "flower of the Russian intelligentsia" was there to a man: famous painters, actors, writers, ministers, deputies, and one high foreign diplomat, namely the French ambassador...I sat at supper with Gorky and the Finnish painter Axel Gallen, and Mayakovsky began his performance by suddenly coming up to us, pushing a chair between ours and helping himself from our plates and drinking out of our glasses. Gallen stared at him spellbound, just as he would probably have stared if a

[1] T. S. ELIOT, *Collected Poems*, Faber & Faber.

horse had been led into the banqueting hall...at that moment Milyukov, our Foreign Minister at the time, rose for an official toast and Mayakovsky dashed towards him, to the centre of the table, jumped on a chair and shouted something so obscene that Milyukov was completely flabbergasted. After a moment, regaining control, he tried to start his speech again, "Ladies and gentlemen..." but Mayakovsky yelled louder than ever, and Milyukov shrugged his shoulders and sat down. The French ambassador rose to his feet. He was obviously convinced that the Russian hooligan would give in to him. What a hope. His voice was drowned by a deafening bellow from Mayakovsky. But this was not all. A wild and senseless pandemonium broke out. Mayakovsky supporters also began to yell, pounding their feet on the floor and their fists on the tables. They screamed with laughter, whined, squeaked, snorted. But suddenly all this was quashed by a truly tragic wail from one of the Finns, a painter, who looked like a clean-shaven sea-lion. Rather drunk, pale as death, he had obviously been shaken to the core by this excess of mis-behaviour, and started to shout at the top of his voice, literally with tears in his eyes, one of the few Russian words he knew: "Mnogo! Mno-go! Mno-go!" (too much, too much...)'.[1]

Twelve short years after the revolution Mayakovsky killed himself. In his suicide note he said: 'There's no need to wake you with telegrams or thunder.'[2]

[1] JOHN LEHMANN, *Memories and Portraits*.
[2] VLADIMIR MAYAKOVSKY, *Poetry and Poverty*, translated and published by Erik Korn, London.

III

For Apollinaire, de Sade was the misunderstood innocent, the ebullient brat who had carried the anal-erotic extravagance of infantile folklore into his adult life and been jailed for it. Morality was, for Apollinaire, the obstruction to innocence:

'Ah! God! how pretty war is with its songs, its long rests. I have polished this ring. The wind is mingled with your sighs.

Farewell! Here is the boot and saddle. He disappeared down a turning and died over there, while she laughed at the surprises of fate.'[1]

In the 1900's and through the 1914-18 war Apollinaire and his friends conducted an explosive party-time of the spirits in Paris. The purpose of the party was the application of the Sadist spirit to culture and conventions. People's beliefs and people's patterns of behaviour were torn up like confetti, burst like party balloons, shattered like furniture in a Keystone movie, and stuck together again (and here lay the movement's disturbing power) not into some makeshift scarecrow but into formal edifices of unprecedented dignity and beauty. 'The plastic virtues, purity, unity and truth, keep Nature in subjugation,' said Apollinaire, and introduced the party:

'So here I am once more among you
I've found my ardent company again
I've also found a stage
But to my dismay found as before
The theatre with no greatness and no virtue
That killed the tedious nights before the war
A slanderous and pernicious art
That showed the sin but did not show the saviour

[1] GUILLAUME APOLLINAIRE, from *The Penguin Book of Twentieth Century French Verse*, ed. Anthony Hartley, Penguin.

Then the hour struck the hour of men
I have been at war like all other men
In the days when I was in the artillery
On the northern front commanding my battery
One night when the gazing of the stars in heaven
Pulsated like the eyes of the newborn
A thousand rockets that rose from the opposite trench
Suddenly woke the guns of the enemy
I remember as though it were yesterday
I heard the shells depart but no explosions
Then from the observation posts there came
The trumpeter on horseback to announce
That the sergeant there who calculated
From the flashes of the enemy guns
Their angle of fire had stated
That the range of those guns was so great
That the bursts no longer could be heard
And all my gunners watching at their posts
Announced the stars were darkening one by one
Then loud shouts arose from the whole army
THEY'RE PUTTING OUT THE STARS
WITH SHELLFIRE

The stars were dying in that fine autumn sky
As memory fades in the brain
Of the poor old men who try to remember
We were dying there in the death of stars
And on the sombre front with its livid lights
We would only say in despair
THEY'VE EVEN MURDERED
THE CONSTELLATIONS
But in a great voice out of a megaphone
The mouth of which emerged
From some sort of supreme headquarters
The voice of the unknown captain who always saves us cried
THE TIME HAS COME TO LIGHT THE STARS AGAIN
And the whole French front shouted together
FIRE AT WILL
The gunners hastened

The layers calculated
The marksmen fired
And the sublime stars lit up again one by one
Our shells rekindled their eternal odour
The enemy guns were silent dazzled
By the scintillating of all the stars
There there is the history of all the stars
And since that night I too light one by one
All the stars within that were extinguished
So here I am once more among you
My troupe don't be impatient
Public wait without impatience
I bring you a play that aims to reform society
It deals with children in the family
The subject is domestic
And that is the reason it's handled in a familiar way
The actors will not adopt a sinister tone
They will simply appeal to your common sense
And above all will try to entertain you
So that you will be inclined to profit
From all the lessons that the play contains
And so that the earth will be starred with the glances of infants
Even more numerous than the twinkling stars
Hear O Frenchmen the lesson of war
And make children you that made few before
We're trying to bring a new spirit into the theatre
A joyful voluptuousness virtue
Instead of that pessimism more than a hundred years old
And that's pretty old for such a boring thing
The play was created for an antique stage
For they wouldn't have built us a new theatre
A circular theatre with two stages
One in the middle and the other like a ring
Around the spectators permitting
But out there there's still a fire
Where they're putting out the smoking stars
And those who light them again demand that you
Lift yourselves to the height of those great flames
And also burn

O public
Be the unquenchable torch of the new fire...'[1]

Alfred Jarry, with his elaborate superstructures of nihilist philosophy called pataphysics, wrote and staged his *Ubu Roi*, a farting knockabout pantomime of the caricatured bourgeoisie, based, like the recent *Macbird*, on the MacBeth plot. Père Ubu, the spluttering apotheosis of all trivial pomposity opens up the play with the first of his frequent exclamations of 'Shit!'—a term then uncommon in serious drama. Jarry himself became utterly involved in his own charade, acted Ubu out of the theatre and into his social life and ultimately became the character to such a degree that no one was certain, least of all Jarry, where the satire ended and masquerade began. Fifty years later the same thing happened with Spike Milligan and his character Eccles.

Max Jacob, heralded somewhat by the fruity imagery of Saint-Pol-Roux, wrote poems of disconnected absurdity: 'A man, a man lost in the middle of trees. Was his mind deranged? He held a standard like a harp embroidered with orange colours. He examines a business deal meticulously or else he carries the coffin of a high personality; he has the air of an Anglican priest, of an angel or a cannibal. He asks for the legendary flower that only grows in Paradise, he has a legendary fortune and does not possess a radish.'[2] The schizophrenic juxtapositions of Lautréamont had been tortured and haunted. The same literary device became, with Jacob and Apollinaire, veritably festive.

Eric Satie wrote the music for this extended party. Jazzy, evocative, brilliant, witty, audacious, it was exactly the dance for the occasion, the appropriate sound to offset Stravinsky's ostentatious dissonances. Diaghilev was in town and, although the extravagant camp of the Ballet Russe was scarcely in the spirit of the Montmartre festivities, Diaghilev had a true impresario's nose for true madness and employed Picasso, Chagall and Stravinsky from among the party guests.

[1] GUILLAUME APOLLINAIRE, 'The Breasts of Tiresias', *The Faber Book of Twentieth Century French Drama*, Faber & Faber.
[2] MAX JACOB, from *The Penguin Book of Twentieth Century French Verse*, ed. Anthony Hartley, Penguin.

The Fauves, the Wild Beasts, plastered on their slabs of unforgivable colour, the pink trees, the vermilion skies; the party exploded into painting. Picasso, sharing a studio with Braque at the Bateau Lavoir, was continuing from Cézanne's Nietszchian beginnings and annihilating the European tradition of art. Gertrude Stein, possibly the greatest poet of the period, in her essay on Picasso, said that in the nineteenth century it became necessary to paint from Nature. In the twentieth century it became necessary not to paint from Nature, which is to say that for Picasso, as for Apollinaire, sovereignty over Nature had been established and, instead of wooing the rapturous sensory experience, he had realized that the greater energy was subjective.

Cézanne had wrestled courageously with the apollonian nude in his classical figure compositions, struggling towards appropriation of the whole Greco-Roman aesthetic. Picasso butchered it with a number of diagonal slashes and stuck masks on the corpses. Thus sculptured and adorned the *Demoiselles d'Avignon* stood stronger than the European tradition that had lasted hundreds of years. It was like scoring a Beethoven quartet for saxophone, kazoo, growl trumpet and cowbell and transforming it into something stronger.

From that point Picasso sailed out on his fantastic voyage. If Rimbaud's drunken boat careened the more severely in the twentieth century it was because Picasso was behind it, pushing it. That Picasso disassembled the classically proportioned torso of Apollo and stuck it together again is beyond doubt. Whether or not in doing so he was conducting some magical re-assemblage of the human form which anticipated, and to some degree precipitated, but in any case prophesied, the concentration camps, the thalidomide disaster and the nuclear mutation, is an interesting point of conjecture. *Les Demoiselles d'Avignon*, the wartime portraits of Dora Maar, the *Guernica* series (Picasso was the only painter whose sensibility *was ready*, knew how to cope, with the major abominations of Fascism) are certainly that late stage in the Montmartre festivities which seem to correspond with R. D. Laing's recollections of end of term in the dissection lab: '...when they had all been dissected to bits—suddenly—so it seemed—no one knew how it began—

pieces of skin, muscle, penises, bits of liver, lung, heart, tongue, etc. etc. were all flying about, shouts, screams. Who was fighting whom? God knows.

'The professor had been standing in the doorway for some while before his presence began to creep through the room. Silence.

' "You should be ashamed of yourselves," he thundered; "how do you expect them to sort themselves out on the Day of Judgement?" '[1]

Norman Mailer points out the same quality in his perceptive essay on Picasso: 'For the last fifty years (if one is to take as his point of departure *Les Demoiselles D'Avignon*) Picasso has used his brush like a sword, disembowelling an eye to plaster it over the ear, lopping off a breast in order to turn it behind an arm, scoring the nostrils of his ladies until they took on the violent necessities of those twin holes of life and death, the vagina and the anus...Picasso is the monomaniac of form, showing us the proliferation of the breast, the eye as breast, the nose as breast, the chin, and the head, the shoulders, knees, belly and toes as a harem garden of breasts—or equally a cornucopia of fecal forms, of genitalia, of buttocks...'[2]

Picasso hangs now in the museums, the schoolrooms, the libraries, and thus the squares sit back, imagining that this beast is safely caged in fame and critical definition. One wonders if, had Ilsa Koch's lampshades of human skin been of brilliant design they too would hang comfortably in the kindergarten. Picasso's *Nude Dressing Her Hair* of 6 March, 1940, is the latest monument which places obscenity where harmony had once rested. 'Apollo is dying', said Nietzsche in *The Birth of Tragedy*. 'I give you a tragic age.' Picasso, Apollo's assassin, was ready with the berserk savagery of total innocence to conjure up the rejuvenated Dionysus in all his formidable power—the Godhead whose formidable phallus Allen Ginsberg choked on.

For innocence, telling, licentious, explosive and gay, was at the heart of the Parisian party, where the twentieth century was lifted, red and squealing, from Columbine's vagina,

[1] R. D. LAING, *The Bird of Paradise*, Penguin.
[2] NORMAN MAILER, 'Picasso', *Advertisements for Myself*, André Deutsch.

82

amidst the coloured streamers, jungle masks, the ragtime oratorios and shattered plastercasts. Innocence was sitting quietly among the brilliance, the wit and the sleight of hand, the blithely schizoid personalities. Innocence was an old customs inspector called Henri Rousseau who said to Picasso in a moment of rainbow-coloured insight: 'We are the greatest painters of the age, I in the modern style and you in the Egyptian'.

The banquet for Rousseau was the crowning event of the Paris festivities. Picasso's studio at the Bateau Lavoir was hung with garlands and a vast banner reading 'Honour to Rousseau'. Under the banner a throne was erected for Rousseau by placing a chair on a packing case. They borrowed a trestle table from the meat market. Marie Laurencin, Picasso, Braque, Max Jacob, and Apollinaire were among the guests. Maurice Raynal wrote in *Les Soirées de Paris*: 'At nine o'clock everything was ready except for the dinner. As the result of circumstances still unknown at the time the dinner which the host had ordered from the caterer was pleased never to arrive at all. We waited patiently first one hour, then two—but in vain. Only after three hours did the host suddenly strike his forehead, realizing that he had made a mistake over the date when he ordered the meal. The dinner would only arrive the day after next.

'When Rousseau saw that everyone was about to run in search of provisions he was seized with sudden merriment and remained gay for the whole evening. Everyone soon came back laden with food. Naturally drink had not been forgotten and, from tinned sardines on, the utmost gaiety reigned. Maurice Cremnitz got up and asked leave to sing: this was refused but all the same he struck up with a song in honour of Rousseau, the chorus of which ran: "This is the painter/Of this Stream/ Who captures Nature/With his magnificent brush!" Presently Rousseau got out his violin, a kind of child's instrument, and played one of his compositions called "Clochette". Soon somebody suggested dancing and the Douanier played a waltz of his own, "Clemence". The warm applause that greeted this filled him with satisfaction…He left his seat and soon began to sing all the songs in his repertory without being asked. At a corner of the table Guillaume Apollinaire, who had found this an excellent opportunity to catch up on his correspondence which was now two months behindhand, improvised a poem and read it out, after Rousseau had finished a song called 'Pan! Pan! ouvrez-moi!"... Suddenly there was a knock on the door. It was Fauvet the barman. With the utmost discretion he had come to announce that one of the ladies had been found sitting on the pavement near his establishment. She had gone out to get some fresh air and, as the result of several falls and upsets, had travelled the whole length of the street as far as his bar. All the ladies present stared at one another and one of them looked at herself in the mirror to see if it could be her; then the party continued, no importance being attached to the episode. At this moment there was a scuffle in the corridor as a result of a regrettable accident perpetrated by one of the guests against the door of the gentlemen's cloak-room. But it was already becoming more and more difficult to disentangle events. The Douanier had the ladies dancing to the strains of his violin; first an accordion and then a harmonica joined in, heads whirled, dawn broke, the bottles were empty and some of the guests had already slipped off...'

Fernand Olivier recalled, 'Rousseau was so happy that, throughout the evening, he received on his head large drops of wax from a large lamp that hung above him without flinching. They ended by forming a small eminence on his head like a clown's hat which he kept right up to the moment when the lamp caught fire. He was made to believe this was the final apotheosis.'[1]

Elsewhere Gertrude Stein wrote:
'In what way do chimes remind you of singing. In what way do birds sing. In what way are forests black or white.
We saw them blue.
With forget-me-nots.
In the midst of our happiness we were very pleased.'[2]

[1] Quoted by JEAN BOURET in *Henri Rousseau*, Oldbourne.
[2] GERTRUDE STEIN, *Accents in Alsace*.

IV

For Tristan Tzara, de Sade was the total permissive who dissolved the structure of morality and thus made absurdity accessible, a man who had clarified the supremacy of the spirit (the libido, ecstasy, in Breton's terms—hysteria) over the material.

Tzara was the waspish and destructive element in that group which gathered in Zurich during the 1914-18 barbecue and opened the Cabaret Voltaire in May of 1916. They were in correspondence with the Italian and Russian Futurists. They displayed Picasso's pictures in the Café Meierei where their cabaret was held. Across the road from the café a Russian called Lenin lodged. Joyce was also to be seen, living frugally while he worked on *Ulysses*. Zurich was alive with ideas.

The original and markedly contrasted couple around whom the Dada movement developed were Tzara and Hugo Ball. Tzara's nihilism had passed beyond the violent extremes of hatred for society to that pitch of absurdity where destruction is the only way back to sense. Hugo Ball was the passive, childlike contemplative who knew that dissolving institutions and definitions by Tzara's savage techniques would be to knock the bottom out of those artificial alignments that prevented men from experiencing and acknowledging their common spirit.

Zurich, in 1916, was an island in the stinking wreckage of society and all its precepts of organization, stability, and security. On that island, as the slaughter wore on, the sureties dissolved rapidly in sensitive minds, and the absurd presented itself as the point from which all decent action must begin. Thus the Dada group were a microcosm of the whole Romantic predicament, the oscillation between the organic and the totally determinant. The sick absurdity of living in the European slaughterhouse was a direct confrontation with the organic. The organic was not, to them, the grandiloquent face of Nature, to be possessed by or to conquer. The organic was simply all that was left to turn to. The correct course, then, was the systematic public dissolution of the fallacious and the corrupt, of all but the organic, and this was to be carried out with some urgency, for rational man would, unless swiftly disarmed (not only of his power but also his faculties), clearly murder everyone without even knowing he was doing it.

Art normally works through slow subliminal channels before it becomes publicly effective. It took hundreds of years for Giotto's humanism to become common practice. Dada wanted to telescope that procedure. It was no good leaving masterpieces around until they started to have effect. The masterpieces had to be immediate and sensational in their nature, had to alter people's minds physically and immediately, and had to do this in a place where people came readily rather than reluctantly or perfunctorily—out of the gallery, into the cabaret. The disruptive gaiety of the Paris party, the calculated lunacy of Jarry and Apollinaire, became an urgent psychological weapon to stop the slaughter.

Tzara started a magazine called *Dada* and expounded his ideas: 'I smash drawers, those of the brain and those of social organization: Everywhere to demoralize, to hurl the hand from heaven to hell, the eyes from hell to heaven, to set up once more, in the real powers and in the imagination of every individual, the fecund wheel of world circus...

Order=disorder; self=not-self; affirmation=negation; ultimate emanations of absolute art. Absoluteness and purity of chaos cosmically ordered, eternal in the globule second without duration without breath without light without control. —I love an old work for its novelty. It is only contrast that attaches us to the past...

Dada means nothing...Thought is produced in the mouth... Art falls asleep...'ART'—a parrot word—replaced by Dada... Art needs an operation. Art is a pretension, warmed by the diffidence of the urinary tract, hysteria born in a studio...'[1]

[1] Quoted by HANS RICHTER in *Dada*, Thames & Hudson.

Simultaneity was the principle that increasingly governed the entertainment at the Cabaret Voltaire. What the amiable Ball had intended as a place where 'a few young people... could enjoy their independence and give proof of it' became an arena where the artists, beside themselves with nihilistic bitterness and hilarity, performed their own work in such a way as to dissolve the work itself into that general chaos in which they placed their faith. Tzara and Marcel Janco read their separate poems together. Huelsenbeck played his tom-toms wearing Janco's grotesque masks, while Emmy Hennings sang her wistful cabaret ballads and Hugo Ball played piano. The poetry of the absurd developed its patterns of scrambled imagery and abstract sound. Says Ball: 'I wore a special costume designed by Janco and myself. My legs were encased in tight fitting cylindrical pillars of shiny blue cardboard which reached to my hips so that I looked like an obelisk. Above this I wore a huge cardboard coat collar, scarlet inside and gold outside, which was fastened at the neck in such a way that I could flap it like a pair of wings by moving my elbows. I also wore a high, cylindrical, blue and white striped witch-doctor's hat.

'I had set up music stands on three sides of the platform and placed on them my manuscript, written in red crayon. I officiated at each of these music-stands in turn. As Tzara knew all about my preparations there was a real little première. Everyone was very curious. So as an obelisk cannot walk, I had myself carried to the platform in a blackout. Then I began, slowly and majestically.

' "gadji beri bimba glandridi laula lonni cadori
gadjama gramma berida bimbala glandri galassassa laulitalomini
gadji beri bin blassa glassala laula lonni cadorsu sassasa bim
Gadjama tuffm i zimzalla binban gligia wowolimai bin beri ban
o katolominal rhinoscerossola hopsamen laulitalomini hoooo
gadjama rhinocerossola hopsamen
bluku terullala blaulala looooo" '

Tzara created the poem of total chance, slicing up newsprint, his own poems and anything else, tossing them into a bag, shaking up the pieces, and allowing them to compose themselves as they emerged. Huelsenbeck adopted the technique:

> This is how flat the world is
> The bladder of the swine
> Vermillion and cinnabar
> Cru cru cru
> The great art of the spirit
> Theosophia pneumatica
> poème bruitiste performed for the first time by
> Richard Huelsenbeck Dada
> or if you want to, the other way around
> birribum birribum the ox runs down the circulum
> Voilà here are the engineers with their assignment
> Light mines to throw in a still crude state
> 7,6 cm. Chaucer
> and the Soda calc. not to forget 98/100%[1]

So did Walter Serner:

> Pottery crashing to the floor:
> o so sweet drank Ninalla's lips Pommery greno first.
> Minkoff, a quite a Russian, deroute on a siding.
> Past us flaps a hand-palm: used besom blows blonde. All-in.
>
> Fall-in.
Mouthful of wine (length: 63 centimetres) into red improved
nostrils

SPAT
Cat!!![1]

In one of the many Dada exhibitions, collections of calculated impertinences in which all sacred cows were victims, not least the artists themselves, the public was admitted through a urinal where they were supplied with an axe to smash up the exhibits that displeased them. This was entirely according to the creative principles of the movement. In the shattered fragments of the pieces new patterns were possible.

So besides lacerating art, society and commonsense the Dada movement had revealed two positive principles, first that of cosmic identity whereby all things are seen as part of the whole of existence and the whole is expressed in every part, so that, once the trivial utilitarian concept of objects is destroyed

[1] Quoted by HANS RICHTER in *Dada*, Thames & Hudson.

the object appears as matter, in cosmic terms, a wonderful rather than a useful entity. One knew that, say, the Belvedere Apollo was 'Art' and one knew that the part one had to play was 'Awestruck'. This prevented any enjoyment. Shatter the Apollo and the pieces, being no longer 'Art', were as wonderful and enjoyable as pebbles on a beach.

The second principle, that of the authority of the senses, followed naturally out of the first. Taste, canons of aesthetics, standards of living, philosophical associations, stood in the way of enjoyment, sheer fun. So people who gawped at masterpieces and missed the world going by, had their senses sharply drawn back to the world, to the bottle-rack, spindly and horned, the bicycle wheel, taut and symmetrical, the urinal, fat and curled, when these objects were presented as masterpieces in Marcel Duchamp's 'readymades', or in the wonderland of Schwitters' Saule, a whole maze of subtly composed objects. Schwitters wrote:

> World needs new tendencies in poeting and
> paintry
> Old stuff is not able to lead further on
> Muses ought to be whisked when mankind
> will survive
> In the very war creative whisky is fallen
> very dry
> We will develop whisky spirit, because we
> see with our ears and hear with our eyes...
> Their phantic contents are so direct, that
> they are placed above the meanings of
> language at all
> Language is only a medium to understand
> and not to understand
> You prefer the language, when you understand
> by it things, which everybody knows by
> heart already. We prefer the language,
> which provides you a new feeling for new
> whiskers to come...[1]

Jacques Prévert, a member of the French branch of the movement, was aware that what they were precipitating had

[1] KURT SCHWITTERS, From *Pin* Gabberbocchus.

been learned from Picasso and the Montmartre party. He wrote:

and the dazed painter loses sight of his model
and falls asleep
It's just then that Picasso
who's going by there as he goes by everywhere
every day as if at home
sees the apple and the plate and the painter fallen asleep
What an idea to paint an apple
says Picasso
and Picasso eats the apple
and the apple tells him Thanks
and Picasso breaks the plate
and goes off smiling
and the painter drawn from his dreams
like a tooth
finds himself all alone again before his unfinished canvas
with right in the middle of his shattered china
the terrifying pips of reality.[1]

'Honour can be bought and sold like the arse. The arse, the arse, represents life like potato-chips, and all you who are serious minded will smell worse than cow's shit.

'Dada alone does not smell: it is nothing, nothing, nothing.
It is like your hopes: nothing.
like your paradise: nothing.
like your idols: nothing.
like your politicians: nothing.
like your heroes: nothing.
like your artists: nothing.
like your religions: nothing.

'Hiss, shout, kick my teeth in, so what? I shall still tell you that you are half-wits. In a few months my friends and I will be selling you our pictures for a few francs.'[2]

That is from a manifesto written by Picabia and read by

[1] JACQUES PREVERT, *Selected Poems*, edited and translated by L. Ferlinghetti, Penguin.
[2] HANS RICHTER, *Dada*, Thames & Hudson.

André Breton in Paris in 1920. It reflects the angry mood of Tzara's provocations.

In Berlin, with the acute bitterness of George Grosz, the caricaturist, as a guiding force, the movement became more committedly political:

'What is Dadaism and what does it want in Germany?

1. *Dadaism demands:*

(a) The international revolutionary union of all creative and intellectual men and women on the basis of radical communism;

(b) The introduction of progressive unemployment through comprehensive mechanization of every field of activity. Only by unemployment does it become possible for the individual to achieve certainty as to the truth of life and thus become accustomed to experience;

(c) The immediate expropriation of property (socialization) and the communal feeding of all; further, the erection of cities of light, and gardens that will belong to society as a whole and prepare man for a state of freedom.

2. *The Central Council demands:*

(a) Daily meals at public expense for all creative and intellectual men and women on the Potsdamer Platz (Berlin);

(b) Compulsory adherence of all clergymen and teachers to the Dada-ist articles of faith;

(c) The most brutal struggle against all directions of the so-called 'workers of the spirit' (Hitler, Adler), against their concealed bourgeoisism and post-classical education as advocated by the Sturm group;

(d) The immediate erection of a state art centre, elimination of concepts of property in the new art (expressionism); the concept of property is entirely excluded from the super-individual movement Dadaism which liberates all mankind;

(e) Introduction of the simultaneist poem as a communist state prayer;

(f) Requisition of churches for the performances of bruit-ism, simultaneist and Dadaist poems;

(g) Establishment of a Dadaist advisory council for the remodelling of life in every city of over 50,000 inhabitants;

(h) Immediate organization of a large scale Dadaist propaganda campaign with 150 circuses for the enlightenment of the proletariat;

(i) Submission of all laws and decrees to the Dadaist central council for approval;

(j) Immediate regulation of all sexual relations according to the views of international Dadaism through establishment of a Dadaist sexual centre.

> The Dadaist revolutionary central council German Group: Hausmann, Huelsenbeck
>
> Business Office: Charlottenburg, Kantstrasse 118
>
> Applications for membership taken at business office.
>
> 1920'[1]

In New York Dada became jazzy. In Barcelona it became stoical and deathly. In Paris, with the Romantic genius of André Breton as a guiding light, it merged and transformed into the subtly different Surrealist movement. What had happened in the lyrical minds of Breton, Eluard and Cocteau, who were direct descendants of the despairing Symbolists, was the idea of Freud's theory of the Id as a new wilderness, a cod-scientific confirmation that the wild wind in Valéry's tree lay not out there, unattainable and separate, but within the human mind, a long-standing prisoner — the Id as a Newfoundland of the sensibilities, to be released like the Bastille prisoners in an immense internal flowering of the mind. Early surrealist manifestoes were as sociologically directed as Dada had been. In 1925 Antonin Artaud, André Breton, René Crevel, Robert Desnos, Paul Eluard, Max Ernst, André Masson, Benjamin Peret, and Raymond (Zazi) Queneau, amongst a great many others, signed a statement saying, amongst other things:

'We want to proclaim our total detachment, in a sense of uncontamination, from the ideas at the basis of a still real European civilization, based in its turn on the intolerable principles of necessity and duty.

'Even more than patriotism, which is a quite commonplace

[1] RICHARD HUELSENBECK, 'En Avant Dada', *Heatwave*, no. 2, ed. C. Radcliffe, October 1966.

sort of hysteria, though emptier and shorter-lived than most—
we are disgusted by the idea of belonging to a country at all,
which is the most bestial and least philosophic of the concepts
to which we are subjected.

'We are certainly barbarians, since a certain form of civilization thoroughly disgusts us...

'It is the turn of the Mongols to bivouac in our squares.
We should never for a moment worry that this violence could
take us by surprise or get out of hand. As far as we are concerned, it could never be enough, whatever happens. All that
should be seen in our behaviour is the absolute confidence that
we have in a sentiment common to us all, the sentiment of
revolt, on which everything of value is based...'[1]

It was the lingering aftermath of Catholicism that drove
the movement away from Dada anarchy towards a kind of
metaphysical Marxism. The whole thing had gone serious
again. For Breton, the long-standing leader of the surrealists,
whose argument with Tzara is one of the significant political
occurrences of the century, de Sade was synonymous with
Blake's Orc. He was the force necessary to blast the Bastille
wall of the Superego and release the 'greater reality' of the
subconscious; for Surrealism meant just that—that the dream
was greater than the material. Artaud, who existentially knew
this assertion as a personal predicament rather than a political
theory, puts it very poignantly: 'Everything in the order of
the written word which abandons the field of ordered and
lucid perceptions; everything which aims at creating a reversal
of appearances, to introduce doubt about the position of mental
images and their relationship; everything which provokes
confusion without weakening the burst of mental energy;
everything which disrupts the relationships of things while
giving this agitated mental energy an even greater aspect of
truth and violence—all these offer death an exit, and relate
us to certain most subtle states of the mind, at the heart of
which death wants out.

'This is why all who dream without regretting their dreams,
without bringing back from the plunge into a fertile unconscious this feeling of an atrocious nostalgia, are pigs. The dream

[1] PATRICK WALDBERG, *Surrealism*, Thames & Hudson.

93

is true. All dreams are true. I have a feeling of harshness, of landscapes as if sculptured, of swaying patches of ground covered with a sort of cool sand, and they mean:

"Regret, disappointment, abandonment, separation, when will we meet again?" '[1] (Note the similarity to George Harrison's 'L. A. Way'). The movement was thus fraught with contradiction. It became a revolutionary movement to which the material evil of European society was of increasingly secondary importance. Yet it continued to proclaim its support for historic materialism.

Issue One of *La Revolution Surrealiste* said, in an Editorial in which Paul Eluard's hand is discernible: 'As the trial of knowledge is no longer relevant and intelligence no longer need be taken into account, the dream alone entrusts to man all his rights to freedom. Thanks to the dream, the meaning of death is no longer mysterious, and the meaning of life becomes important...

'We declare the surrealist exaltation of mystics, inventors and prophets, and we go on...

'Revolution...Revolution...Realism is the pruning of trees, surrealism is the pruning of life.'[2]

The Editorial for Issue Two indicated the social application of these principles: 'The idea of prison and the idea of barracks are commonplace today: those monstrosities no longer shock you. The infant lies in the calmness of those who have got round the difficulty by various moral and physical abdications (honesty, sickness, patriotism...)'[2]

The tone of Breton's own first *Surrealist Manifesto* in 1924 was predominantly inward-looking:

'SURREALISM, noun, masc., Pure psychic automatism by which it is intended to express, either verbally or in writing, the true function of thought. Thought dictated in the absence of all control exerted by reason, and outside all aesthetic or moral preoccupations.

'ENCYCL.*Philos*. Surrealism is based on the belief in the superior reality in certain forms of association heretofore

[1] ANTONIN ARTAUD, *Collected Writings*, City Lights.
[2] Quoted by PATRICK WALDBERG in *Surrealism*, Thames & Hudson.

neglected, in the omnipotence of the dream, and in the disinterested play of thought. It leads to the permanent destruction of all other psychic mechanisms and to its substitution for them in the solution of the principal problems of life.'[1]

What Breton did then, in transforming Dada into surrealism, was disarm it on two scores, the metaphysical and the political. The first he handed over to Freud and the second to Marx. Small wonder that five years later, when he published the second *Surrealist Manifesto*, he reiterates the old line with somewhat less aplomb—'Surrealism should not be at the mercy of this or that man's whim; if it declares that it can, by its own means, deliver thought from an ever harsher bondage, put it back on the path of total understanding, restore its original purity, then it is enough to justify its being judged only by what it has done and by what remains to be done in order to keep its promise.'—and is ultimately reduced to political silence—'They asked me to give a report on the Italian situation in the "Gas" cell, specifying that I was to rely upon statistical facts alone (steel production, etc.) and *especially no ideology*. I could not.'[1]

These dead ends illustrate the fundamental difference between Tzara's use of chance and Breton's. Tzara's was carried out as access to the cosmic, to the total identity of Being, a submission, if you like, to Nature, whilst Breton's automatic writing, Masson's compulsive calligraphy, were seen as access to the human subconscious, a considerable narrowing of scale and possibility, far more humanist in its pretensions than Tzara's work, an appropriation, if you like, of Nature.

Thus, if Tzara wished to denude the human mind so that it played, oceanic, in the wonderment of innocence, Breton, as he states, wanted to develop the human mind so that it rose to a situation of improved control and power. Breton's Communism was therefore contradictory but inevitable. It followed Romanticism. Tzara was meanwhile on the only firm political ground for art. He was an anarchist.

Artaud said: 'And if there is one hellish, truly accursed thing in our time, it is our artistic dallying with forms, instead of being like victims burnt at the stake, signalling

[1] Quoted by PATRICK WALDBERG in *Surrealism*, Thames & Hudson.

through the flames'.[1] Nevertheless, despite their separate intentions, objects were left behind by these desperate magicians. The released Id, the progressive subjectivity of art, had produced abstraction; pictures, sculptures, poems that were best and most properly enjoyed as simple material forms, which would then serve as fetishes of immense power and beauty. The Cantos of Ezra Pound are often abstract juxtapositions of language fragments, exquisitely co-ordinated. The Viennese composers Schoenberg and Webern, passing through serial techniques, showed Boulez, Stockhausen and Barraque the way to the 'sound object'. Boulez spoke, very much with Nietzsche in mind, of the collective delirium into which the human mind must move, and contrived this delirium by exquisitely ordered works.

Kandinsky's painting, I think, best illustrates how reference and definition, rational thought and reasoned communication being altogether abandoned, the cohesion of unattached life and energy in systems of aesthetic unity can stand as evidence to an area of Being perpetually accessible, a common denominator among men and things, to which men can turn when attitudes destroy themselves and reason curls whimpering in the desert.

[1] ANTONIN ARTAUD, *Collected Writings*, City Lights.

V

The bible of the subconscious is James Joyce's *Finnegan's Wake*—a book written not only about dream, in the language of dream, adopting the voice of a dreaming man, but also written for dream, a book whose aural richness is lost if the multiple puns are approached analytically, and whose puns only open out properly into a succession of concentrically flowering image-nuclei if they are taken automatically. The only way to experience *Finnegan's Wake* is to allow the relentless patterns of sound and syntax to mesmerize the perceptions in such a way as to make the puns accessible as the lightning puns were made accessible by the delirious speed of the radio programme ITMA. Thus, ultimately, the mind expands and becomes the collective mind of all men, as the hero Earwicker's mind is indeed the mind of Man asleep in a Chapelizod pub. Joyce avoided the limitations of Freudian surrealism by conceiving his dream in Jungian terms. But ultimately his faith lay in Nature. Annalivia Plurabella, the green and fecund female river, was the antidote to the crippling guilt of the Phoenix Park crime. It was the Romantic attitude granted a new technique by psycho-analysis, a new significance imparted to the old jingling patterns of folklore and common speech. The English Apocalyptic poets of the war years, Barker, Thomas and Gascoyne, were very much followers of Joyce. The complexity and profundity of *Finnegan's Wake*, together with the fact that the ideas of Freud were amplified and strengthened by those of Vico, made the work less prone to vulgarization than surrealism and subjective abstraction.

After the Second World War a vast network of small galleries sprang up throughout the Western capitals and abstract painting became a paying game. The squares decided to re-establish contact with the alienated visionaries by defining the patterns of their subjective adventurings as 'Decoration', as 'Art', and using it accordingly. The art schools chimed in with this scheme of things, harnessed their trainee artists first to the gallery system, secondly to industry and thirdly to industrial design, so that the current output of art students, in London at any rate, is in the machine language of industrial design, while individual vision is laughed off as a sentimentality. Thus abstract painting and sculpture became corrupt and would have remained so had it not been for the fusion of ideas which occurred in New York and San Francisco in the post-Hiroshima years.

For Americans the Marquis de Sade was an urban Captain Ahab, the hero of Melville's *Moby Dick* who stamped his quadrant to fragments that he might dominate the very sun by the power of his own will. For Americans Jung was Whitman who had declared himself all men—indeed a microcosm of the Universe. The Symbolists had not been slow to acknowledge Whitman. Indeed the total freedom of his verse had inspired their own relaxations of form.

American artists had, however, two other sources of spirit: the East, whose culture had already influenced West Coast painters like Morris Graves and Mark Tobey; and the hipster, whose creative pragmatism in improvization surpassed the most successful surrealist excursions into the subconscious. It was rather like Hesse's outsider hero, Steppenwolf, being instructed by his saxophonist rival—'You see, in my opinion there is no point at all in talking about music. I never talk about music...I am a musician, not a professor, and I don't believe that, as regards music, there is the least point in being right.'[1] For American artists de Sade was embodied in the psychopathic genius, Charlie Parker, whilst the cosmic absurdity of Tzara's fortuitous juxtapositions had long been anticipated in the One-Is-All-And-All-Is-One-So-What-The-Hell religion called Zen Buddhism. 'Magnificent! Magnificent!/No one hears the final word/The ocean bed's aflame/Out of the void leap wooden lambs' was not written in Paris or Zurich during the 1914-18 war, but in Japan in the fourteenth century.

[1] HERMANN HESSE, *Steppenwolf*, Penguin.

In New York, in the late forties, a nervous hypnotic man seemed to synthesize all the conjoining cultures in his unique personality. A heroin addict and a familiar of the underworld, he had something of the hipster. The son of an ultra-respectable middle-western business family, he had something more of the hard-willed independent puritan aghast at the abominations of his time, and yet, within that same puritan framework, he had an old-fashioned sceptical business acumen that gave him a quick nerve for the changing localities of power. A westerner, he prided himself on his accuracy with a pistol and valued freedom as highly as Whitman and Wild Bill Hickock. As a sensitive and lonely child, he had, like William Blake, seen visions and become curiously familiar with the supernatural. A homosexual, his consequent approach to human relationships had the psychological insight of a Proust or a Gide. Indeed his cold eye and thin lips gave him a remarkable similarity to the latter. His voice, like Pound's, had the rasping, down-home tones of the cracker-barrel philosopher. His humour was as sour and colloquial as Mark Twain's. He was, at that time, known only to a handful of students, Allen Ginsberg, Jack Kerouac, Carl Solomon, and he was, to them, a combination of mentor and magical character. He used several names. The real one was William Burroughs.

Just where Burroughs' convictions lay in those years immediately after Hiroshima is uncertain, but it is clear from letters and accounts of that time (for instance the famous descriptions by Jack Kerouac in *Time of the Geek* and *On the Road* and the notes to Ginsberg called *The Yage Letters*) that a murderous hatred of the bomb, of Harry Truman, of John Foster Dulles, of the *Time-Life* organization, of the materialism and bureaucracy of American life, was predominant in his mind. In this facet of his thinking he was the direct descendant of Henry Miller, Nathaniel West, Kenneth Fearing, Kenneth Patchen, a clear American tradition of masochistic social criticism. Also it's clear that his life was a meandering search for that timeless spiritual life where human communication was possibly telepathic and perfect and the strange planes of being in his childhood visions could be revisited. Long before the current psychedelic movement began Burroughs had tried and rejected drugs as a means of achieving this. Rather did his experience of drugs lead him to a bitter understanding of how the human metabolism is subject to exterior controls and how a man seeking vision and enlightenment becomes doubly prone to those controls. He ultimately reached a pitch where not only society but Nature itself appeared as a confidence trick, a chronic imposition.

Certainly the quality of flight informs all post-Hiroshima American art. The Moment, the psychopathic Now in which man was imprisoned when the future became improbable, was the launching point from which the creative missiles were hurled into chance winds where they were played along like gliders. Now was the point from which Charlie Parker's phrases were thrown in a flurry of semiquavers and gritty inflections, spreading out like gliding eagles of long sour notes over the subsequent eight or twelve bars. Now was the brush and paint in Jackson Pollock's hand and the place where he stood and sent his lariats of Ducol snaking out across the prairie canvas leaving a trail for Kline, Motherwell, Francis, Hoffman, Still, Guston, Rothko, and De Kooning. Now was the New York from which Kerouac and Dean Moriarty (Neal Cassady) set out on those long flights to Denver and San Francisco described in *On the Road*. Now was the left hand margin of Charles Olson's typewritten breath-lines as he expounded his dogma of projective verse from the short-lived Black Mountain College. Now was the word 'Who' in Ginsberg's saxophone-inspired *Howl*, a repeated syllable that sends the Fearing-style paragraph-line spinning out through its syntax, losing punctuation in the sheer volition of flight:

I saw the best minds of my generation destroyed by madness, starving hysterical naked,
dragging themselves through the negro streets at dawn looking for an angry fix,
angelheaded hipsters burning for the ancient heavenly connection to the starry dynamo in the machinery of night,
who poverty and tatters and hollow-eyed and high sat up smoking in the supernatural darkness of cold-water flats floating across the tops of cities contemplating jazz,

who bared their brains to Heaven under the El and saw Mohammedan angels staggering on tenement roofs illuminated,

who passed through universities with radiant cool eyes hallucinating Arkansas and Blake-light tragedy among the scholars of war,

who were expelled from the academies for crazy & publishing obscene odes on the windows of the skull,

who cowered in unshaven rooms in underwear, burning their money in wastebaskets and listening to the Terror through the wall,

who got busted in their pubic beards returning through Laredo with a belt of marijuana for New York,

who ate fire in paint hotels or drank turpentine in Paradise Alley, death, or purgatoried their torsos night after night...[1]

Ginsberg's generation, the Beat Generation, adopted, finally, the bare-foot, bearded modes of 'existentialist' Paris. Their alienation, however, was of a significantly different kind. The Parisians were to be taken as intellectuals and were remarkable for the cultivated sterility of their feelings. The Beats were bewildered American middle-class kids whose preoccupation with philosophy and the arts was largely incidental to their symptomatic delinquency. In fact it was here, amongst this group, that the delinquent came to be revered not only as a creature liberated of morality and superego, but as a person whose way of life served as a protection against the massive public guilt of the Korean war and the H-bomb. He, like the hipster whose descendant he was, showed an alternative way of life to that of society. Gregory Corso and Ray Bremser, therefore, excellent poets though they both are by any standards, were both adopted by the group largely for their delinquency and the special frisson which it created.

The generation centred its life around a nomadic tribe which travelled between Berkeley, Denver, and Columbia University, with occasional excursions into Mexico. The real centre of the group was, however, the West Coast, where they set up a community in the seedy waterside suburb of Venice West. Important figures were Ginsberg, Kerouac, who originated

[1] ALLEN GINSBERG, *Howl*, City Lights.

the typical writing style, Corso, Snyder, Whalen and the half-legendary Herbert Huncke and Neal Cassady. Alexander Trocchi, also, was an early Venice resident.

On the West Coast the Beats did all that the current community of hippies have done and more. They experimented wildly with all available drugs and set down intelligent observations on their consequent discoveries. The drug writings of Ginsberg ('It is electricity connected to itself, if it hath wires/it is a vast spiderweb'),[1] of Rosenthaal ('Heroin is the first night in this new season...Cocaine is the startle of sunshine on a turbulent sea...Pot is theater'),[2] of McClure ('...For days it lightens the black interiors of the body and lends an ivory cast of sleekness and luminosity to the senses...')[3] are particularly brilliant. Also on the West Coast Beats painted action paintings, studied Eastern religion, yearned back, like the hippies, to the days of the redskins (Bremser: '...drooling to turn you, Mother America, back into/the one-time-great Shoshonee magnanimous squaw/to the decadent Indian poet—lost god of the plains...'),[4] created the cool jazz style of Al Cohn, Gerry Mulligan, Shorty Rogers, and pioneered the now universal reading of poetry to jazz in public.

They also, significantly, established a vital and fundamental independence quite early when Laurence Ferlinghetti, another excellent poet, set up his own shop and publishing firm in San Francisco, City Lights, and put it at the disposal of the Beat community.

Behind all the anti-academicism and the Huckleberry Finn soliloquizing there was a very familiar objective. Michael McClure wrote:

> —A barricade—a wall—a stronghold,
> Sinister and joyous, of indigo and saffron—
> To hurl myself against!
> To crush or
> To be a part of the wall...

[1] ALLEN GINSBERG, *Kaddish*, City Lights.
[2] I. ROSENTHAAL under nom-de-plume H. Sheeper in *Gnana* magazine.
[3] MICHAEL MCCLURE, *Meat Science Essays*, City Lights.
[4] R. BREMSER, *Poems of Holy Madness*.

Spattered brains or the imprint
of a violent foot—
To crumble loose some brilliant masonry
Or knock it down—
To send pieces flying
Like stars!
To be the chalice of the hunt,
To handspring
Through a barrier of white trees![1]

Now was the commencement of the flight perpetually re-commenced. It was the Romantic/Symbolist/Dada/Surrealist quest continued with a big-shouldered frontier panache and a bland Oriental clarity.

[1] MICHAEL MCCLURE, from *The New American Poetry*, ed. Donald Allen, Grove Press.

IV
Sick

'When will the veil be lifted?
When will the charade turn to Carnival?
Saints may still be kissing lepers.
It is high time the leper kissed the saint.'

R. D. LAING

I

The decline of the anti-bomb movement in 1962 left us stranded in the unbearable. The unbearable was now clearly visible. The one thing the protest movement had achieved was to tear down all artificial comforts. We knew for certain that governments had nothing whatsoever to do with the morality they preached and enforced, that society had lost its appetite for life and looked forward to the death it had contrived (how many times had I stood on ordinary doorsteps with black and white leaflets, arguing down through the levels of the deterrent theory and lingering patriotism until the householder blurted angrily 'Well what difference does it make if it does come? So long as we all go quickly the sooner the bloody better I say'), that we ourselves lacked even the will of colonial dissidents, that none of us was sufficiently alarmed about extinction to force the murderers to put down their weapons, that society commanded nothing but contempt, much less dedicated labour or respect for law, that love, honour, faith, selflessness were as false in ourselves as in our elders, that the only effective thing to do was what we daren't do—riot and destroy the death machine in a demonstration of serious protest, that the only thing we *could* do was sit in humiliation and wait for extinction.

The question, then, was practical. How best could one go about the business of waiting in humiliation for the end of man? One could, to begin with, become more passive. Young people ceased to be garrulous. In schools children stopped playing games and in dance-halls and clubs fewer people danced. At all events one avoided work. Young people had worked hard against the bomb. They had been snubbed. They were not likely to work again, except in the interests of their own sensationalism. Two passive people are isolated from one another. We became isolated.

Another thing we could do was live for sensation, as the hipsters and the teds had, but we could do it deliberately, live for sex rather than love, for speed rather than safety, for kicks. It is my experience that a large number of teenagers became then, and remain, incapable of thinking more than half an hour ahead. Things like promises and responsible undertakings, honour, indeed any principles at all, are, of course, impossible in minds so conditioned. Clearly, in a way of life devoted to the sensation of the moment, drugs were of considerable use and began to be used. That they may be addictive or lethal was comparatively irrelevant because such dangers belonged to the future and the future was, to say the least of it, not a safe bet, too improbable to be taken seriously into account. Domesticity became regarded as rather wistfully old-fashioned and, like the world, temporary.

An anti-gestalt became prevalent among young people, an instinct to leave nothing complete, to half-close doors, to half-finish letters, to do three-quarters of the washing up, to leave the cinema partway through the film, for an act completed is an identity established, and an identity established is a relationship acknowledged, and no entity outside ourselves and our implicit instincts was to be trusted. Who cares to finish the building when all the ground is quicksand. Work may sometimes pass the time—no more.

Finally, for five years we had been politely informing government and public that their policies were directed towards inconceivable horror far beyond the scale of the previous two world wars. How were we to live with the thought of that horror so clearly in our minds, whilst knowing that our own indignation had proved impotent? Obviously an affectlessness had to be cultivated. Morality, pain and compassion, the whole business of identifying with other people and thus sharing and helping their discomfiture, had to be dissolved in humour, as it had been dissolved in humour by the soldiers at Ypres blithely bawling, 'Where's Tommy Atkins? 'Angin' on the wire. 'Angin' on the wire...' Our means of doing this was the sick joke.

A story goes that when a famous cartoonist produced his recurring joke—nurse with new baby confronting young mother: 'Will you have your supper now or later?'—it was a signal for him to be taken away. Such humour, in which values are totally negated, had been a sure sign of certifiable madness. Sick humour was the humour of someone who was ill, sick. Living with the bomb had made us all ill. Those most aware of the bomb showed the symptoms most clearly and used those symptoms as a last banner to brandish under the noses of the squares as a syphilitic might display his chancres to a puritan: ' "Mummy I don't like little brother." "Shut up and eat what you're given."—You see, we are ill. *We are ill*. You laughed. You've admitted it'.

This was ultimately the distressed and utterly serious message which Lenny Bruce had to impart. A very different thing from the fashionable 'satire' of *Private Eye* and the *Establishment*, which had nothing to say except that the public school/Oxbridge clan could now use 'satire' as an alternative career to the church, the army and broadcasting. Commencing as a sexually obsessed cabaret comedian with the diabolic charm, the improvisatory genius, the perfect delivery and the heroin habit of an archetypal hipster, Bruce's cabaret act became increasingly a flagellation of himself and his audience, as every single sacred, serious thing, every single thing held in love and reverence was revealed as lost in the winces that accompanied his compulsive, self-abusive situation monologues, and, indeed, his wry and actual public self-abuse. His death was one of a long and significant line—James Dean, Jackson Pollock, Charlie Parker, Billie Holliday, Fats Navarro, Clifford Brown, Bud Powell, Marilyn Monroe, Lenny Bruce, Brian Epstein, Joe Orton…casualties…

But the real burst blister of sick humour was William Burroughs' slaughterhouse carnival *The Naked Lunch*. Since his early appearance in New York Burroughs had ventured into South America after wonder-drugs, been deported from Mexico, had stayed briefly in London and Paris, and settled in Tangiers where his heroin habit got worse. During the bad stages of his habit and his consequent withdrawal through apomorphine he scribbled ceaselessly what was taking place 'in front of his senses at the time of writing'. Allen Ginsberg, finding Burroughs in wretched circumstances in Tangiers, gathered the fragments from the squalid corners of the room. They were eventually assembled to form a collage novel in which the paranoid fears of withdrawal wove themselves into a fabric of sado-erotic hallucination, a nightmare satire about the manipulation of humanity through the creation of need. What makes the free spirit prone to need and therefore manipulable is the craving flesh. *The Naked Lunch* is an angry circus in which the sick joke is not only a weapon against society but against human physical existence itself. Its implication is that we have been conned into our nauseous vulnerable bodies. It sets out to dislocate the mental norm that keeps us there, in the flesh, by schizoid juxtapositions of humour, nausea and (this, like Francis Bacon's paint-surface, is its really extraordinary quality) an exquisite grace of prose.

It is unlikely that any previous literature has the direct physical effectiveness of *The Naked Lunch*. As Francis Bacon's *Figure In A Landscape* caused a schoolgirl to faint on the floor of the Tate Gallery, so *The Naked Lunch* actually caused at least one unprepared square to vomit on the carpet and leaves the mind of anyone who reads it redirected sexually. It depicts the world and existence as a nightmare obscenity and it describes accurately how we felt the world to be at that point, the early sixties, when *The Naked Lunch* was finally published.

The nightmare was shared and a number of us described it— R. D. Laing in his *Bird of Paradise*, Alden Van Buskirk in his Oakland poems, Christopher Logue, Edwin Brock, George MacBeth, Peter Porter whose *Annotations of Auschwitz* is surely one of the best English poems since the war, Adrian Mitchell, William Wantling, Charles Bukowski.

And, as we were mentally ill, mental illness itself became of interest in a curious way. Schizophrenia was ill-defined. At best it meant, means, someone who was isolated and therefore not adjusted to the patterns of society. The language was anyway familiar to artists:

> SMITH: What do you do for a living, little fellow? Work on a ranch or something?
> JONES: No, I'm a civilian seaman. Supposed to be high mucka-muck society.

S: A singing record machine, huh? I guess a recording machine sometimes sings. If they're adjusted right. Mn-hm. I thought that was it. My towel, mm-hm. We'll be going back to sea in about—eight or nine months though. Soon as we get our—destroyed parts repaired. (Pause)

J: I've got lovesickness, secret love.

S: Secret love, huh? (Laughs)

J: Yeah.

S: I ain't got any secret love.

J: I fell in love but I don't feel any woo—that sits over—looks something like me—walking around over there.

S: My, oh, my only one, my only love is the shark. Keep out of the way of him...[1]

Not Becket or Joyce or Artaud—two schizophrenics recorded chatting in a New York madhouse. If the patterns of society centred around the H-bomb was it not possible that schizophrenia was a tortured means to a fuller existence, to a life more properly human, to complete being? This echoed the Romantic/Surrealist attitude to madness, the vision of de Sade, Van Gogh, Lautréamont, Artaud, all of whom were certified at some point in their development. R. D. Laing, David Cooper and a number of associates, began to approach this point of view through their long experience as practising psychiatrists. Cooper set up an annexe to Shenley mental hospital called 'The Villa' where certified schizophrenics were permitted to act out their madness as fully as possible and arrive at a point on the other side of the experience rather than being shocked and drugged back to the point from which they began. Laing and Cooper did extensive derogatory analytic work on the fundamental units of society, the lovers, the family, and the neighbourhood. Their perpetual guide in this was the philosophy of Sartre, particularly his analysis of Being-For-Others. Finally it was Laing who stated the position most lucidly:

'When all has been said against the different schools of psychoanalysis and depth psychology, one of their great merits is that they recognize explicitly the crucial relevance of each person's

[1] J. HALEY, *Strategies of Psychotherapy*, Grane & Stratton.

experience, especially in the so-called "unconscious", to his or her outward behaviour.

'There is a view that is still current that there is some correlation between being sane and being unconscious, or at least not too conscious of the "unconscious", and that forms of psychosis are the behavioural disruption caused by being overwhelmed by the "unconscious".

'What both Freud and Jung called "the unconscious" is simply what we are, in our historically conditioned estrangement, unconscious of. It is not necessarily or essentially unconscious. I am not merely spinning senseless paradoxes when I say that we, the sane ones,'

—in this case it was the delegates of the 6th International Congress of Psycho-therapy—

'are out of our minds. The mind is what the ego is unconscious of. *We* are unconscious of our minds. Our minds are not unconscious. Our minds are conscious of us. Ask yourself who and what dreams our dreams. Our unconscious minds? The dreamer who dreams our dreams knows far more of us than we know of him. It is only from a remarkable position of alienation that the source of life, the Fountain of Life, is experienced as the It. The mind of which we are unaware, is aware of us. It is we who are out of our minds. We need not be unaware of the inner world.

'We do not realise its existence most of the time.'

'But many people enter it—unfortunately without guides, confusing outer with inner realities, and inner with outer—and generally lose their capacity to function competently in ordinary relations.

'This need not be so. The process of entering into *the other* world from this world, and returning to *this* world from the other world, is as "natural" as death and childbirth or being born. But in our present world that is both so terrified and so unconscious of the other world, it is not surprising that, when "reality", the fabric of this world, bursts, and a person enters the other world, he is completely lost and terrified, and meets only incomprehension in others...

'Why do almost all theories about depersonalization, reification, splitting, denial, tend themselves to exhibit the symptoms they attempt to describe. We run the constant risk of being left with transactions, but where is the individual? The individual, but where is the other? Patterns of behaviour, but where is the experience, information communication but where is the pathos and sympathy, the passion and compassion?...

'We psychotherapists are specialists, as they say, in human relations. But the Dreadful has already happened. It has happened to us as well as to our patients. We, the therapists, are in a world in which the inner is already split from the outer, and before the inner can become outer, and the outer inner, we have to rediscover our "inner" world. As a whole generation of men, we are so estranged from the inner world that there are many arguing that it does not exist; and even if it does exist, it does not matter. Even if it had some significance, it is not the hard stuff of science, and if it is not, then let's make it hard. Let it be measured and counted. Quantify the heart's agony and ecstasy in a world in which when the inner world is first discovered we are liable to find ourselves bereft, and derelict. For without the inner the outer loses its meaning, and without the outer the inner loses its substance...

'When our personal worlds are rediscovered and allowed to reconstitute themselves, we first discover a shambles. Bodies half-dead; genitals dissociated from heart; heart severed from head; heads dissociated from genitals. Without inner unity, with just enough sense of continuity to clutch at identity—the current idolatry. Torn body, mind and spirit by inner contradictions, pulled in different directions. Man cut off from his own mind, cut off equally from his own body—a half-crazed creature in a mad world.'[1]

And elsewhere Laing wrote: 'Our sanity is not "true" sanity. Their madness is not "true" madness. The madness of our patients is an artifact of the destruction wreaked on them by us, and by them on themselves. Let no one suppose that we meet "true" madness any more than that we are truly sane. The madness we encounter in "patients" is a gross travesty, a mockery, a grotesque caricature of what the natural healing

[1] R. D. LAING, *The Present Situation*. Paper addressed to the 6th International Congress of Psycho-Therapy and published in sigma Portfolio.

of that estranged situation we call sanity might be. True sanity entails in one way or another the dissolution of the normal ego, that false self competently adjusted to our alienated social reality: the emergence of the "inner" archetypal mediators of divine power, and through this death, a rebirth, and the eventual re-establishment of a new kind of ego-functioning, the ego now being the servant of the divine, no longer its betrayer...

'We can no longer assume that such a voyage (schizophrenia) is an illness that has to be treated...Can we not see that *this voyage is not what we need to be cured of, but that it is itself a natural way of healing our own appalling state of alienation called normality?*'[1]

That there was a necessary era of therapeutic lunacy at hand had long been an idea continuously present in Beat writing. The first public mention of *The Naked Lunch* was in 1956 when Ginsberg dedicated *Howl* to Burroughs with the joyous announcement that the 'endless' book he was writing would 'drive everybody mad'. Jack Kerouac, even earlier, in *Time of the Geek* had come to some disturbing conclusions: 'Everybody in the world has come to feel like a geek...can't you see it? Can't you sense what's going on around you? All the neurosis and the restrictive morality and the scatological repressions and the suppressed aggressiveness has finally gained the upper hand on humanity—everyone is becoming a geek! Everyone feels like a Zombie, and somewhere at the ends of the night, the great magician, the great Dracula-figure of modern disintegration and madness, the wise genius behind it all, the Devil if you will, is running the whole thing with his string of oaths and hexes...

'You feel guilty of something, you feel unclean, almost diseased, you have nightmares, you have occasional visions of horror, feelings of spiritual geekishness—Don't you see, everybody feels like that now...

'It's the great molecular comedown. Of course that's only my whimsical name for it at the moment. It's really an atomic disease, you see. But I'll have to explain it to you so you'll know, at least. It's death, finally reclaiming life, the scurvy of

[1] R. D. LAING, *The Politics of Experience*, Penguin.

the soul at last, a kind of universal cancer. It's got a real medieval ghastliness, like the plague, only this time it will ruin everything, don't you see?

'Everybody is going to fall apart, disintegrate, all character structures based on tradition and uprightness and so-called morality will slowly rot away, people will get the hives right on their hearts, great crabs will cling to their brains…their lungs will crumble. But now we have only the symptoms, the disease isn't really under way yet—virus X only…

'Listen! You know about molecules, they're made up according to a number of atoms arranged just so around a proton or something. Well the just-so is falling apart. The molecule will suddenly collapse, leaving just atoms, smashed atoms of people, nothing at all…as it was in the beginning of the world. Don't you see, it's just the beginning of the end of Geneseean world. It's certainly the beginning of the end of the world as we know it now, and then there'll be a non-Genceseean world without all the truck about sin and sweat of your brow. He-he! It's great! Whatever it is, I'm all for it. It may be a carnival of horror at first—but something strange will come of it, I'm convinced.'[1]

It was the psychopath, the ted, the mod, become policy. It was the post-Hiroshima evils stripped down and acknowledged. It was the napalm-scorched world. It was the filth of our humiliation and it was the point of cultural development at which all three previously separate traditions of pop, protest and art began to merge. We heard the sound Ginsberg had prayed for:

> Your clean sonnets?
> I want to read your filthiest
>   secret scribblings,
>   your Hope,
> in his most Obscene Magnificence.
>   My God![2]

[1] JACK KEROUAC, 'The Time of the Geek', from *The Town and the City*, Eyre & Spottiswoode.

[2] ALLEN GINSBERG, from 'To An Old Poet in Peru', from *Outburst*, ed. Tom Raworth.

II

Up to the point of the failure of CND it would be broadly true to say that pop was the prerogative of working class teenagers, protest was the prerogative of middle class students, and art was the prerogative of the lunatic fringe. The pop fans despised protest as being naïve and art as being posh, the protesting students despised pop as being commercial and art as being pretentious, and the artists despised pop for being tasteless and protest for being drab.

There had, however, been occasional bridges. The hood, the rocker, the ted, had long been idolized by artists who saw him as the champion of the oppressed class (Sillitoe), the incarnate will (Gunn), the noble savage (Brando), the free libido (Kerouac), or a good lay (Ginsberg). When trad jazz became widely popular it was enjoyed, in one form or another, by all three groups. Skiffle, an offshoot of trad jazz, was folksy enough for the protesters, creative enough for the artists, and twangy enough for the pop fans. When the West Coast Beats and Horovitz and Brown in England started to perform poetry informally, with jazz, that was a further bridge. When they did it under the auspices of CND that was yet another.

Ray Gosling sensed that something was changing in 1961. He wrote in an open letter to an old friend: 'You finish off your letter by saying, "Don't change. I know I won't." Well, Howard, my old duck, I think I have. The way I look at it is that the whole world's changing out here, and I'm moving with it because I like the way it's changing all the way. Oh, you don't see it in the papers, but you wait five, ten, fifteen years' time when you come back. You won't know this little old island. Perhaps I won't either. But I know I'm loving every minute of this changing, seeing a whole way of life come through, seeing a world change right in front of my eyes and knowing I'm part of it, caught right in the middle, helping to change it all and being changed by it all at the same time.

'Remember when we were at school. Oh, don't worry, the school hasn't changed one little bit. The change hasn't gone that far. But remember the old crowd. Mo (he's in New York now) with that face and the haircut—all straight and floppy and unstyled. And Jerry (he's got this play coming off in Coventry some time next year) with those black unused jeans, tight in all the wrong places, and that curly black hair all over the place. Remember the talk all about Tennessee Williams and James Dean and "I wanna go to America", and Music with a capital M, and bringing Culture to the People and all that. The way we all took the rise out of the Pops and the People and Politics.

'Well, Howard, now there's a new crowd. The new arty-crafties are different. They're still the same terribly conscious lot, getting all worked up over what's happening. They're still the all brain and no sport, still looking and listening and talking and laughing in all the right places, but you want to see the way they dress. They've got all tight in the right places and their hair's all sharp and well razored and they're as much involved in things as the secondary modern kids. It's not just looking and listening and talking and laughing any more. They have got mixed up in things, all involved. I tell you if you lined this new generation up with the same age lot from the sec. modern, you'd have a job to tell one from tother. The superior air has got left behind. They've got their feet on the ground. The capital letters for art and music and culture have been missed out. You remember the fifth formers, the old teddy boy lot when we were in our last year in the Sixth. Well, this new lot have taken over from there. They're all keyed up and with it all and in. For them things have become a whole way of life. It's De Beat generation all Europeanized, with Banning the Bomb and Jazz and De popular arts. And the point is that down in the beer and piana bars and in the jazz rooms they really are mixing. Howard, they're all right.'[1]

Perhaps the most important bridge, though, was 'The Goon Show', a radio comedy programme that ran throughout the late fifties and went a long way towards preparing the ground

[1] RAY GOSLING, 'I Like You Full Stop', *Queen*, 13 September 1961.

for the current hybrid sub-culture. The origin of the Goon Show and its curious humour lay, I believe, in British National Service. National Service in the time of the H-Bomb, when all defence was geared to massive nuclear retaliation anyway, was an imposed absurdity which English teenage conscripts sustained by forming their own sense of humour, a combination of corny music-hall comedy, the humour of English comic papers like *Dandy* and *Beano*, hatred of war and the officer classes—the army is one place where class distinction is imposed by law—and a wild nihilistic surrealist element which derived from the absurdity of the army itself. Polishing bootstuds and painting coal black were, after all, masterpieces of Dada. The International Christmas Pudding rolled along inevitably. We all heard our Barrack Room fantasies articulated and performed perfectly by the Goon Show team of Spike Milligan (also a trad trumpeter), Michael Bentine, Harry Secombe, Peter Sellers and the bop drummer, Ray Ellington. The Goon Show catchphrases and the Goon Show caricature voices spread into everybody's conversation and provided us all with schizoid subterfuges, vocal disguises. Our attitudes became inflected with Bentine's manic hatred of war and governments (he had been among the troops who released the Belsen prisoners), with Spike Milligan's socialism (a founder member of the Committee of 100 and the Direct Action Committee) and his public conduct (a radio discussion on the nature of humour when he suddenly dried up and refused to speak—another radio interview when he claimed that the Goon show farces were an accurate representation of the world—a fabled public reception where he sat on the steps outside and peppered the arriving guests with inane remarks—the time he sent his wife a telegram asking her to please pass the marmalade). The Goon Show was protest. The Goon Show was surrealist and therefore art, and the Goon Show was every National Serviceman's defence mechanism, was therefore pop.

Two alien traditions had tentatively come together. The influence was widespread.

The chaotic paintings and novels of John Bratby give a graphic picture of the world of the London art schools at this time. Throughout this world the prevailing mood was pure

Goon and the prevailing sentiment was anti-bomb. The crowning expression of both mood and sentiment was the comedy-trad of two bands, the Temperance Seven and the Alberts. The Temps, who started off with a brilliant freak-clarinettist called Joey, finished up in the Top Twenty.

The Alberts, far wilder than the Temps, with disturbing elements of genuine lunacy in their make-up, consisted of the Grey Brothers and Bruce Lacey. The Grey Brothers owned an extensive collection of Edwardian clothes and redundant wind instruments, all of which Dougie and Tony could play with disarming skill. They appeared on all anti-bomb demonstrations and most Communist rallies, Dougie in Norfolk jacket and plus-fours, or white ducks and yachting cap, his cornet and his lecherous greyhound both on golden chains. When they performed at Colyer's, ravers staggered back from the blinding explosives flashing from the bells of the instruments and the sight of Dougie's magnificent genitals hanging in splendour as he sat in kilt and tam-o'-shanter with pheasant plume, blowing the guts out of 'Dollie Grey', while Professor Lacey accompanied on the amplified penny-farthing bicycle. Before their legendary San Francisco engagement (where they flopped miserably–'Now listen mac, what the act needs is a little polish'–and escorted a stuffed camel back through the lost motels of the Western Desert) they performed their riotous 'Evening of British Rubbish' in London and sank a boat in which they were being interviewed by the BBC, or so the story goes. Bruce Lacey made his magnificent hominoids, sick, urinating, stuttering machines constructed of the debris of the century, always with pointed socialist/pacifist overtones but with a profound sense of anger, disgust and gaiety that goes far beyond any simple political standpoint. The hominoids, radio-controlled, began to appear in the act.

Screaming Lord Sutch, with his pop-adaptation of sadistic melodrama, Jack-the-Rippering up his volunteer victim to the thunder of steel guitars, took some of the Alberts' lunacy into the rock-'n'-roll clubs. With his bid for Parliament he took the same spirit into the General Election.

Dick Lester, the director of the Beatles films in which Lacey played, also the producer of films with Spike Milligan, the

Bonzo Dog Doodah Band, and Arthur Brown, swinging down to the stand with a flaming hat, the face of Queequeg and the voice of Michael Bentine, all owe a good deal to this privately run looneybin of Goon Show humour. Other corners of the same madhouse contain the 'Wham' cartoons of Leo Baxendale (simultaneously Secretary of Scottish CND) and the anarchic plays of John Antrobus whose *You'll Come to Love Your Sperm Test* worked nicely on the guardians of Edinburgh morality. His *Bed-Sitting Room,* co-written with Milligan, is possibly the most moving and uncompromising of works about the Bomb. Like Milligan, Secombe and Lacey, Antrobus lives and works in a state of near-manic deadlock with society.

Plays like 'Sperm Test', with its outrageous audience involvement, Lacey's environments—the desolate room with a turd on the easy chair—the total anarchy of Alberts performances, the satiric collages of consumer debris, the public tatty practical jokes, all had certain things in common with what was happening in American art.

Action painting was an art of 'finds'. The painter didn't make the splash of paint, he allowed it to happen and then 'found' it. Cigarette ends, fragments of cartons, were 'found' and left clinging to the canvas. It wasn't such a long step to Rosenquist's paintings of ad art spaghetti against fellatio lipstick, Jasper Johns' bronze beer cans and American flags, Lichtenstein's blown-up comic-strip fragments. It was an extension of the Duchamp 'readymades', the Cubist and surrealist 'found objects', as Action painting had been an extension of surrealist automatic writing, Masson's compulsive calligraphy (automatic writing dissolving into pure calligraphy in Burroughs' work with Brion Gysin). The found objects of Bruce Conner and Kienholz, like Lacey's hominoids and my own constructions, had overtones of social comment.

Having 'found' splashes of paint, having 'found' urban-commercial objects, American painters went on to 'find' human action. A man walking, if presented in a certain way (the way the San Francisco Mime Troup used walking, for instance) related to the dance in the same way that beer cans related to sculpture. Thus the early 'happenings' of Allan

Kaprow, Claes Oldenburg and Jim Dine were by painters and were a direct development from action painting. Happenings were simply three-dimensional paintings in which the movements of painter and public were incorporated into the design. This obviously had a good deal to do with the Cabaret Voltaire, with Janco's masks and Ball's Corinthian column. But the existential difference between the Zurich wartime environment and the smart New York gallery environment makes a significant difference in the nature of the work, no matter what the artist's intention.

The term 'happening' was quickly imposed on the work of a number of people presenting unusual public events. It was applied to the situations by which Ken Dewy in America, Mark Boyle in England and Jean-Jacques Lebel in France provoked their public into acting freely in a given environment. It was applied to the Skoob Tower ceremonies of John Latham. It was applied to rail crashes engineered by Wolf Vostel, to the blood-orgies of Otto Muhl, Gunter Brus, Herman Nitsch and their Vienna Institute of Direct Art, to the Japanese Zero Dimension Group and their erotic demonstrations, to the didactic political events of the International Situationists, the New York Black Mask anarchists and the Amsterdam Provos, to the musical use of action in compositions by John Cage, Cornelius Cardew and recently Stockhausen, to Adrian Henri's romantic collage-events in Liverpool's Cavern Club, to the cool detached exercises of Robin Page and the Fluxus Group with their murdered violins and their public defecation, eventually to wide-open LSD parties where paints and noise apparatus were at hand for anyone to play with, parties which were the fore-runners of the San Francisco Be-Ins and the current mixed-media light shows.

Many 'happenings', those of Ralph Ortiz, Gustav Metzger, Yoko Ono, Al Hansen and others, involved the principle of transformation by destruction. Create a sculpture by tearing up an armchair, a piano, a typewriter, your own clothes, and mount the result as a found object. Clearly when The Who, a particularly violent pop group, went berserk and smashed up their amplifying equipment, and that was subsequently kept in as part of the show, when The Move obliterated effigies of politicians as they played, there was a close connection between the popular music world and the previously separate world of art.

This was no accident. With the work of Lichtenstein and Rosenquist, in which pop commercial images are presented as found objects, a curious coming to terms with pop-industrial culture had been attempted. Art stopped flirting with Nature, as it had since Rousseau, and decided to look its arch enemy, mass production, squarely in the eye. Rosenquist said he painted 'to stop the sky coming in at the window'. Lichenstein said he painted to 'come to terms with' something he 'despised'. But Lichtenstein also wished to paint something unacceptable to the fashionable art world that had clustered round action painting. His paintings were intended as something just too garish and nasty for the snob collectors. The only one it worked on was Peggy Guggenheim. On the whole his intention backfired. Lichtenstein was interpreted as a piece of elaborate camp and was bought up. In England pop art rediscovered a kind of whimsy of the commonplace in Peter Blake's assemblages and David Hockney's gay illustrations. *Dodo, Trad* and other shops up and down the Portobello Road, which was, by now, a place where the three separate traditions could literally be seen intermingling and merging, followed as the outcome of pop art, selling fetishistic bric-a-brac for idiotic prices. Art, then, had moved towards pop.

The members of The Move and The Who, of The Pretty Things and The Rolling Stones, were vastly different, socially and psychologically, from the hard-case rock 'n' rollers. Ex-art students, many of them, who came into pop by way of R & B, they had memories of anti-bomb protest, of the Alberts and the Temperance Seven. They knew about modern painting and sculpture, indeed their counterparts were already creating the current school of English sculpture, smooth, mechanistic, brightly coloured and kinky, so they consequently enjoyed an appreciation of the modern movement as a whole. They broke away from traditional twelve, sixteen and thirty-two bar patterns. They composed their own increasingly sophisticated and imaginative lyrics. They increasingly ignored the mistaken dictates of managers and promoters. They introduced wild fashions which obviously owed a lot to the art school fancy dress rave. They, with their fashion designer parallels, also from the art schools, took popular culture by the scruff and whipped it far ahead of the square administration. Pirate radio, broadcast from ships, islands and bizarre marine structures all around the British coast, whipped the culture, significantly and for the first time, out of reach of the law. It should be made clear that there was nothing of deliberate protest about pirate radios until the extra legislation against them. Radio Caroline, heroically remaining at the time of writing, immediately becomes an underground institution. But initially pirate radio was a purely and brashly commercial enterprise even though it reflected exactly the speed, rhythm and flavour of the maturing alternative culture.

Pirate disc jockeys became trend-setters, known and reputed as such, appointed by the public. In those wild days of 1963-4 they would appear at the Scene, the original mod club in Ham Yard, the premises of the old Cy Laurie Jazz Club, in fantastic clothes, dyed hair, make-up, dictating a new fashion and a new dance every Saturday night. John Lennon's little piece 'At The Neville' sketches in the club scene of the period.

Carnaby Street boutiques opened within a few short months. Tiny shops, run by kids making their own clothes, opened all over the country throughout 1965-6. *Vogue* and *Harpers* were strangers at these places. High fashion, overnight, began to look what it had always been, stilted, pompous and silly. Only Mary Quant among the squares had her ear to the ground. Recently she said, 'The Beautiful People are non-violent anarchists, constructive anarchists. They are the real break-through. But I have been worrying about the way they dress. It can't be called a fashion because it's old clothes, and it's always depressing to wear clothes of the past. Whenever I see that happening I feel we designers have failed to supply the answer.' She needs to worry. Most of her sensational lines so far have been taken from art school jumble-sale fashions— the daisy motif, kitchen curtain materials, granny clothes....

Fashion then, became an applied art. As much inventiveness and creativity was employed there as in the action paintings, the collages and assemblages. The colours were delirious. England had stopped being grey.

The use of optical illusion in painting, a response surely to Boulez's demand for a progressive delirium, became quickly translated into clothes. The use of electronics and stroboscopic lights drove pop music further and further towards public trance.

When Zen, psychedelic drugs, and beat poetry became prevalent the fusion of the three cultures was complete. American Groups like the Mothers of Invention, the Grateful Dead and Jefferson Airplane, playing for 48 hour freakouts in San Francisco's Longshoreman's Hall, had the Beatles on one hand, Bob Dylan on the other, and Ginsberg and Burroughs very close to centre. The whole scene looked like the final arrival of Dan Propper's 'Final Hour':

'In the 10th minute of the final hour the Daughters of the American Revolution applied lipstick to their cunts and mascara to their pubic hairs. Contemplating their handiwork, they decided to sign up for correspondence courses in ventriloquism;

In the 16th minute of the final hour a band of inscrutable indians in full battle regalia filed silently back and forth past a telephone booth in front of the ASPCA;

In the 18th minute of the final hour 6 drunken juvenile delinquents became stupefied on the subway and were carried to Canarsie where they awoke to evening uncertainty. They commandeered a rowboat and headed for open water, and were last seen just outside Sheepshead Bay, rowing erratically and mumbling energetic prayers to Jean Genet;

In the 39th minute of the final hour the president had a wet dream and the navy was ordered into Algiers;

In the 42nd minute of the final hour the indians made their final appearance, stalking up to the candy counter of the New York Paramount wearing football uniforms. They gathered up armfuls of popcorn and grunted up to the balcony, never to be seen again;

In the 45th minute of the final hour there was an abundance of nakedness and hopeful uncertainty;

In the 46th minute of the final hour the first transparent clothing was worn out of doors;

In the 47th minute of the final hour prostitution became un-
 necessary;
In the 48th minute of the final hour all the road signs were altered
 to GO!;
In the 49th minute of the final hour all women's magazines were
 turned into semen;
In the 50th minute of the final hour the Boy Scouts joined with the
 Girl Scouts in a new era of joy and experimentation;
In the 53rd minute of the final hour Jesus Christ appeared on the
 cover of Time magazine along with Donald Duck and J. Edgar
 Hoover...'[1]

The Beatles were and are the biggest single catalyst in this
whole acceleration in the development of the sub-culture.
They robbed the pop world of its violence, its ignorant self-
consciousness, its inferiority complex. They robbed the
protest world of its terrible self-righteous drabness, they
robbed the art world of its cod-seriousness. They reflected
the scene from which they came, where all this fusion of art,
protest and pop had happened previously, in microcosm, for
the world to follow; so that Allen Ginsberg, visiting Liverpool
a year after the Beatles left, was moved to pronounce it 'the
centre of consciousness of the human universe', a statement
more perceptive than extravagant. In Liverpool, however, the
peaked caps, mini-skirts, long haircuts, drugs, happenings,
collages, poetry readings and pop clubs generated a significantly
different atmosphere from that of the London Scene. Liverpool is a roaring, seedy, working-class port. It has something
of the old red-nose Lancashire comedian about it. It has the
crumbling grandeur of the nonconformist north. It has the
whimsicality and drunken recklessness of an Irish docker. It
lacks completely the 'Swinging London' feeling, the Kings
Road, debby, two-seater, sports model element. There's
nothing toffee-nosed about Liverpool. Marcel Duchamp
once said that his life had been devoted to removing the preciosity of art. Liverpool was the place where his idea paid off.
Already it had produced Billy Fury and Clinton Ford. It went
on to produce Cilla Black and Gerry and the Pacemakers

[1] DAN PROPPER from *The Beats*, ed. Seymour Krim, Fawcett Publications,
1960.

besides the Beatles. Freddy and the Dreamers, a scatty surrealist group, came from nearby Manchester. The so-called Mersey beat was a Lancashire version of the heavily negroid Tamla Motown sound. The Liverpool Poets, Adrian Henri, Roger McGough, Brian Patten, Mike Evans, Tonk, and their many local followers, formed a style for public reading with pop groups which, like the work of Milligan and the Alberts, constituted a sort of gentle music-hall surrealism. The music/satire group, The Scaffold, thrived on a local audience. John Lennon of the Beatles wrote in a far more savage mood with pungent sick overtones and illustrated his work with sophisticated little drawings. As The Beatles went their own way more and more, their lyrics more and more reflected the Liverpool spirit—'Yellow Submarine' is a perfect example. On the same album *Revolver*, the Beatles introduced influences of Indian music, electronic music, chamber music and brass band music, a collage technique which is borrowed completely from Liverpool pop art and happenings. 'She's Leaving Home' and 'Eleanor Rigby' both have a strong Patten influence. Brian Patten, the outstanding poet of the whole group, has moved on to a far more individual style. Nevertheless the religious nature of his recent work, derived from meditation and LSD, follows a curiously similar pattern to that of the Beatles' public image.

In 1960 this poem of Adrian Henri's would have seemed unthinkable:

Paul McCartney Gustav Mahler
Alfred Jarry John Coltrane
Charlie Mingus Claude Debussy
Wordsworth Monet Bach and Blake

Charlie Parker Pierre Bonnard
Leonardo Bessie Smith
Fidel Castro Jackson Pollock
Gandhi Milton Munch and Berg

Belà Bartók Henri Rousseau
Rauschenberg and Jasper Johns
Lukas Cranach Shostakovitch
Kropotkin Ringo George and John

William Burroughs Francis Bacon

Dylan Thomas Luther King
H.P. Lovecraft T. S. Eliot
D. H. Lawrence Roland Kirk

Salvatore Giuliano
Andy Warhol Paul Cézanne
Kafka Camus Ensor Rothko
Jacques Prévert and Manfred Mann

Marx Dostoevsky
Bakunin Ray Bradbury
Miles Davis Trotsky
Stravinsky and Poe

Danilo Dolci Napoleon Solo
St John of the Cross and
The Marquis de Sade

Charles Rennie Mackintosh
Rimbaud Claes Oldenberg
Adrian Mitchell and Marcel Duchamp

James Joyce and Hemingway
Hitchcock and Buñuel
Donald McKinlay Thelonius Monk

Alfred Lord Tennyson
Matthias Grünewald
Philip Jones Griffiths and Roger McGough

Guillaume Apollinaire
Cannonball Adderley
René Magritte
Hieronymus Bosch

Stephane Mallarmé and Alfred de Vigny
Ernst Mayakovsky and Nicolas de Stael
Hindemith Mick Jagger Durer and Schwitters

    Garcia Lorca
        and
            last of all
                me.
By 1965 such a poem was inevitable.

III

The point of view was stated with the greatest honesty and clarity by Norman Mailer in his play, *The Deer Park*. The hipster hero, Marion, has failed to allow the girl Elena to kill herself, has, in fact, permitted her to telephone for help when he might have prevented her.

ELENA

...Please call the hospital...Have them send an ambulance over here...to Marion's.

(She hangs up)

I'm sorry, Marion, I'm so sorry, but I don't want to stop.

(She begins to weep)

(It is at this moment that the bomb goes off a hundred miles away—far across the desert. But the light through the window is intense, a white shuddering light. Elena screams and Marion does not move. He merely looks at his hands. When the light has gone, a red glow is left in the sky. Then he begins to speak in a little private voice, a murmur away from the delicate voice of the sensitive gone mad.)

MARION

Dorothea, my mother, she made money from men when she was young, and I was her bastard, a passing gift from a passing prince, no more—because the salmon of his seed did not have such a vast desire to gain the rapids of a janitor's daughter. Yes, I was her bastard, and I grew up while she was doing her gossip column. The cruellest gossip column in the country. An assassin. She used to print the American flag next to her face. So I knew what it was all about. I mean I knew early. She wanted me to be a priest. I was to be her sacrifice—do I have to spell it out? I have this idea so deep in my head

(Striking his forehead)

that the center of hell must be in here, yes I have this idea that I am a saint, and I feel what God feels, and He is an extremity beyond mine because there is an extraordinary destiny He has to achieve and He does not know if He will succeed or not because He is a part of Us. He is failing because We are failing, because We are too cowardly, because We want to move too slowly, and hold to what We have, when the world, the tangible substance of God is ready to be blown beyond existence in those radiations of hate which none of Us can contain any longer. There is a torment coming when the being of all of Us will depend on whether there is a man brave enough, bold enough, to go further in his mind than anyone has ever gone and yet communicate his vision. And I am not that man. I am too weak. I have failed God again...[1]

We were eaten up by repressed violence and we were soured by the constant terror of inconceivable violence being committed on ourselves and the rest of man. From this we had strugglingly produced a culture. It's possible to get hysterical over the obvious connection between that culture, as it stood in 1965, and the Moors Murders. I did. It's possible to get carping about it. Pamela Hansford Johnson did. It's possible to pretend there isn't a connection. That's rubbish.

Romantics, Symbolists, Dada, Surrealists, Existentialists, Action painters, Beat poets and the Royal Shakespeare Company had all applauded de Sade from some aspect or other. To Ian Brady de Sade was a licence to kill children. We had all, at some time, cried 'Yes yes' to Blake's 'Sooner murder an infant in its cradle than nurse an unacted desire'. Brady did it. There were other connections.

Both Brady and Hindley were working class libertines in a world where the working class libertine, from Sillitoe's Arthur Seton to Genet's Claire and Solange, had been eulogized by the rebel culture.

The similarity between Brady and Hindley and Genet's maids is the stronger because the Moors murderers had fallen in love, made their love into a delusion of inviolability, and, as I believe, made a fetish of the licence they thought this afforded them. There were a good many of us doing the same

[1] NORMAN MAILER, *Advertisements for Myself*, André Deutsch.

thing at the time, daring, sexually and emotionally, what would have been unthinkable in the fifties, when we still had our political hopes. A good many of us were trying, like Mailer, to move out of deadlock by breaking all taboos.

Titillatory Nazism was by no means peculiar to Brady and Hindley. We had all applauded and romanticized the American leather-jackets, particularly Hell's Angels, with their swastikas and cheesecutters. There were numerous Nazi overtones in literary life, like the distinguished writer who sent his mistress iron crosses and photos of Hitler signed by himself. Private fantasy, of course, but so was life for Brady and Hindley until the fuzz came calling. Where, in love and sex, does permissible fantasy end as an innocent game and begin as impermissible reality? Had not the surrealists taught us to follow the dream?

Besides this there was Roger McGough having a fantasy girl-friend address a valentine to Ian Brady in one of his poems.

There was the Glasgow tenement background which Brady shared with the Scots who were so active in the London underground, Trocchi, Laing, Telfer, McCafferty, McGrath.

There was the way in which Brady referred to ordinary folk as 'animals', meaning, surely, something very like what we meant when we talked about the 'squares'.

Further, if Brady had had a greater intelligence and a literary talent might he not have written very much like Lautréamont? Lautréamont, whom we had all praised?

Besides this there was the Goon Show adulation. The reverse of the screaming tape was filled with Goon Shows recorded off the radio.

There was the Romantic pantheism, the moonlight trips to the wild moors on amphetamine and cheap wine, no rare combination. There were the overtones of witchcraft, cabbala and bestiality.

There was the sick sense of humour—the grafting of jolly Christmas songs onto the end of the tape of little Leslie Downey whimpering, pleading and screaming; Brady's remark, 'He's a brainy bastard isn't he', as he and Smith carried the butchered Evans upstairs. Both ideas worthy of the best sick comedians. Jokes that not only said, 'We are ill' but also said 'We are ill and so what. We love it'. It was precisely that step that we were all trying to take in our humiliation and despair.

There was the shared enthusiasm for sado-masochistic spy thrillers–'The Man From Uncle', 'The Avengers', the James Bond series, in all of which affectlessness is cultivated as a means to dignity, to be cool; in all of which freedom is blithely appropriated by the hero by the simple technique of not feeling compassion.

There was the widespread rash of sado-masochism in the arts. When Brady and Hindley were carrying out their first murder plans Otto Muhl and Herman Nitsch had already carried out their first ceremonials with entrails, flesh and smeared food. Keith Musgrove and I were discussing publicly disembowelling a human corpse and hurling the guts at the audience. Nitsch lamented the fact that corpses were available to medical students but not to artists. So did we. Del Foley showered the audience with offal at the first Notting Hill Gate festival, and I, with Musgrove and other members of the sTigma team, did a fake disembowelling in Better Books basement. 'I thought you'd murdered her', said Tony Godwin. 'It'll come to that', said John Calder. It was certainly a razor's edge between the public ritual and the private ceremony. At that time we were never quite sure whether what we were doing in happenings was demonstration or personal therapy. Frequently a savagery that began as satire, depicting, say, a politician engaged in some fantastic foulness, changed midway to sadistic participation on the part of the artist, as he expressed himself in the mood of the piece. This was always happening to Lenny Bruce.

We were in a common consciousness, a point of awareness the sharing of which knit us into one mind. Brady and Hindley were the part of that mind that fell separately on the wrong side of the razor's edge.

Moral shame, moral absurdity, moral abuse, moral paradox and moral outrage had frozen us at a point of almost total negativity. The way out was the numbing of the moral sense and the use of the sensation, the pain, and the anger as propulsion. In the perilous adventure towards movement and construction there was the possibility of terrible catastrophe. The catastrophe fell on the heads of Brady and Hindley, who were less sophisticated and less prepared, who did not yet really know how viciously ill they were. The catastrophe fell, God forgive them and us, on the bodies of their defenceless victims, on the spoiled lives of the relatives.

A poet, when told of the first rumours of the Moors Murders, nodded and said 'Ah, it's started.'

Later the same poet said 'You see—there's little doubt, if the twentieth century is the twentieth century, Hitler was the twentieth century politician. But when it comes to it, you just don't do things like that.'

When Pamela Hansford Johnson suggests that Brady and Hindley were the obscene emanation of a widespread sickness in society she achieves a masterpiece of understatement. My own conviction at the time, albeit hysterical, was that Brady and Hindley were the scapegoats, the necessary low point that someone had to plumb before progress was possible. A press photographer I know had to be taken off the case, not on seeing the face of Hindley or hearing the tapes, but on forming the impression that the crowd outside the Court of Inquest at Hattersley stood there in envy rather than indignation.

Pamela Hansford Johnson's mistake was her diagnosis of the sickness, which is not a facile sensationalism with its roots in commerce, but a state of dis-Grace with its roots in the compulsive suicide of the species. The obvious evidence of this lies in the very obvious fact that Miss Hansford Johnson missed, that Brady was a footling amateur, a whimsical eccentric, compared with any decorated, lauded us bomb crew in the Vietnam war, that any judge and jury in support of one and condemnation of the other is the sickest joke of all, that if the Vietnam bombing and the H-bomb are a fair price to pay for the free trade of the West and the survival of Communism, then our journey to the deepest place of hell, though intolerably expensive, did not cost so dear.

In the same year Adrian Mitchell wrote:

ONE: we were swaddled, ugly-beautiful and drunk on milk.
Two: cuddled in arms always covered by laundered sleeves.

THREE: we got sand and water to exercise our imaginative faculties.

FOUR: we were hit. Suddenly hit.

FIVE: we were fed to the educational system limited.

SIX: worried by the strange creatures in our hands, we strangled some of them.

SEVEN: we graduated in shame.

EIGHT: World War Two and we hated the Germans as much as our secret bodies, loved the Americans as much as the Russians, hated killing, depending on the language in the Bible in the breast pocket of the dead soldier, we were crazy-thirsty for Winston Superman, for Jesus with his infinite tommy-gun and the holy Spitfires, while the Jap dwarfs hacked through the undergrowth of our nightmares—there were pits full of people-meat—and the real bombs came, but they didn't hit us, my love, they didn't hit us exactly.

My love, they are trying to drive us mad.

Make love. We must make love
Instead of making money.
You know about rejection? Hit. Suddenly hit.
Want to spend my life building poems in which untamed
People and animals walk around freely, lie down freely
Make love freely
In the deep loving carpets, stars circulating in the ceiling,
People like honeymoon planetariums.
But our time is burning.
My love they are trying to drive us mad.

Peace was all I ever wanted.
It was too expensive.
My love, they are trying to drive us mad.

Half the people I love are shrinking.
My love they are trying to drive us mad.

Half the people I love are exploding.
My love, they are trying to drive us mad.

I am afraid of going mad.[1]

[1] ADRIAN MITCHELL, from *Out Loud*, Cape Golliard Press.

IV

Sickness was, then, for many, a will to enact some definitive ceremony of violence that would spend the aggression inherent in the collective subconscious, exorcise it and thus leave society cleansed of fear, with a clear way out for our over-accumulated frustrated energies. Some impulse of this nature informs Gustav Metzger, Ralph Ortiz, and the Vienna Institute of Direct Art.

Sickness was also, then, the confrontation of taboo, daring the uncountenanceable only to discover that no harm is done—'God has not said a word'. The feeling of exhilaration following the first act which violates the previous restriction, the moment after leaving the Church, committing buggery, making love to one's own sex, when new areas of freedom open out limitlessly like vast meadows. How Leonardo must have felt dissecting his first procured corpse, or Renaissance dukes defying the Pope, or Masaccio painting his earthy, naked Adam and Eve after the draped formalities of the Byzantine convention. The operation proves sick when an early triumph leads headlong into a later folly—marihuana and cocaine into heroin, pederasty into child murder, sado-masochism into permanent harm, psychedelics into mutations and so on.

But sick is also simply what it says, an illness and therefore undesirable. The most sinister possibility remains that the subculture has merely found a different excuse for exactly the same destructive drives as the so-called squares. This is a broad view, cutting across all declared standpoints, based on simple marked similarities.

It seems to me however that these similarities, if they are similarities, are constituted of those elements that are symptomatic reflexes in response to the post-Bomb situation, rather than the elements that constitute deliberate psycho-therapeutic measures—that those elements are the self-appropriated margin of freedom which the hipster manufactures for himself and which the alienated young adopted as a defence measure, the margin of uninvolvement, disengagement, affectlessness, 'cool'. We only really resemble the squares in our defence mechanisms, in our fear.

The cool element prefers the casual fuck, which is an extension of masturbation, to a mutual sexuality which impairs his autonomy; the cool element exchanges passion for movement; the cool element rejects compassion as a burden, as psychologically false; the cool element is the element that responds to James Bond; the cool element feels strengthened rather than assaulted by sick humour; the cool element wears dark glasses, is faceless.

The cool element is also reinforced by drugs which produce an even greater inviolability. Alex Trocchi once told me he first took heroin for the sense of inviolability it gave him. If the cool hipster is severed from identificatory processes and thus from other people's pleasure and pain, he is nevertheless an athlete of time. Cool jazz musicians swing more than hot jazz musicians because cool jazz musicians, their tone clear of vibrato, unburdened by any emotional nuance which may prolong their note unnecessarily, are more mobile around the beat, which is, of course, a measurement in time, and can swing better because of their temporal skill. The same principle applies to Cassius Clay and the Harlem Globetrotters. But this in itself is an enslavement, an enslavement to action and time, an over-awareness of the clock. Drugs, all drugs, even aspirin, will sever this. No user is punctual. All users understand perfectly their own time and their own events, provided they use the same drug. Events outside this awareness are severed from them completely. The alarm system by which appointments, distribution of energy, schedules, are maintained, emergencies met and suffering people relieved, is silenced and from the safety of the silence, ridiculed as 'paranoia' or even 'fascism'. Thus a Hatfield youth, on an LSD trip, sat and watched a baby drown in three inches of water. He may have just seen spiders eating through the walls or a pterodactyl at the window. An experienced tripper, he knows that all before his senses will pass, avoids the alarm which would signify a 'bad' trip and 'keeps his cool'. The baby dies.

A similar dislocation is implied when David Medalla says, as he did recently, that he subscribes to the Eastern belief that reality is an illusion. So does Burroughs. So do a good many others, although, in their adaptation, the belief is substantially sentimentalized and coarsened. The point is that, illusion or not, it is an illusion we live by and is therefore more real, in the sense of being more vital to our self-maintenance, than any metaphysical reality, merely an enrichment but not a necessity to our self-maintenance. By Medalla's belief life and death are of no importance, compassion is a pathetic error, the bomb, by the logical conclusion to which almost no one progresses, is your best friend. It will, after all, liquidate 'illusion' and leave 'inner truth' unimpeded. Possibly the gravest of the psychological gashes inflicted by the bomb is the way in which the hunger for regenerative spirituality becomes discoloured into a vapid pseudo-oriental anti-materialism which says 'Why worry about the world and the human species? They're not real anyway.' 'Let the bombs fall,' writes Joe Berke, 'the biggest bombs, and so a great mandala will unfold, and in one micro moment, all that can be, will be; and all that need be stated, will be stated; and western man will have achieved full and everlasting expression of what no longer need be expressed.'[1]

The end result of such a disengagement can be interpreted as identical to the attitude of the firmly engaged; the rebels can be held to be the same as the entrenched establishment in a different guise. The drug of one is LSD, the drug of the other is patriotism; the one inflicts mutation on his young by LSD, the other by nuclear fallout; the one, if he's a Hell's Angel, roars through the border towns raping and wrecking in motorized battalions, the other, with more vicious equipment, does the same thing in Vietnam; the one suffers from the faceless loveless sex of the psychopath, the other suffers from the faceless loveless sex of the puritan, anal-restrictive bourgeois, the sex of the Playboy Club and the

[1] JOE BERKE in *Fire*, Poets and Painters Press.

strip show. The one courts Nothing as a religious principle by drugs, the other courts Nothing as a political principle by nuclear physics—or so the argument can run. It's vehemently and coherently put in a recent pamphlet by G. Legman— 'The Fake Revolt.' Certainly the obsessive concern of both is death and cruelty while both cultivate a similar affectlessness and both, in America particularly, share the same community neuroses, the aftermath of puritanism.

But even in their reflexes, even in their self-protective devices, there are significant differences marking the rebels off from the squares. We are not sufficiently orientated to Freud or Laing as yet to be able to discount deliberate intention. It would be false to look at the symptomatic diseases of the subculture without their being illuminated by the declared intentions of the people involved, who have said with desperate urgency again and again that they are concerned for the health of man by the removal of restriction and the re-establishment of ecstasy as the pivot of living. Their final cry of policy and underlying alarm, no matter how it may contradict their religious ideas, is 'Ban the Bomb'. There seems no little indication then (being as objective as one can when one is sympathetic) that the affectlessness of the rebel is, as I have said, the toleration of a vast, profound and honest alarm, and an alarm at no projected phantom but at the fact of imminent nuclear destruction which the square persistently ignores. Afflicted by identical neuroses maybe, and with similar effects on his psycho-sexual metabolism, the rebel is honest with his affliction. He advertises whatever is twisting in his mind and testicles with a desperate honesty. He says, '*We are ill.* Admit it'. His gesture and honesty might even lead to public murder.

The square pretends, pretends, pretends. He rationalizes, and rationalized patriotism as a drug merely serves to enlarge the gap between belief and self, between belief and truth. The rebels may burn out that gap by sheer intensive exposure of the neuroses which constitute it.

Legman puts it that such policy invalidates revolt. I can't speak too closely for Americans but I can only repeat that in England the failure of CND looked like the end of effective revolt unless we were prepared to move, as the American

Negroes were, to wholesale political murder. Left with this situation we could, as Burroughs advocated, dismantle the destruction machine, disassemble society. This being the situation, our very sickness and humiliation was a virus which we could spread. We could spread it by inflaming it and acting it out publicly, whereby squares could either recognize it in us and themselves and cure it, cure this terrible destructiveness, or they could contract it, have it spread within and amongst them until they were incapable of human communication, punctuality, honesty, until all sense of property, identity and morality was dissolved. A desperate measure and one which required our own self-sacrifice. This, I believe, is what society is now witnessing. If the squares want to stop the rot, save their children and believe in their society there is one and only one utterly indispensable first step—nuclear disarmament at any price, whatever the risk to the nation.

V
The Underground

The atmospheric colours have changed from negative to positive when disaffiliation from the original majority is discovered to constitute affiliation to an international minority holding more internal understanding and cultural power than any government or group of governments.

I

May 1965. They have been bombing Nicosia. Criton shows me his drawings. Why are Criton's curtains always closed? You leave Ballard's Lane at Finchley Central, you say 'hello' to the newsboy on the corner who you once taught. He grins. Old Nutty don't change much, do 'e?

You walk down the road and over the bridge and you see this court of post-war jerrybuilt flats, the exposed plumbing, the raw brick and tile, the bourgeois pretensions of front gardens (unkempt, carrying fragments of sweet wrappers, bus tickets, on the sodden stumps of flowerbeds—maggots in the rose) and the stained glass front doors and windows. And Criton's flat, in the other used open family flats, is closed like a blind face. Curtains drawn. Will he answer the door? Is he ill or dead? Is the blindness of the house the same as his eternal blandness—Criton's irremovable grin set like a garden gate across his violated sensibility.

He is home, grinning. He shows me his drawings. They are much better than his previous work. The pedestrian, self-conscious cubist-pacifist designs are still visible, stacked in a corner of his studio. These new drawings twist in a summary of shock—one line, wiry, poised, feeling its way along the contours of the bombed, terrified figures. The drawings are formally ambiguous—a disconcerting uncertainty about whether volume or recession is described—you can read the line two ways too often. Often the drawings are grotesquely erotic, with a kind of berserk sarcasm. Criton talks guardedly. He wants to get us all together. He serves tea and biscuits. He is going to invite me to a meeting, an exhibition, a party. He is working with Dave Trace and an architect friend. There'll be a meeting-exhibition at his pad. There'll be a maquette of his planned environment, an extension of the sTigma. There'll be a book to describe it. There'll be Issue Two of Amaranth. He wants something from everybody. Yes, yes, sure Criton. I have this urge to go away from Criton. I've had it for two years. The whole damn project is directing my dream. My dream belongs to my preserved otherness from things, God, nature, all men and most women. My dream is aimed, I suppose, at God but if it were to turn in another direction I wouldn't stop it or have anyone else determine which way it is to face. Criton pulls at my dream, he pulls me from women, he competes with my family-life like the jazz band used to, like CND used to.

We sit and drink tea. There is this cold polished surface on what Criton says—no humour, no irony, except that ineradicable grin of goodwill in the midst of his pride.

I agree with Criton. Our ideas coincide. CND failed. The sTigma failed. The facts are there. We must do what little we still can. But we face one another over tea and as I undertake to write for Amaranth, to provide constructions for the exhibitions, to attend the meeting, my sensibilities turn away. We part, having made extensive plans, with no common feeling. Back up the hill. Finchley Central. Crazy.

In 1962 I went to Salzburg, a long way on a dull train. No buffet. No bar. No other English-speaking person. My first hours alone for any length of time since childhood. I went to Salzburg with a CND badge on, and on the way back, at one fixed point along the night journey, I quite firmly saw that the Campaign had failed, that I must use the bomb as an evolutionary spur, and I took my badge off.

It was all now a question of becoming, of accelerating evolution beyond the point of special suicide. And I had to explain all this to Criton a few short weeks after my return—the first meeting with Criton, the first meeting between us.

We may not have met if Currel-Brown hadn't gone to Gloucester. Currel-Brown wrote his letter to *Peace News* in the previous July: 'I would like to contact a few *Peace News* readers who share my concern. I shall be as brief as possible as I have a feeling that all this has been discussed in your columns before.

'I believe that art is not a small remote compartment of human experience, like croquet or spider-watching, but a vital activity, a communication to all men about, for instance, life and death, good and evil, war and peace within and without the individual. The imagination can be at least as explosive a power for peace, love and individualism as any there is for war and oppression, as every dictator has had to know.

'But in the contemporary art world it is very unfashionable to be "committed" even in the broadest sense. While this can be seen as an amply justified revulsion against what has happened, for instance, in Communist countries, it saddens me that when thousands of pictures are sold in London every year, which are concerned solely with "texture" and "tension" and similar purely technical problems, the only "committed" works which are at all well-known are a few cartoon-like variations on a theme of mushroom clouds and crosses and emaciated, sculptured marchers.

'Great galloping rampaging imaginations are needed to create an idiom as all-embracing and as hard-hitting as the Dada movement that took organized society by the scruff of the neck during the First World War. They must combine the ruthless honesty of Francis Bacon with the vision of religious painters; they must shout and shock and pray and never resign themselves to Armageddon.

'I am, at present, painting with such things in mind and would like to contact three or four artists, amateur or otherwise, to whom these ideas appeal with a view to an exhibition in London in, say, six months time. A large proportion of any profits could be given to the Committee of 100 and to Oxfam, and the exhibition would be as large and well-advertised as possible. A statement of basis of the group might be published. Would any one interested please write to me at this address.'[1]

I answered the letter and a second letter before going to Salzburg. I had a hundred or so big paintings, seven novels and a number of sculptures piled up in my studio. Bond Street and straight publishing had rejected me thoroughly and repeatedly and I had, by now, rejected them. The letter seemed to indicate where and how I wanted my work to reach a public. When I got back from Salzburg I wasn't so sure. Was 'commitment' going to help me to jump off the end of the limb, or was that jump in itself a commitment?

[1] From *Peace News*, 13 July 1962.

Brown had cracked up. Before this point all one's friends had been idealistic, balanced, articulate. After this point breakdown was common. Everybody's self-maintenance collapsed. Currel-Brown passed the replies to his letter on to Criton Tomazos, then retired to Gloucester to write *Smallcreep's Day*.

Criton called a meeting. With misgivings at being dragged back into the peace movement, I went.

The house was semi-detached in Golders Green. There was an acid sunset spilled across the sky behind the television aerials. The Tomazos family had given their son the ground floor front room. Besides me there was a sixth-form schoolboy and his pot-headed friend. I had never met a schoolboy pothead before. He was a dark, good-looking schoolboy pothead.

Criton conducted the meeting with a perilous efficiency. He qualified everything he said and he qualified every qualification. Behind him was a mural, a sentimental Guernica, his work-in-progress. I explained my position. I agreed that there was common ground—we all wanted to wake people up. We agreed on an exhibition, an environment exhibition. We agreed to pool ideas in a book which we could show round. We planned the exhibition for the crypt of St Martins in the Field where several pacifist events had taken place and we made a date to meet there. Then we went and got drunk—one of those too quick adolescent piss-ups. The schoolboys got hysterical and rolled on the floor. I got avuncular and giggly. Criton sat cold sober with his grin correctly fixed in place across his face. Rocking sickly on the bus home I felt some nightmare naïvety pinning me down in adolescence. Condemned for life to play and plan with kids while manhood remained somewhere out there to the eternal north, unattainable even by the hardest pessimism.

Bright autumn day. A CND march going by, almost like hard sunlit ghosts, a passing dream. Incalculable remoteness, now, after Aldermaston. A kid gave me a handout and I stopped myself wanting to cry. Stop. Definitely. Just like that. Stop.

The man who showed us the crypt seemed sympathetic. It was cool. The Dick Sheppard Memorial Chapel seemed to me an opportunity for some rich sour work. How could I explain the shriek I wanted to smear across the public face? Criton was all virginity and silence. He excused his optimism continuously like an eager student. He was anxious to please, eager and humble. I could explain my position and describe the twisting pain in my skull to Criton and he would say 'yes' because he was intelligent and more than articulate but he wouldn't and couldn't understand. Not with an innocence as wide and seemingly invulnerable as his.

We measured the crypt, made our floor plans, drawings, maquettes and scale models. The Vicar of St Martins took one look at our ideas and said, 'This is not for St Martins'—sanctimonious nasal voice, music-hall vicar.

Something about Criton's ideas angered me, big dumb rounds of plaster—silence, always silence. It wasn't an aestheticism that avoided the point. It wasn't the student immaturity of his vision and technique. It was, and remained, something to do with the bland guiltless Apollonian spirit that informed him. He seemed informed by the idea of everything and never by its physical presence. As Mozart always unfailingly makes me want to smash things, so Criton gave some savage impetus to my own ideas for the exhibition.

We sent the folio of ideas to Bryan Robertson at the Whitechapel. He ignored it. It became obvious that he intended to go on ignoring it after he'd had it a year without reply. I said, 'Let's do a magazine. Keep us occupied until we do the show'. I had just duplicated a book of poems with Keith Musgrove. The possibilities of duplicating (mimeographing) yawned invitingly. I turned out *My Own Mag: a Super-Absorbant Periodical* in November 1963, as an example of the sort of thing we might do. My intention was to make a paper exhibition in words, pages, spaces, holes, edges, and images which drew people in and forced a violent involvement with the unalterable facts. The message was: if you want to exist you must accept the flesh and the moment. Here they are.

The magazine, even those first three pages, used nausea and flagrant scatology as a violent means of presentation. I wanted to make the fundamental condition of living unavoidable by nausea. You can't pretend it's not there if you're throwing up as a result. My hope was that a pessimistic acceptance of life would counteract the optimistic refusal of unpleasantness, the optimistic refusal of life, the deathwish, the bomb. I was miles away from the utopia of Criton or anyone else. I was close to the blues, to Picasso, to Sartre. Criton didn't like the Mag, thought it negative and disgusting. I felt a little shamefaced.

The French teacher at the school where I worked duplicated the first mag for me. He liked it. He said, 'Do it again'. He was called Bob Cobbing.

I circulated the first Mag to twenty or so people who I thought might be interested. Better Books took the rest and sold them at a penny each. I determined then, and kept to it, that I would run the project as I had painted and played jazz, within the capacity of my earnings as a teacher, utterly independently, ultimately printing, editing, assembling, drawing, writing largely, and distributing the thing myself, always at a deliberate loss so as not to form a dependence of the smallest kind. I got replies from Ray Gosling, Anselm Hollo and William Burroughs.

Like most people then, I only knew Burroughs through magazine extracts from his novels. I had read *The Naked Lunch* extracts in *Big Table* particularly often, and misunderstood them. The similarity to my own imagery showed that we were in the same place but Burroughs was travelling in the opposite direction. It took me some time to realize this. Beyond acceptance, my direction was towards the aesthetic of obscenity. Clearly what is called beautiful is merely what was called ugly previously. It was time to step up the pace. Circumstances left us with unrelieved obscenity. So, I thought, let us take that obscenity and make beautiful things with it, as Picasso had with bombed people, as blues saxophonists did with all the anal-erotic grunts and squeals of sexual discord. But let's first (and this, I thought, was my common ground with Burroughs) let's show people where they stand in such a way as to force them to acknowledge the unalterable elements in their condition. Let's force people to accept life and live it.

But the obscenity of *The Naked Lunch*, far from being a device for contriving the acceptance of life, was intended as a device for obliterating life as it had ever been known. Mr

Bradley Mr Martin stood not only for Left and Right politically, but for left and right physically, not only for East and West politically but for east and west physically, not only for right and wrong but for good and bad. The composite figure BradleyMartin and the hilarious replica sequence satirized all opposites and dualities by which man is trapped in space, time, in both existential and sociological identity. Opposites are linguistically defined. Dissolve language, said Burroughs, and opposites drift into harmonious unity. Man has been cheated of oneness. His way back to it was by the dissolution of language, the dissolution of definition, the dissolution of individual identity and the formation of a society with one harmonious mind telepathically informing all bodies in an interminable life out of time. 'Junkies of the world united on a string of rancid jissom', said Burroughs, perversely guying his own concepts. If the Romantics believed man's province was the sublime, Bill Burroughs believed, believes man's province is the subliminal. It was a logical extension of the surrealist belief in the greater reality of dream, of Tzara's onslaught on the conventional concepts of reality, of de Chardin's belief in the consolidated Noosphere, of Dunne's belief in the illusory nature of time, of the ancient communities of the Mayas who existed in a common consciousness precipitated from the Gods through the priests, of the ego-dissolution of Zen. Burroughs in fact was not only saying, 'You must become God by dissolving yourself into timelessness—otherwise you perish as a species by your own hand' —he was also prepared to force, contrive and trick people into the dissolution of self. He was prepared to do the dissolving:

'The Human Being are strung lines of word associates that control "thoughts feelings and *apparent* sensory impressions". Quote from Encephalographical Research Chicago Written in TIME. See Page 156 Naked Lunch Burroughs. See and hear what They expect to see and hear because The Word Lines keep Thee In Slots...

Cut the Word Lines with scissors or switch blade as preferred The Word Lines keep you in Time...Cut the in lines... Make out lines to Space. Take a page of your own writing of

143

you write or a letter or a newspaper article or a page or less or more of any writer living and or dead...Cut into sections. Down the middle. And cross the sides...Rearrange the sections...Write the result message...

No one can conceal what is saying cut up...You can cut The Truth out of any written or spoken words//

Cut up and spray back of all minds living...The human are being strung lines of In when you cut it up...

No one can con Cut Up...Cut your own where...Humans are struction to thought feel all minds...Cut the'[1]

The first step then was the dislocation of the word, the main line of power control. A writer, Burroughs was well situated to sabotage language. The irony when critics take a Burroughs cut-up and 'expose' its 'lack of literary merit' is rich indeed. Rather like criticising a murdered corpse for not being healthy.

The cut-up method, already announced in *Minutes To Go* and *The Exterminator*, two Underground booklets, already demonstrated at the Edinburgh Writers' Conference organized by John Calder in 1962, already constituting large sections of the novels *The Soft Machine* and *The Ticket That Exploded*, was first launched as a programmed assault on reality in the Moving Times section of *My Own Mag*.

June 1965. At the meeting there are a lot of people I don't know. I don't know the girl with pink trousers. I think she's close to Criton. I hope she is. If Criton gets his oats more often, or at all, I might get closer to him.

Outside Criton's flat the evening is warm and mellow. A liquid golden light drowns the valley of red-roofed suburbs between Totteridge and Ken Wood. I am in love and ashamed of it. My control has gone. Does Criton understand this? Will he? Can he understand that this kind of love dismantles your machinery like a habit? That I can make no promises?

Wilcocks is there and Bruce Lacey is there and John Latham is there and John Rowan is there. The Musgroves haven't come. Neither has Trocchi or Cohen or Watkins.

We sit round and talk. Criton shows his drawings, his plans

[1] WILLIAM BURROUGHS, *The Exterminator*, Auerhahn Press.

and his maquettes for his environment. We have seen the flat which has itself been made an environment for the purpose of the meeting. Violent constructions stand in the corners with sarcastic little plastic ornaments distributed over them. We discuss the question of money for Criton's project. It involves a multi-storey building, would cost thousands. I quell my anger at the old protective trick : plan outside your pocket if you want to avoid being effective.

The plan carries out all that Criton felt lacking in the sTigma, the moral seriousness, the wit, the confrontation with self and nothingness rather than with the plethora of nausea we had constructed in Better Books basement. It illustrates the eloquent and architectural use of space and proportion rather than the angry claustrophobic impositions of the sTigma. I avoid a central position in the discussion. I still fear that my ebullience will offend and disrupt the team. I haven't yet clarified in my mind that the disagreement in the sTigma came from our working at cross purposes. Criton, Wilcocks and I were moralists with CND backgrounds. The others were antimoralists with no background of social protest.

As Criton talks on I wonder how to tell him that he is avoiding action, that ultimately he'll be confronted with the vapidity of his own idealism.

Then I make my excuses and get out. I want to swim in guilt and evening light. I want to get drunk.

Burroughs sent his first testing letters from Tangiers. In the bitter winter of 1964 he came to London. He was stopped at the customs and his visit was limited to fourteen days, no reason given. I went to meet him. The hotel in Bayswater was as unremarkable as a Wimpy bar. The room was what you'd expect. A pale boy came in partway through our conversation. He looked younger than he was, had button eyes and a button nose. He was ill with junk.

Another friend came in—Tony Balch. Tony and Bill talked about films. They were unimpressed by Jack Smith's *Flaming Creatures*—Tony had seen a Brakhage birth film at Knokke, was enthusiastic. He had passed out watching it. Both were very concerned for subliminal effect—the direct impact on the nerve, the dislocation, redirection of the neuro-psychological complex. McLuhan militant. Through the casual drift of the conversation Bill interspersed testing, hinting remarks, nudging me towards an understanding of what he was doing with cutup, 'The whole damn thing—cutup—establish a schizophrenic relationship with a typewriter'. He spoke elliptically, shyly. He was careful to see that his sentences reached your ears in fragments. He perpetually dealt in clues and hints, never in explanation. It seemed something of an irritation to him to have to communicate verbally at all. His stoop, his thinning hair, his thickening impassive businessman's face dissolved periodically in the force of his tiny pebble eyes and the mobility of his exquisite lips and he became a creature of unnerving purity and energy, a quicksilver thing, all nerve, weightless. '—Innarested in—Mag—noospaper format— columns—juxtaposition—headlines. Could take a walk—recording— what I call *innersection point*—an' y'have a little picture—Might be—uh—streetcorner—name of the street. On y' go—get on a bus—Little picture, number of the bus—Recording, recording. Then cut it up, grid it, shuffle it, fold it in. Feed it back.'

Coupling this with a later understanding of the intersection point indicates the hard fact that for Burroughs the passing events of time were timeless. A horizontal walk down an ordinary street was for him an unaltering existence, perpetually simultaneous out of time, uncontinuing.

'—All go—pub—drink maybe—', and so we went. There was floral wallpaper up the stair well. Wordlessly we passed down the stairs, out into a cold, clear night. Above the amputated trees in the square the stars were like spilled sherbet. I had a terrible quick sense that I was losing them. The saloon bar was full of whacks burbling over jolly pints of E. We found a table in the public bar. There was a lot of bright glass and a dart game. My customary sentimentalization of the crowd ran on to very dry ground. 'F'r instance—party. Have a party, 'joy yerselves. Everybody comes, writes an account of the evening to come. Tape record the evening. Cut accounts in with tape, grid, shuffle, see what comes up…'

Tony and Bill talked on. I started to get drunk, amiable puppy drunk. When I asked Bill if I could buy him another gin and It he said, 'Yes, I want more', like that—sort of old-fashioned. A plain dry statement of a physical fact.

I got drunker, piling down pints of sentimentality. Burroughs' personality cut across me like a diamond.

We left. The boy went to the hotel. We chose the drabbest of the egg-and-chip cafés along Queensway, went in and ordered a meal. By now I was effusive and a little maudlin, went to the lavatory, walked into the Ladies, came back and made a loud beery joke about it. Went on to clumsy chat about queers and drag shows. Burroughs nodded, played me along nicely. Balch was bent over with hilarity and embarrassment. A disengaged observer in my brain who never never gets drunk but always watches for fun was impressed by the intelligence of Burroughs' tolerance and a little sadistically satisfied at Balch's discomfiture. Balch and the boy had both got my grammar school blood up a little with their Senior Quad drawls. I was half-determined to be as gauche and butch as possible.

We finished the meal and split. I shook Burroughs' hand warmly. I felt considerably honoured. I think I said so. I meant to. Then I went and drank more in the grimy bar at the top of Bayswater Tube Station. An old woman muttered to herself and the lights swam in the beer. Music. Two short months later it dawned on me fully what Burroughs was attempting. It was like the earth opening under your feet.

October 1965. There is a special peculiar atmosphere to these Better Books functions, a sort of curious mixed atmosphere, part Quaker, part Anarchist, part decadent. The crowd usually consists of idealistic figures in publishing, up and comings, amiable potheads, one or two celebrities, and a rash of kids of all three sexes.

There is always a lot of cheap red wine, chat in the upstairs room and something happening in the basement. This time the Musgroves have come. Alex is talking to a man from Millbrook. Calvin Hernton and John Keys, homesteaders in the newly opened Kingsley Hall, are there, Keys jiving with a thin, closed, dark girl. Criton has his grin with him. Had I known I would have brought my Noddy mask.

The basement is divided into compartments with ironic Christmas decorations. Criton is ironic. I am sarcastic. Constructions, some adopted from the Group H exhibition, some specially constructed, are lying around like a picnic of cadavers.

Under the arch, in a screened off room, Criton is showing the maquette for the cage, the book of photographs illustrating its aims. He is still hoping to drum up contributions. I wonder whether to ask him what he proposes to do with his time until the funds are there. I decide not to.

Gradually the party moves upstairs and finally out into the street. The wine is churning redly in my guts and I have decided to make a scene somewhere.

I put *Mr Watkins* together wrongly, treated the idea like a wild way of making a word object. That was okay but Burroughs meant the project as the dissolution of time.

Mr Watkins Got Drunk And Had To Be Carried Home was, is, though, a fair record of Writers' Forum. Officially a committee ran 'Arts Together' but really it was Bob Cobbing. 'Arts Together' was the far-out division of the Finchley Society of Arts. Finchley Society of Arts, a pretty typical collection of public virgins, divided themselves from their far-out division over the inclusion of the new youth group in the ranks. This was a bunch of kids taught by John Moate and I, finally by Cobbing as well, mostly from the Alder School, a forbidding secondary modern in East Finchley. They did possibly the finest junk sculpture I've ever seen, together with fantastic erotic paintings and drawings. They wrote an odd wayward kind of pop-poetry.

In 'Arts Together' Writers' Forum was the literary platoon. They published duplicated monographs, a magazine called *And*, held mutual butchery sessions every week, winter readings in the library and summer readings in the park. At different times regulars were Lois Heiger, Nancy Taylor (long-suffering Nancy), Gerda Meyer, Jean Salisbury, me, Bob, Barry Cole, Keith Musgrove, Heather Musgrove, Dick Wilcocks, John Moore, Bill Butler, Jeff Cloves, Lee Harwood, Mike McGrinder, and, the best of the English beat-imitators, Derek Roberts, still unpublished but for a WF booklet. The atmosphere was, again, that odd mixture of middle class liberalism and flat-out mad. This was because of the conjoining of professional with amateur, of totally committed artists with do-gooders, a nice working mixture that has never happened in Centre 42 and isn't likely to while Wesker continues to whine about professionalism as though it were equated with creative merit. Ultimately it was Writers' Forum that first published Ginsberg's *The Change* (a poem whose colossal importance has scarcely yet been realized) and made available a good deal of work in the 'concrete' field, notably that of Dom Pierre Sylvester Houédard, the anarchic monk who bombards the world with classic Dada from Prinknash Abbey, and B. P. Nichols, a Canadian poet whose work goes parallel with the more expressionist concrete poetry of D. R. Wagner and D. A. Levy. Concrete poetry, elsewhere published by the Wild Hawthorn Press of Ian Hamilton Finlay, and the sound poetry of Cobbing and Ernst Jandl is, in fact, a development of the aesthetic potential in the leavings of Dada. Its message, finally, is close to that of Tzara, of Burroughs, of Rothko, of Laing, of John Latham. No Thing (no particular thing, no defined thing, no isolated thing, all-inclusive totality, total spirit) is Everything. Everything is Nothing. To live completely you must acknowledge the significant void.

The visual platoon of 'Arts Together' was called Group H. It held frequent exhibitions wherever anyone would let it. Regular exhibitors were me again, Rowan and Cobbing again, John Latham, Bruce Lacey, Brian Wall, Gaby Weissman, Islwyn Watkins, Criton Tomazos, but our pieces were invariably overshadowed by the jangling barrel-organ jazz of amateurs like John McCarthy, Colin Shorter, Jeff Cloves, Frank Taylor, Alan Baker, and the brilliant David Rothman. Dave Warren is possibly the finest sculptor working in England at the present time. The average Group H exhibition looks something like a cross between a carousel and a concentration camp. Barbara Wright, writer and translator of Jarry and Queneau, was our solitary critical champion.

There were theatre, music and cinema platoons as well which featured at one time and another the budding talent of Lionel Bart, the British première of Genet's *Love Song* and the first happenings to be performed in London. Currently Cobbing is opening his own arts centre in the newly pulsating Covent Garden area. It promises to be good. After all, for the past three years John Calder, Arnold Wesker, Alex Trocchi, Joan Littlewood, Martin Bax, Miles and the Greater London Arts Council have been promising creative recreational centres for London, but the only place in London where that kind of thing has been regularly going on (until the recent UFO and Haynes' Arts Laboratory) has been Better Books, the Charing Cross Road shop where Cobbing was manager and would be still if Collins, who own Better Books, hadn't wised up to the scene.

The people I invited to write their accounts and come to the party were from Writers' Forum and Group H. They seemed handy and literate. Keith, John, Bob, Lois, me and Nick Watkins provided accounts and Nick set it as a subject at the school where he was teaching, so provided some marvellous copy a good long time before Brian Johnson used the same technique in *Albert Angelo*. The result, sieved and shuffled, was *Mr Watkins*. I ran off a handful of copies and distributed them around WF.

April 1966. The phone goes. Criton. I don't want to see or speak to anybody. I've recently had a nervous crack-up and managed to pass it off to the family as flu—three wincing days bound in the sheets, trying to dull my screaming nerves. I want to hibernate. And now Criton rings.

He speaks like a gnome, the way he spoke coming away from the Maudsley after seeing John. This doesn't help. He asks if he can come and see me and of course I say yes. The hell of it is I agree with the man. He'll come now, he says, and there is really no good reason why he shouldn't.

I open to his knocks. He looks even more gnomish, impressively solemn much of the time and the grin changed from the old amiable five-bar gate to a new aggressive coyness—a you-know-and-I-know-and-we've-all-known-all-along kind of grin.

I ask him how his fund is going and I suppose it must sound sarcastic but I don't mean it that way. Whatever way he takes it, he doesn't reply. I realize that the conversation is to be carried on in hints and signals which for the moment I prefer. I am, in any case, in an unrelieved delirium in which the reorientated systems of gravity and proportion are big and simple voices and temperatures, common reference points for minds dissolving into one another.

The simple interpretation of what we agree upon, squatting on my living room carpet, grunting, grinning, tittering and probing, is this: Eternity is God. The barrier to God is ego, will and fear. The route to God is insanity, the dissolution of identity through the dissolution of rational relationships. Psychosis has been the common language of art since Rimbaud. We all dwell in Eternity in the more significant parts of our being. The temporal parts of our being deny this. We are agreed on this. What there is some disagreement over is whether or not to dissolve completely our temporal separate existence or to maintain that separate existence as a penance until death. However there is sufficient agreement between us for us to decide on a little project.

This then is what Criton is doing with his time while he waits for the funds. He has also been spending a good deal of his time at Kingsley Hall.

The first job I have to do for Criton is duplicate a circular for him. I get the skin through the post and nip in after school hours to turn it out. It is an invitation to the people living around Kingsley Hall to attend an event. It is simply phrased for the general public. Criton's more complex invitation he duplicated and circulated himself.

MY. FLOWERS. GROW
WITHOUT. WHOSE. PERMISSION
FOCUS. THIS. WAY.

SO...IT...HAPPENS...ON APRIL 1st...PRECISELY... 7-8PM...inside or outside...Kingsley Hall...Powis Road... Bow E3...Advance 2532....The world knows already...the neighbours will/have been informed...THE CROWDS WILL/ invade...at the appointed T.I.M.E....the police WILL/HAVE BEEN there to contain any disorder Please listen carefully... before you evacuate...and lock THE DOORS:
(1) Request the Ground Grand Hall for MY HAPPENING...

NOBODY PLANS MY HAPPENINGS...They just...
I am seeing Bruce Lacey at 2pm. today asking him to install
2 loud SPEAKERS and one...round-the-neck microphone...
Please lock him out...because he may not come at all...

(2) I will/have made alternative arrangements with local/church
authorities for another hall...in case IT RAINS OUTSIDE...
if it does...THE WEATHER STOPS NOBODY'S
TEARS as they watch the tely...to find out WHATS GOING
ON...GOT IT?SO BE IT...

(3) Everybody HAS BEEN INVITED few/many/nobody
WILL COME

(4) I suggest you do/do not invite doctors and patients from
FLOWERING HOSPITALS at a moment's notice...

If Ronnie is still suffering with flu...entza...give him a kiss from
NOBODY'S LIPS...Ask him to CALL ME JUDAS

MY. LOVE. TO. ALL.

I deliver the copies to Criton. The curtains are drawn but inside
the air is crackling with mischief. I join Criton in the joke. I walk
into his house. I lean against the jamb of the kitchen door while
he makes a cup of tea. There is a corpse at my elbow. Yellow,
emaciated, lolling head, eyelids puffed. The mischief drains
away. My legs are water.
Only Criton's flat mate—Chinese student, dopey with sleep.
What a giggle. Nevertheless I get out fast. Quicksand.

The first copy of the *Moving Times* reached me in May, ready
for the special Tangiers edition of *My Own Mag*. It was in
three columns—the first of the column cutups—cod-newspaper
format. The first column contained the explanation:

> ' "We will Travel not only in Space But In Time as Well."
> A Russian scientist said that. Let's start travelling. Form the
> words into columns and march them off the page. Start with
> newspapers like this: Take today's paper. Fill up three columns

with selections. Now read *cross* columns. Fill a column on another page with cross column readings. Now fill in the remaining columns with selections from yesterday's papers and so on back. Each time you do this there will be less of present time on the page. The page is "forgetting" present time as you move back in time through word columns. Now to Move forward in time. Try writing tomorrow's news today. Fill three columns with your future time guesses. Read cross column. Fill one column on another page with your cross column readings. Fill the other columns with tomorrow's newspaper. Notice there are many hints of the so-called future in your cross column readings. When you read words in columns you are reading the future, that is you are reading on subliminal level; other columns on the page that you will later experience consciously you have already read. "You don't remember me, Mister?"

You will see "me" tomorrow and tomorrow and tomorrow to the last syllable of recorded time because you have written and read "me" today. You still don't remember? Your memory of the future will improve in columns.'

The second column was cross-readings from the *Tangiers Gazette*. The third was phrases from *Nova Express* cut in with fragments of the *New York Times*, both newspapers very old copies.

COLUMN TWO: 'For beginners today we are going to study the verb *fix*. I fix I fixed I have fixed. The general meaning of *fix* is to fit together or put in place as I fixed the notice to the board…'
COLUMN THREE: 'Mr Bradley Mr Martin stood there in dead stars heavy with his dusty answer drew September 17, 1899 over New York that morning giving you my toy soldiers put away steps trailing a lonely dining room cool remote Sunday…'
CROSS COLUMN: 'A Russian scientist said for beginners today Mr Bradley Mr Martin said that lets start there on dead stars form the word into verb *fix*. I fix I fixed I heavy with his dusty columns have fixed the general answer drew September off the page…'

'…you can write your dreary walk before you take it. Until you find the only walk is out…'

I read it. Very good. Crazy. Too much. Then I typed it on to the skin and read it again. Jesus Christ.

The future was present in the subliminal. Cross-column readings, shuffle-ups, cutups, were an utterly incorruptible voice, not belonging to any self-interested individual, not attached to any needing, habituable body, an accessible truth beyond the trivial statistics of time and matter. 'No one can con Cut Up.'

If you want to get to the root of your behaviour cutup, I quickly discovered, is a better way than hypnosis or auto-suggestion. Whatever the truth in Burroughs' assertions (and I believe there is considerable having seen his by now extensive evidence) when scanning across three columns of print the phrases you select from the scrambled words are selected by a part of your mind that has no direct voice. The idea then goes on to say that that part is the common mind, the mind you share with previous ages, the Jungian racial subconscious through which Artaud communicated with the so-called dead, the mind we share with one another, the chain of consciousness along which information sometimes races like a bolt from —well, from where? Where does the information start?

One thing was becoming a severe, close point of concentration between a number of us. Rational communication comes nowhere near this area of mind. If your communication is to result in action, in change of direction, then argument, McLuhan's 'hot' information, the communication used by CND, by all political protesters, ostensibly by all politicians, is useless. The advertisers had the people moving their way. What was required was an explosive planted straight into the human subconscious to blow it off course. I became excited. There were elements about the whole thing that contradicted my nauseous pantheism. Was our violence aimed at showing people their location or at dislocating them? Whichever aim here was a chance and anyway there was little to lose—'All is not yet lost Moriarty'. I began to glimpse an end to the sickness. From the middle of violence, cruelty and complete writhing despair there seemed a possibility of light...

Beyond this there was a further and more serious possibility—that matter follows information, that the thing that is lied about will ultimately act the lie, that the thing that is masked will cease to exist. Burroughs currently attempts control of people's lives by playing tapes of obscene or pleasant sound in their vicinity, spells of aesthetics. Lives take on the quality with which they are surrounded. The evil spirits follow the evil sounds.

This, then, was the region in which Burroughs was operating. Nothing new about it. Zen. Dada. Surrealism. Even Christianity. Any line of thought which derogated matter in the face of the spirit was echoed here. The unnerving thing that made the *Moving Times* like a cataclysm was that this was not preached or put forward as a legitimate flight of the imagination. This was being applied to reality in order to destroy reality. Not theory—lab work, the psychological equivalent of germ warfare. As Burroughs so merrily quoted, 'Let petty kings the name of party know/Where *I* come I kill both friend and foe'.

No sooner had the signals gone out in that fifth issue of *My Own Mag* than they started to come back. Carl Weissner in Heidelberg, Claude Pélieu and Mary Beach in San Francisco were ploughing their poems in with fragments of newsprint, drifting scraps of telecommunication. Harold Norse was on the wavelength. So were Dan Richter and Philip Lamantia. Other voyagers—the word 'cosmonaut' was coined about this time—were sending the record of their mental impulses and cosmic readings to Burroughs and to one another. Weissner published the first issue of *Klactoveedsedsteen*. Most of it was devoted to column cutups.

For myself—I was beginning to drift, to lean on the dream more than I ever had, and to lean on some really berserk and intrapersonal typhoon beyond the individual dream. Intersection points—the recurring phrases, words and numbers which tied one incident to another, one person to another, one time to another, were carrying me along on a tidal pattern of inevitable events. The idea of the exhibition had by no means been abandoned but the rock-hard convictions I maintained about fact and aggressive realism were beginning to leak at the corners and letting in the strange perfumed winds. I was part of an inevitable complex and I watched each image reveal itself to my senses, each sensation impinge itself, with wonder and delight.

Letters were pouring in from all over the world. My mind was everywhere. Lovers were my other selves. Coloured electric tremors seemed to be passing through humanity, flashing liquid across my perceptions. Nightmares walked my house—familiars. All things coming under my senses quivered with a crazy potential.

I spent a lot of time with Keith Musgrove. We went to Writers' Forum meetings. We planned and performed happenings in North London. We did a book together. We sat and talked. We roared and raved and were expelled from a number of pubs and restaurants. Mostly we just drank. I remember a party at Nick Watkins' studio. Travelling there, the shop signs flashing across the car windows strung themselves together into messages. Thoughts rattled across my brain like disconnected bursts of machine-gun fire and the snide bastard in me that watches me for kicks capered about in eldritch delight, had me hurl Keith into a hedge, had my life thronging through the world and the world rattling through my senses like a motor-driven rosary.

I woke up one morning at this time, early summer 1964, to find a loosely packed parcel thrown on my bed, thrown by my wife with a certain amount of resignation. It contained two typescripts from Alexander Trocchi—*The Invisible Insurrection of a Million Minds* and *Sigma, a Tactical Blueprint.*

I read through them quickly:

'We are concerned not with the *coup d'etat* of Trotsky and Lenin, but with the *coup du monde*, a transition of necessity more complex, more diffuse than the other, and so more gradual, less spectacular. Our methods will vary with the empirical facts pertaining here and now, there and then.

Political revolt is and must be ineffectual precisely because it must come to grips at the prevailing level of political process. Beyond the backwaters of civilization it is an anachronism. Meanwhile, with the world at the edge of extinction, we cannot afford to wait for the mass. Nor to brawl with it.

The *coup du monde* must be in the broad sense cultural. With his thousand technicians Trotsky seized the viaducts and the bridges and the telephone exchanges and the power stations. The police, victims of convention, contributed to his brilliant enterprise by guarding the old men in the Kremlin. The latter hadn't the elasticity of mind to grasp that their own presence there at the traditional seat of government was irrelevant. History outflanked them. Trotsky had the railway stations and the powerhouses and the "government" was effectively locked out of history by its own guards.

So the cultural revolution must seize the grids of expression and the powerhouses of the mind. Intelligence must become self-conscious, release its own power, and, on a global scale, transcending functions that are no longer appropriate, dare to exercise it. History will not overthrow national governments; it will outflank them. The cultural revolt is the necessary underpinning, the passionate substructure of a new order of things...

...We must reject the conventional fiction of "unchanging human nature". There is in fact no such permanence anywhere. There is only *becoming*...

...Meanwhile our anonymous million can focus their attention on the problem of "leisure". A great deal of what is pompously called "juvenile delinquency" is the inarticulate response of youth incapable of coming to terms with leisure. The violence associated with it is a direct consequence of the alienation of man from himself brought about by the Industrial Revolution. Man has forgotten how to play. And if one thinks of the soulless tasks accorded each man in the industrial milieu, of the fact that education has become increasingly technological, and for the ordinary man no more than a means of fitting him for a "job", one can hardly be surprised that man is lost. He is almost afraid of more leisure. He demands "overtime" and has a latent hostility towards automation. His creativity stunted, he is orientated outwards entirely...

How to begin? At a chosen moment in a vacant country house (mill, abbey, church, or castle) not too far from the City of London we shall foment a kind of cultural "jam session"; out of this will evolve the prototype of our *spontaneous university*.

The original building will stand deep within its own grounds, preferably on a river bank. It should be large enough for a pilot group (astronauts of inner space) to situate itself, orgasm and genius, and their tools and dream-machines and amazing apparatus and appurtenances; with outhouses for "workshops" large as could accommodate light industry; the entire site to allow for spontaneous architecture and eventual *town planning*...

...We envisage an international organization with branch universities near the capital cities of every country in the world. It will be autonomous, unpolitical, economically independent...

...The cultural possibilities of this movement are immense and the time is ripe for it. The world is awfully near the brink of disaster. Scientists, artists, teachers, creative men of goodwill everywhere are in suspense. Waiting. Remembering that it is our kind, even now who operate, if they don't control the grids of expression, we should have no difficulty in recognizing the spontaneous university as the possible detonator of the invisible insurrection.

...Now and in the future our centre is everywhere, our circumference nowhere. No one is in control. No one is excluded. A man will know when he is participating without offering him a badge...

...We can write off existing universities...The university... will have much in common with Joan Littlewood's "leisuredrome"...will be operated by a "college" of teacher-practitioners, with no separate administration...

...In looking for a word to designate a possible international association of men who are concerned individually and in concert to articulate an effective strategy and tactics for this cultural revolution, it was thought necessary to find one that provoked no obvious responses. We chose the word "sigma." Commonly used in mathematical practice to designate all, the sum, the whole, it seemed to fit very well with our notion that all men must eventually be included.

In general, we prefer to use the word "sigma" with a small letter, as an adjective rather than as a noun, for there already exists a considerable number of individuals and groups whose ends, consciously or not, are near as dammit identical with our own...

...The basic shift in attitude described in the foregoing pages must happen. IT IS HAPPENING. Our problem is to make men conscious of the fact, and to inspire them to participate in it. Man must seize control of his own future: only by doing so can he ever hope to inherit the earth.'[1]

The web was connecting up its separate strands. Between Criton, me, Burroughs in Tangiers, Trocchi, Weissner, Pélieu, something was clearly happening.

I answered Trocchi by return, saying simply, 'What do you want me to do?'

[1] ALEXANDER TROCCHI, 'The Invisible Insurrection; sigma, a Tactical Blueprint,' *City Lights Journal*, no. 2, ed. L. Ferlinghetti.

II

To a certain degree the Underground happened everywhere spontaneously. It was simply what you did in the H-bomb world if you were, by nature, creative and concerned for humanity as a whole. Not concerned just for self and friends or for any corny abstract humanity thrown up by church, charity or politician, but concerned for the business of being human in whatever happened to be the conditions surrounding humanity, convinced that the business of being human and the continuation of that business is intrinsically, not relatively, important, possessed by a sense of warm and sensuous well-being in one's membership of everybody else.

The predicament was, in fact, the re-alienation of the artist in far more stringent circumstances than those of the nineteenth century. The nineteenth-century artists were faced with the collapse of Christianity and the end of Hellenism. We are faced with the end of man.

It was a particularly subtle alienation by this time, not an easy position to maintain. The old rebel groups and rebel movements, Cubism, Surrealism, Dada, had been incorporated into the international art racket where they were partially emasculated (a) by misinterpretation through liaison between the commercial galleries and newspaper critics, (b) by sale within a cultivated price range that ensured work only reached people in the upper income bracket who could treat outrage as amusement according to their well-tried methods, (c) by the presentation of art in an aura of plum-coloured carpets, morning suits, toffee-nosed smalltalk platitudes, a presentation which narrowed the social range of the art public still more, (d) by financially compromising the artists so that galleries could dictate their styles of work.

The rebel styles in literature were blocked out of publishing, out of libraries, out of serious discussion, by the extensive influence of the universities who are too idle to reform their critical axioms and therefore try to preserve the critical status quo. The new music was opposed by most of the established orchestras for a similar reason—musicians would have to change their concepts to meet it and they couldn't be bothered. The anti-life was protected on all fronts and if the situation really got threatening the establishment could always get crude and use censorship.

The suicide pact had, with elaborate speed and alacrity, preserved its pattern of demolition. A simple move in a simple war, really. Society was subconsciously determined to destroy mankind. The artists were consciously determined to destroy society. So society bought them off. Many a good man fell. The money was so plentiful in some quarters that theft became the imperative act of integrity.

All over Europe, America, then, artists, creative people, stepped aside into a deliberate sell-it-yourself amateurism. This was the beginning of the Underground.

John Rowan wrote in the third issue of *And*: 'Still, it's a funny thing that no live stuff ever gets printed in this country unless the writers themselves get busy and do something about it.

'The poems and other writings that interest us most are unacceptable to publishers, editors and programme planners. And at least some of the writing in this magazine is utterly unacceptable to almost everybody. That is why we put it in. It seems to us that one of the functions of a magazine that doesn't make a profit is to print stuff which is incomplete, tentative, naïve, idiosyncratic and thoroughly irritating—so long as it has enough life to stand up and answer for itself…'

When Cobbing, Musgrove, Rowan and I were putting on our shows in hired rooms, exclaiming our poetry in public parks, swinging the duplicator handle throughout the long Saturday afternoons of 1963 we had no idea that the same thing was happening all over the world.

Nevertheless the characteristic pattern was set in the United States. Since 1956 City Lights had shown what could happen if you ignored the professional middlemen and set up in business yourself. You immediately got all the profit, sidestepped the critics, and were your own censor. The most intolerable stuff got to be published—at last. At long long last 'standards' went to the wind.

Together with City Lights in the late fifties came New Directions, Auerhahn, and Grove, all sympathetic publishers knowledgably committed to publishing nothing but work of experiment and consequence. Grove was the publisher of the *Evergreen Review*, veritably the showpiece of the finest Beat writing coupled with adventurous work from everywhere else.

Other little magazines followed, *Yugen, Big Table, Kulchur*. These were, nevertheless, printed from type and were therefore reliant on a backer, although they began to demonstrate that the only thing preventing poetry becoming a mass commodity (as it had been in medieval times, when it was oral, before it became the prerogative of literacy) was orthodox publishing. In England Migrant (Shayer, Turnbull and Fisher), Wild Hawthorn (Ian Hamilton Finlay), and Matrix Press (Tom Raworth) set themselves up in the early sixties.

The current popularity of Beatles lyrics, Lennon's poetry, public poetry readings, the popularity of a lyric like 'A Whiter Shade of Pale', indicates that the old trade-cry of the literary agents and publishers—'Too obscure for the general public'— meant simply 'Too obscure for me, hampered as I am by a public school, Oxbridge conditioning'. I once asked Edward Lucie-Smith why his year at Oxford turned to the Movement poets for their example. He replied, 'They were the only contemporary poets we knew'.

Similarly American theatre groups, American painters, were doing things for themselves off their own bat. Barnett Newman organized his Artists' Workshop where painters criticized each other's work and exchanged ideas—brilliant revolutionary ideas. Theatre was presented in tiny pads, living rooms, studios, barns. The first happenings were presented in painters' studios, very much in the same way that elaborately prepared parties take place (Bruce Lacey did some of the best.) The Living Theatre had existed for some time and had become as much a tribal unit as a creative one—a family of disaffiliated people living in the theatre where they worked.

Writes Kenneth H. Brown, author of *The Brig*, which the Living Theatre presented in 1963, 'The nature of the play (*The Brig*) and the squalor of their living conditions naturally unified the company to an extreme degree; and intensified their alienation from society. It was at this time that I began to sense a certain sado-masochistic quality which pervades through all the work done by them. The fact that their apartment had become a shambles, that they had been ejected from the Cherry Lane Theatre for negligence, that my play was deteriorating before their eyes, that this building which they themselves had constructed was collapsing under them, and that they were beating their breasts because the world was doing them grave injustice became, in my eyes, the very thing which held them together…

'It is not enough to say that here lies a community bound together by its alienation from the world, that within this communal structure is to be found a devotion to work and a way of life awful and desperate in its extremes out of which grow hideous sado-masochistic fungi which are an integral part of their massive personal and theatrical undertakings. It seems that the price they pay for their mutual involvement is often a loss of perspective, a collective insanity, an Artaudian madness that fills a theatre with hollow foreboding and shattering presence. There is no moderation in this corner of life. The personal and professional being is blended and becomes one. The theory on which this is based is Platonic and, as such, seems beautiful, but when put into practice, dark and mysterious areas of man's essence are uncovered which produce results that greatly resemble monastery life in the middle ages.'[1]

In all these ventures the audience was presented with a take-it-or-leave-it attitude. Increasingly they took it.

The strong element of pacifist protest and bomb-anxiety in the Living Theatre, however, made it clear ultimately that the Underground was not exclusively concerned with the arts outside the commerce-and-criticism machine. It was also concerned with world unity, world peace, current conflagrations, over-authoritarian government, nuclear disarmament and,

[1] KENNETH H. BROWN, from *City Lights Journal*, no. 3, ed. L. Ferlinghetti.

above all, the appropriation of the maximum freedom for the individual, whereby he could strike and appropriate those levels of ecstasy that would provide him with a reason for living —thence to offer that ecstasy to other people in the hope that they too might start to want to live, might not wreck the whole boat through their own distaste for the voyage. Thrown out of their theatre by the New York police, the Living Theatre went on tour, messengers and reluctant evangelists of an attitude and a way of life.

The attitude was, is, one in which despair, neurosis, mental unbalance are all part of the day-to-day norm, everybody's starting point, at which all former reference points—society, morality, religion—are eradicated, where the individual may move to establish his own values and relationships according to his own experience. It was, of course, a maturing of the hip point of view. There was present, in the step-by-step adventure to the next kick, a growing common appetite for a common spirituality, a commonly acknowledged need for certainty, love and God or something just as good, for the old Christian virtues without any of the Christian trappings of morality, puritanism, orthodoxy, liaison with the state, body hatred. Sex, beyond the footloose hit-and-run casual fuck of the psychopathic hipster, the defensive brutalism of the ted and the rocker, the kinkiness of the mod, the Freudian fundamental of the Surrealist, became a purchase on the spiritual, a direct contact, in orgasm, with whatever might exist that might be called God. The perfect orgasm as studied and preached by Wilhelm Reich, was seen simultaneously as a holy union with the cosmos and a cure for the squares, who, it is assumed, are largely so suicidal because they never get a good fuck.

Drugs also could conceivably be the means to values beyond the ordinary comparative scales of society, politics and commerce. The Negro hipster took his drugs for kicks. The Underground, guided by the writing of Ginsberg and McClure, took them as a means to the experience of something in which one could place something like belief and faith. In 1963 the mere mention of the God concept was good for a laugh. By 1965 it was many people's most serious concern.

Delinquents and misfits began to work at their delinquency with a veritably Wesleyan zeal. Defensive amateurism became a messianic crusade, defensive switched to offensive; this offensive was the Underground. It was marked off from the previously described hybrid culture by its self-awareness and deliberation. It was decided upon and acted out, praxis not process. It ran parallel with the process-developments in popular culture which happened automatically. It was perhaps this neck-and-neck race between praxis and process that brought about such a fantastic pace of development.

The word Underground was still, in the early sixties, not yet in common use. It probably came into use in New York around 1964. Two main activities defined it, finally. Duplicated magazines and home movies.

Both movies and magazines were called Underground because they were so totally divorced from the established communicating channels, and because they were intensely concerned with the use of the obsession for sex and religion as a weapon against the spiritual bankruptcy which begat the bomb. There was a good deal of concern for immediate points of protest like Vietnam and the Civil Rights Campaign, an idolization of political protest figures like Dylan and Baez, but the concern was more for the wider issue; for the fact that, with appetite for living so depreciated, collective suicide by some method or other was inevitable until the deeper illness was cured in oneself, amongst one's friends, finally publically.

There was an unprecedented concern to air all taboos as blatantly as possible, to confess and sing from the rooftops all the most impermissible desires, a strange merging of the titillatory pornographic with the avant-garde absurd, and, mixed in there in the ring-fucks and the gobble scenes, among the toe queens and the coprophiles, the gods of Ancient Egypt and Mexico, of India, Tibet and the Pacific Islands fornicated hilariously, evoking Madame Blavatsky and Aleister Crowley rather more strongly that their own pre-historic temple orgies. Drugs became almost a social obligation.

OK Motherfuckers! come out of your
freak-skulls blaring Nothingness. Heave

Your piles out the touring car window!
This is the time for THE SPRAY OF THE
BRAIN. Rip Brain Valves! Gobble Gobble
        Resist Hate Lines!

                    Gobble Gobble!

Total Assault!
    Forward with Brainvalves
turned to SPRAY ALERT,
as when a Tom Cat unloads in a
Wet-dream: Yellow River Yellow River
Get the enemy on your freak-beam

                    Gobble Gobble!

This is the waiting Guerilla Pretzel
of America. Get the money. Get
The Power. Braid their piles into
magical lavaliers! MASS ALERT!

GOBBLE GOBBLE! INsect fuzz upon us!
Resist hate lines! Stomp!Freak!
Gobble! Phil Whalen! Calling gentle
flame brains into the Arena. Piles out the
Touring Car.

            In the dawn raids outside the bunkers
            we spray vast Love Hunks!

Ankle-grabbers of the Universe
This call to Gary Snyder, Michael
Cock-eagle McClure, Lawrence Freakinghetti!
Forward with mind-beams spraying! Lob Alert!
Lob Alert! Get the beams planted into
their minds! Toe Queen Lessons Learned
at last: Tillie the Toe Queen in Times Square
to the Broadway Arcades No matter
what the fuck hating dingleberry cops
say/do/think/want. More Auden rim
jobs in FUCK YOU/!

Come on all You shining Genius Poets,
piles out the Touring Car! Get
disgorged on the spokes of the wheels
as they wrap you up. Get caught.

Goddammit! The worst you can get
is a flame-job from an Ant Colony or
Tholh's beak into your tuchas. Get
There! The FUGS are doing McClure
Rock 'n Roll Ghost Tantras all over
New York!

Get the Universe back in the SUN-BOAT!
Come on Whalen, stop worrying about
your alpha Rhythms. Get out on
that tight rope between coma
and convulsion, waving a speech!

Out the touring car. Out the touring
car. Big draggy speeches &
power scenes? TOTAL ASSAULT!
Get the money. Get
the power. Get the liaisons!
Big beautiful faces flashed on the
screen. Toe Grope Toe Grope
Piles out the touring car.

> This is bunker ♯ Sanders…
> New York Amphetamine Terror
> Roger 'n Out Roger 'n Out!
> April 1, 1965 – PEACE EYE BOOK
> STORE drop your drawers
> Midnight.[1]

The best of the duplicated mags and shoestring movies were
made in New York. Ed Sanders, a graduate bum, poet, anti-
bomb demonstrator who had served a prison sentence for his
part in the New York Harbour swim-ins, who eked out a
living selling newspapers etc to the junkies and trans-
vestites of Times Square, collected a number of otherwise

[1] ED SANDERS, from *Bulletin from Nothing*, no. 1, ed. Pélieu & Beach, 1965.

unpublishable poems from the leading Beat writers including Ginsberg, Snyder, Whalen, Burroughs, Mailer, put them together with the best of the poets of his own generation, Szabo, Harry Fainlight, Ted Berrigan, himself, duplicated the lot on to big furry tinted sheets of paper, stapled them together with an introduction, and called the lot *Fuck You, a Magazine of the Arts*. This was the commencement of Fug Press. The editorials of *Fuck You* were the manifestos and rallying point of the Underground. In typical Sanders expletives they exhorted queers and junkies, lovers and dropouts to defend themselves against police harassment through effective legal channels. Ginsberg and Fainlight, at this time, conducted a kind of layabouts' legal advisory service.

Sanders' distribution centre was the bookshop he opened in his own apartment—the Peace Eye Bookstore. Although Better Books, City Lights, and Asphodel stocked *Fuck You* under the counter it was largely distributed by mail. The most notorious issue was the one with the still from Andy Warhol's orgy film on the cover, a three-part sucking scene. Other publications were *Bugger—an anthology of anal-erotic poetry*, and *The Fug Songbook*. Besides these Peace Eye put out a list of collector's items for sale, like the collected pubic hairs of the major literary figures of New York, and a jar of cold cream used by Ginsberg and Orlovski as a lubricant before intercourse, both items signed on the containers.

The Fugs, a burlesque rock-folk group led by Sanders, featuring not only lyrics by himself and Kupferberg but also musical settings of Shelley and Blake, are indefinable in their quality. The conscious irony of their twanging and swinging hillbilly sound is an American parallel to the music hall element in the Alberts' makeup. They share, as well with the Alberts, an anarchic messiness of presentation, irritating to squares who frequently miss the joke. The lyrics, however, are the important thing, for their sexual audacity and Sanders' wild execution of them in public performance. All Sanders' activities took place under CND symbols decorated with little drawings of the Egyptian Gods fucking merrily in different positions.

Tuli Kupferberg, a member of the Fugs with rather more

political ideas than those of Sanders, had launched his *Birth Press* slightly before *Fuck You*. *Birth Press* was produced by photo-litho and ran, first, into an examination of sex, then drugs, then children's poetry.

All copies but the last were collages of snippets, quotations and antiquated illustrations, cut from the magazine or manual where they had been found. The drug booklets constitute the most informative I've seen on the subject, with every possible attitude covered and the same dire warnings being issued in the nineteenth century against alcohol, tea and tobacco as are now issued against marihuana. Shortly afterwards came *True Confessions*, incredible collage collections laying the American cancer as naked as an onion:

'Afraid? Ha-Ha! I'll Make You Bristle With Fighting Courage in 48 Hours'—'In Color: The Vicious Fighting in Vietnam'—'NU-TECH CIRCUMCISION CLAMP'—'New Sexual Deviation Cure Seen. Technique Uses Electric Shock 75 Times a Day...'

Ted Berrigan's C Press published the other distinguished duplicated mag, called *C*. Its contents were more consciously literary than those of *Fuck You*, with a fair proportion of cutup—not the semantic clairvoyance of Burroughs (of which Berrigan published a fair amount in his *Time*) but whacky dislocated collages of original writing and corny old novels shuffled together into strange distorted narratives. Charlie Plymell's *Now Now*, predominantly pictorial, was a third important 'mimeo'.

Closely associated with Sanders in the first days of the movement, Andy Warhol already enjoyed a reputation as a pop painter. His style, slight variations played across total symmetry (for instance, a silk-screened still of Marilyn Monroe repeated four-by-six in different colours) proved itself as adaptable to happenings, movies, pornography, as to anything else. With Warhol the subject matter is finally of no importance. To use material superficially sensational—the movie camera left running in the sex orgy, by the sleeping man's bedside, on a series of Underground faces, ten minutes on each, the identical helium-filled pillows in silver floating their different ways, and so on, all emphasize the aesthetics of bore-dom through repetition. The ultimate effect on the audience is that of tricking them into prolonged meditation. Their crowded minds empty and they examine the Nothingness within. Warhol's frequent sadistically amoral public remarks reflect this standpoint as John Cage, the composer, had re-flected the same standpoint in his compositions (extremely similar to Warhol's in their use of mathematical regularity, repetition and total fortuitousness). Cage said of Rauschen-berg's painting-constructions:

'To Whom:
Rauschenberg's paintings

no subject   no image   no taste   no object
no beauty   no message   no talent   no technique   (no why)
no idea   no intention   no art   no feeling
no black   no white

'After careful examination, I have come to the conclusion that there is nothing in these paintings that could not be changed, that they can be seen in any light and are not destroyed by the action of shadows.

'Hallelujah! The blind can see again; the water's fine.'[1]

Warhol merely took these elements and chose to impose them on the art public by every sensational means. In doing so he made himself a curious public figure. Smart, camp and seem-ingly possessed of perpetual youth (although in his middle-age, he looks like a teenager) he became the darling of the young and rich. His studio, where a team of a dozen bright young artists turned out products to his design, was a necessary port of call in the social round. He stood for all the qualities that marked off the American Underground from its English counterpart, for hip exclusiveness as opposed to aggressive egalitarianism, for huge commercial success set against the English firm socialist attitudes, for modish camp as opposed to the butch attitudes of class warfare no English rebel can ever really lose. Very few donkey-jacketed YCL and Anarchist

[1] JOHN CAGE, from *New Departures*, no. 4, ed. Michael Horovitz.

League members could ever realize that in democratic, pioneering, whiskey-swigging, pseudo-masculine America, where every man is self-made, the nonconformist attitude is the effeminate. Lester Young with his hair ribbons had discovered this. So had the bop musicians with their floppy velvet bows, for there is a raving queen at the heart of the Yankee badman that no conventional American likes to be reminded of, Ishmael in bed with Queequeg, Whitman who was just too big to be straight, the beautiful Indians and the mountain men whose odd similarity to drag-queens the Haight-Ashbury hippies were quick to discover.[1]

Despite the priesthood awarded Warhol, however, the classic Underground movie is *Flaming Creatures*, a tattered romantic documentary-fantasy about a Tangiers drag-club where septuagenarian queens drift around in their lace and stained satins, clinging to magical fetishes and drunken sailors. Its maker, Jack Smith, says of his films: 'How I adore Maria Montez with her stunning 1935 padded shoulders, that marvellous creature, that sheer gossamer goddess, I have seen the *Cobra Woman* twelve times in my life. All during my childhood she was my ideal of sheer filmy beauty, and all I want my photographs to do is recapture what she exuded.'

Other important Underground movies were Kenneth Anger's *Scorpio Rising*, Tony Balch's and William Burroughs' *Towers Open Fire*, the entire work of Stan Brakhage, films by Carson Davidson and Bruce Conner in the States, Yoji Yurio and Yoko Ono in Japan, Steve Dwoskin and Jeff Keene in England.

The New York Underground of that time, 1963/4, was in contact with an army of expatriate Americans wandering, active, in the wake of the Living Theatre throughout the whole of non-Communist Europe, wandering either from choice or legal necessity. Some had been drifting since their demobilization in 1945. For them Paris remained the centre where they circulated around Maurice Girodias's erotic Olympia Press and Gait Froge's English Bookshop. In the fifties a nexus of young writers including Trocchi, Terry Southern and Simon Vinkenoog, worked on the important magazine *Merlin*.

[1] See *The Return of the Vanishing American* by Leslie Fiedler, 1969.

For the later expatriates the European capital was Tangiers. Permanent residents in Tangiers were Paul Bowles, Jack Smith, Ira Cohen, Irvin Rosenthaal (Cohen and Rosenthaal produced *Gnaoua*, a magazine devoted to exorcism, from Tangiers, and followed it up recently with *The Great Society*), Brion Gysin, Michael Portman, Ian Sommerville and William Burroughs who lived with his son in his own house in the Calle Larachi Marshan. By this time Burroughs was the god of the Underground, looming obscure and fabulous behind his high priests, Ginsberg, Kerouac and Ferlinghetti (Corso, essentially irreverent, had quarrelled with Burroughs on visiting Tangiers in 1963). What Burroughs thought of many of his followers he says pretty clearly in *Nova Express*: 'And now I have something to say to all you angle boys of the cosmos who thought you had an in with The Big Operator–'Suckers! Cunts! Marks!–I hate you all–And I never intended to cut you in or pay you off with anything but horse shit–And you can thank The Rube if you don't go up with the apes–Is that clear enough or shall I make it even clearer? You are the suckers cunts marks I invented to explode this dead whistle stop and go up with it.'[1] I trust I understand William correctly. I usually do.

Another outpost of the New York Underground was Dan Richter's bookshop in Athens. The Richters produced the excellent magazine *Residu*, probably the finest anthology of the writing of the early sixties. George Andrews and Harold Norse, both formidable and adventurous writers, were frequent visitors. All along the Mediterranean coast drugs and sex were varied, cheap and often legal. The content of the writing was distinguished from that of the New York Underground by its incredible voluptuousness and the relative absence of either Buddhist or jazz elements. The Beat community in Ibiza had even continued the Venice West phenomenon and anticipated Haight-Ashbury.

In San Francisco, where City Lights bookshop still thrived, the wild men of the fifties had taken on an almost grandfatherly air. By 1964 a new generation had arrived in San Francisco and made City Lights their rendezvous. Claude Pélieu, a young Frenchman with a thorough understanding of Sur-

[1] WILLIAM BURROUGHS, *Nova Express*, Calder & Boyars.

realism had arrived with Mary Beach, the daughter of Joyce's publisher. Both were aware of the fact that cutup was an adventure which extended on the one hand the psychic adventure of surrealist automatic writing and on the other hand the purely aesthetic juxtaposition of language fragments begun by Pound and the Imagists. Friends and co-operatives of Pélieu were Charles Plymell, a jazzy poet from Kansas, one-time editor of *Now Now*, who did sadistic collages, Norman Ogue Mustill, also a collagist, and Dave Haselwood of Auerhahn Press. There was/is a funky expressionist spirit about much of their work. The two *Bulletins From Nowhere* and *Grist* from Wichita give the prevailing mood.

Two other natives of Kansas are active in San Francisco: Bruce Conner, the artist whose constructions of nylon, cheap lace and wax that looks like sperm or mucus have simultaneously a raw horrific impact and a certain macabre glamour, and Michael McClure, the Beat poet, who has now extended his monumental vision towards theatre, giving readings of his beast-sound poems naked but for a lion's head, turning on LSD in public and displaying the effect on his behaviour, finally writing his play *The Beard* which incorporates public cunnilingus and was chased from theatre to theatre by the San Francisco police.

Another exciting playwright in the San Francisco second generation is Bob Burleson. *City Lights Journal*, Numbers 1, 2 and 3, give a fair survey of other local talents.

'Funk' is a jazz expression. Like the term 'jazz' it was used before the music. It meant originally the thick pungent odour given off by the sexually aroused female. It ultimately came to mean the aesthetic of obscenity—the aural equivalent of sheer stench. The term usually implies in jazz a good deal of heavily vocalized tone, grotesquely slurred notes, growling phlegmy anal-erotic distortions. Funk in San Francisco, rather different from Ed Sanders' blithe scatology and the total sexual gluttony of Tangiers, has at least something to do with the tough spirit that Kansas gave to the West Coast. A similar spirit was reflected briefly in the duplicated magazine *Olé*. Edited and distributed by Doug Blazek, it specialized in a gritty poetry of sex, dirt and torment. Blazek was perceptive in pointing out the connection between funk and Lorca's 'duende'—'the moribund duende dragging her wings of rusty knives along the ground'. *Olé* was the testing ground and ultimate platform for William Wantling, Charles Bukowski, Marcus J. Grapes, Harold Norse and Blazek himself.

Funk poetry contrasts strongly with the Black Mountain tradition of free verse. This was also carried on mainly in mimeo magazines, rather distinguished ones with nicely balanced type patterns. Ed Dorn's *Wild Dog* was one of the best.

Different again, and owing something to both funk and Black Mountain writing, were the productions of the *Marawannah Quarterly*. D. A. Levy, a fine and exciting poet[1], first appeared in them. Despite the harassment of police and the derision of academic critics mimeo magazines continue and currently promise to survive the psychedelic newspaper craze.

In Europe the Underground, whilst connected with American expatriate groups, reflected regional differences in terms of interpretation, although the fundamental purpose was identical: the current technological/commercial/industrial/rational civilization is suicidal, it must be destroyed; a new culture, based on total freedom, extended sensibility, and spirituality of some kind re-established in the place of politics must be developed at breakneck pace and spread among the people; human communication must be freed of the limitations of language; people must be induced to identify with humanity rather than with class or nation; fear for security must be shifted from the centre of human affairs and aspiration towards human fulfilment in terms of vitality, ecstasy, and delight be put in its place: thus the wish to live must be rekindled in the species and the drift to suicide redirected.

The Underground in France consisted of a group of young men who could remember a childhood under the Nazis, an adolescence in the Algerian war with its attendant horrors, who had the collosal pomposity of de Gaulle for an Aunt Sally. Their biggest traumatic spur was the maudlin negation of democratic principle whereby de Gaulle came to power. The International Situationists, centred in Paris, profoundly

---

[1] Since time of writing, after years of harassment by the Cleveland Police, D. A. Levy has killed himself.

Marxist in spirit, began operations in the fifties. Their programme, under the secretaryship of Jaquelin de Jong, has consisted of commando activities enforcing Breton's Marxist-Surrealist point of view—political correction through the dislocation of prevalent moral attitudes. They held well-attended international conferences and formulated rigid policies. Unlike the Maquis, the Communist Party and other effective political organizations, they had no internal means of discipline and were therefore ineffectual. When, for instance, they wrote to American members instructing them to secure the release of Alex Trocchi who had been arrested in New York on a drugs charge, the instructions were about as realistic as the Committee of 100's repeated intention to 'take over' various American rocket bases. The sum of their achievements is, finally, a number of witty and pointed public events and the *Situationist Bulletin* which contains collages, comic strips, and articles of an unusually high quality.[1]

The younger wave of the French Underground assemble round the publications of J. F. Bory, Julien Blaine and Henri Chopin (*Approches* is about the best) and the happenings of Jean-Jacques Lebel. This group, closer to surrealism than to Marxism, closer to the American movement than the Situationists, besides making considerable headway in exploring the hinterland between painting and literature in concrete poetry (a fine international exhibition was organized in 1967) have conducted a number of seasons of happenings in Paris under the general auspices of Jean-Jacques. The last and most dynamic included a happening by Jodorowsky that left everyone stunned:

'I get inside the frame with my back to the audience.

The woman lashes me with her whip.

I draw a red line on her right breast with a lipstick.

A second lash of the whip. I draw a line on her left breast.

A last blow of the whip. The line begins at her solar plexus and goes down to her vagina…'[2]

Since these events Jean-Jacques has put on the notorious

[1] This is no longer true. Situationists were very active during the Paris student riots.

[2] JODOROWSKY, from *City Lights Journal*, no. 3, ed. L. Ferlinghetti.

production of Picasso's play *Desire Caught By The Tail* and continued to paint his whacky Picassoid pictures. The typical Lebel event places powerful emphasis on public sex, as do the Japanese events of Hijikata and of Kato with his Zero Dimension Group. A morbid sexual preoccupation informs the posters of the Japanese artist Yokoo and the film maker Adachi.

It was a similar aggressive preoccupation with the earthier aspects of sex and life which caused the members of the Indian Hungry Generation Group of writers to be arrested. Malay Roy Choudhury, Debi Ray, Samir Roy Choudhury, Saileswar Ghose, Subhas Ghose, Pradhip Choudhury and Subimal Basak have pioneered an expressionist style of which the best known example is *Stark Electric Jesus* by Malay Roy—'Why wasn't I lost in my mother's urethra/Why wasn't I driven away in my father's urine after his self-coition/Why wasn't I mixed in the ovum-flux or in the phlegm'[1]—for which Choudhury was convicted and ruined.

The similarity between *Stark Electric Jesus* and *Howl* is quickly apparent. Also in the same mode is the *Human Manifesto* of Yuri Galanskov: 'No one will tread/The white, shredded veil/Of my soul./People!/Leave me, forget it.../Don't bother to comfort:/There is nothing to breathe with/In your inferno!/ Welcome Famine and Paltriness now!' Whether there is direct communication or not it seems clear that the emergent Russian Underground of the imprisoned Galanskov, Ginsberg, Dobrovolsky, Laskova, Daniel and Sinyavsky is on exactly the same mental wavelength as the Underground elsewhere. The significant division is no longer between east and west but between square and hip all over the globe.

In Australia there was Richard Neville, Dave Duncan, J. J. Wake, Albie Thoms, Gordon Lasslet. Says Lasslet, 'There has grown up here a group of people who have been given the nickname of the "push". They are thinkers and innovators of new standards...consist of one of every kind of scrag in the community so there is always a good cross-

[1] MALAY ROY CHOUDHURY, from *City Lights Journal*, no. 3 and *Klactoveedsedsteen*, no. 4, d. Carl Weissner. See also *Intrepid 10*, ed. Alan de Loach, 1968.

section of opinion. they have their patron saint, his name being "sebastian scragg"…

You will note that the leader of the anti-viet war demonstration in front of australia house in london gave his name to the press as "sebastian scragg".[1] Sebastian Scragg's own magazine was *Obscenity*.

In Vietnam there were the poets of the National Liberation Front and their representative in Czechoslovakia, Pham Van Chuong. Jiri Valoch carried the concrete poetry banner in Czechoslovakia. In Romania there was the *Romanian Review*. In Switzerland there was *Poesie Vivante*. In Italy there were Carlo Betaha and Donatella Manganotti who translated Burroughs into Italian.

In bywaters of America and Britain there was Day Parsons and Ray Gosling (Nottingham), Alex Hand (West Hartlepool), Ian Breakwell (Bristol), Dave Cunliffe and Tina Morris (Blackburn), Pete Hoida (Cheltenham), Dom Sylvester Houédard (Gloucester), Arthur Moyse, Chris Grey, Charles Radcliff and Ted Kavanagh (London Anarchists), Bill Butler and Jeff Keene (Brighton), Ivor Davies (Edinburgh), Victor Sloane (Belfast), Dan Georgakas, Benn Morea, Ron Hahne, Everett Shapiro, Bruce Elwell and Murray Bockchin (New York Anarchists), 'Copkiller' (New Orleans), Frank Goldsmith (Pittsburgh), Morgan Gibson (Milwaukee), 'Limbo' (Vancouver), D. Keirdorf (Detroit) and a host of others.

Alexandro Jodorowsky was the leader of the Mexican PANic movement. His manifesto is aggressively explicit:

> 'In order to comprehend the idea of the "efimero" it is necessary to explain PANic philosophy. Yet this is impossible because PANic is *action*, more than anything else. There may be men capable of thinking PANically but unable to act. On the other hand there are those who—in the archaic sense of the word—act 'panically', i.e. without thinking. The real PANic individual tends to *idea-action*. Therefore, it is anti-PANic to write public proclamations. The only possibility of *explanation* lies in MAXIMS and STATEMENTS:
>
> —The PANic individual "is" not but "is being".

[1] GORDON LASSLET, from a letter to Dan Georgakas published in *Smyrna Newsletter*.

177

—The PANic intelligence is capable of stating two contradictory ideas at the same time as stating infinite ideas, then stating nothing at all.

—Before PANic, thought came in *anxiety* and led to *aloneness*. PANic, on the other hand, comes in *euphoria* and leads to collective *entertainment*.'[1]

Another Latin American group, the Nadaists of Columbia, have an even more violent policy. Their manifesto cries, 'Ever since our Nadaist appearance in the hell of Colombian society, a rosy wave of evil has grown in our spirits... We've reviled our loves, beliefs, fanaticisms, hopes, memories and happinesses, not for other idealisms but in exchange for nothing or for an oceanic indifference...'

The PANic movement of Jodorowsky is tied up with the German PANic group, led by Carl Weissner from Heidelberg. PANic has mounted chaotic public events—'shortly after Word/Sound?Playback Pissoir Event in local Heidelberg yellow-green urinal had drawn crowds of paralysed burghers/ tourists/bums into crystal scent of PANic public bladder-howl-policemixup-TalkViaThePenisApocalypse-Dan Georg-akas materialized in grey cyst of neckar fagtown coming from rome/detroit/peloponnesus poet/writer/celebrator—of Society to Save God, Phallus Soc., and Countless others—for allnight manifesto session:—Manifesto For the Grey Generation'[2]— and has consistently produced *Klactoveedsedsteen*, a magazine named after one of Charlie Parker's best known numbers, featuring largely the cut-up and tape-recorded exchanges between Weissner and Burroughs. *Klacto* is, however, a vital European gathering point for a number of talents, publishing regularly a strong international mixture of writing and draw-ing—Alex Hand, Dick Wilcocks and myself from Britain, Pelieu, Beach and Plymell from San Francisco, Bukowski and Blazek from the *Olé* stable, Georgakas of the New York anarchists and De Prima and Berge of the New York beats, Bory of Paris, Belart and Vinkenoog of Amsterdam, and writing from all over Germany, Belgium and France.

[1] JODOROWSKY, from *Klactoveedsedsteen*, no. 4, ed. Carl Weissner.
[2] From *Smyrna Newsletter*.

The other leading German mimeo was *Mama* from Munich, with a good deal of American writing, including pieces from members of the Living Theatre, sigma propaganda from Trocchi and myself in London, and the brilliant strip drawings of Uwe Lausen. The editor of *Mama*, Klaus Lea, has since formed a liaison with the Verlag Petersen Press and published a number of the original Dada documents in facsimile.

In Berlin and Vienna Muhl, Nitsch, Vostel, Brus, Peter Veibel, Werner Schreib were carrying out happenings of incredible destructive power—a fractured man walks through the streets, nudes are suspended in plastic, released and spattered with freshly disembowelled entrails. Elsewhere in Europe Jean Toche (Belgium), Gianni Simonetti (Italy), Pablo Serrano and Marco and Marchetti of the ZAJ group (Spain) carried out aggressive art work.

But by far the most powerful Underground activity in Germany comes from the Berlin Commune I (called the Horror Commune) which has carried out a number of didactic public events including a mass love demonstration in which all the girls touched up the police and another in which a pamphleteer emerged from a coffin. The central figure of the Commune, Fritz Teufel, currently awaits trial for meeting police bullets with stones. Whatever the court's decision, it will be turned to propagandist advantage by the remaining members of the Commune.

Much of their activity is a Marxist application of the techniques employed by the Amsterdam Provos. This enormous tribe, consisting, finally, of every member of the Beat community that had gathered in Amsterdam since the fifties, modelled its activities on the one-man political happenings of painter Robert Jasper Grootveld, who once spent a number of days on a raft in the middle of one of Amsterdam's main canals. He had furnished the raft as a bourgeois sitting room and sat through the days reading newspapers.

The Provos, with their apple symbol, exploded into the public eye in 1966 with their violent demonstration when Claus von Amsberg married into the Dutch royal family. Since then their activities have included a happening in which hundreds of young people lay in the public square in blood-stained bandages, a campaign for free public bicycles to be painted white and left around the motor-free city, giving birth-control pills to adolescents, procuring a barge for a pad and playroom for itinerant Provos.

An odd aspect of the Provos is their emphasis on a kind of anti-romantic purity—the white denims and the white bicycles, Grootveld's campaign against tobacco smoking, their concern for elementary civil liberties, the odd and disruptive presence of old-fashioned left-wing liberals at their head (who, incidentally, show increasing friction with the genuine beat and hoodlum element in the movement), their representation on the local government. Nevertheless, behind the declarations and the high civic intentions the same clouds of potsmoke drift and the same painful dislocation exists: 'To climb the social ladder, to have a job, means: to collaborate in the next atomic destruction, to collaborate with the Authorities and their Strategic Propaganda—the television…We are supposing that neither President Johnson nor Mr Koscygin will listen to us, but we are freed by that to do what we want. We understand that a demonstration will finally be inept. That is just why it is so important to make this demonstration all that can be made of it…If God created this society we will do well to tie up with the devil…'[1]

Perhaps through the extraordinarily forthcoming attitude of Amsterdam authorities, under whom public funds seem more easily accessible and less likely to be frittered away on drugs, and definitely because of the energy and optimism of Simon Vinkenoog, a Situationist veteran of the fifties in Paris, Amsterdam is the place where sigma has taken root and been productive. A publicly endowed sigma centre exists, incorporating gallery and theatre, where activities have been continuous for more than a year.

Tjeb van Tijen, the current leading figure in sigma, has organized the open-air display of Geoffrey Shaw's PVC illuminated dome in Amsterdam and a continuous drawing that started in London, spread along the streets to a taxi, thence to a plane, from the plane to an Amsterdam taxi to the Stedelijk

[1] ROEL VAN DUYN, from *San Francisco Earthquake*, no. 1, ed. Herman, Dusenberg, Bastian, Leonni.

Museum. A number of the draughtsmen involved, including John Latham, were arrested in London and subjected to heavy fines.

sigma, however, was Alex Trocchi's name for the cultural tendency to progressive alienation and for his own ideas. It was a term he applied to both praxis and process of the whole movement. It was also a bid to convert a stage in social evolution into an international spiderweb with himself at the centre. Since then it has become evident that the movement is linear rather than concentric, that there are no power figures, and that there is no centre for such a figure to occupy.

Trocchi arrived in Britain in 1963 from the United States, accompanied by his wife and child. At Edinburgh he was joined by Burroughs for the International Writers Conference organized by John Calder. At the conference Burroughs gave the first public demonstration of his cutup technique. Together he and Trocchi moved down to London.

In London they became the pivot round which a number of people revolved—Charles Hatcher, Tom Telfer, McGrath, Philip Green, myself.

They were not, however, the beginning of the Underground in England. Towards the end of the great days of Aldermaston certain of the whackier and younger CND followers had gathered in the Peace Cafe in the Fulham Road, eventually closed through notoriety for drugs, and formed a cultural nucleus that looked mainly towards America and the Beats for its model. Prominent figures to emerge from this group were Dave Cunliffe, Lee Harwood, Ian Vine, Neil Oram, Spike Hawkins, Miles and, most important, Mike Horovitz and Pete Brown. In those days inseparable, Horovitz and Brown, who had met at the Beaulieu Jazz Festival where the beats ran amock with fire and water, combined on the magazine *New Departures* (three issues, very glossy and very far-out), the jazz-and-poetry road show *Live New Departures* (a marvellous season at the Oxford Street Marquee in 1963— any lively poetry available and more or less orthodox hard bop) and an endless mutual poem called 'Blues for the Hitch Hiking Dead'. Horovitz's finest hour to date, however, has been his chaotic Festival of the New Moon at the Albert Hall in 1966, when Spike Milligan introduced a note of true anarchy into the proceedings.

Horovitz's concern is reflected in his Goon-inflected poetry, particularly the long 'Declaration' published in 1963. He wants to see the arts reinstated as public festival, gay, simple, stripped of obscurity and, above all, stripped of sour, perverse overtones. Continuously he works towards this end.

Trocchi launched sigma; Better Books, owned then by Tony Godwin, opened its paperback shop with a wild mod décor and a succession of influential managers, Bill Butler, Miles, Bob Cobbing; Jim Haynes launched his Edinburgh bookshop and his theatre, the Traverse; Dave Cunliffe started his *Poetmeat* magazine from Blackburn, and deliriously, within about twelve months, everything started to grow together. Jimmy Johns' Peanuts Club, all that was worth saving of CND, with the brilliant Mike Osborne Quartet and hellroaring left-wing poets like Dick Wilcocks and Del Foley, was a favourite meeting place.

The first Edinburgh Writers' Conference was followed by a series of conferences and carve-ups at which different groups converged. The unofficial Edinburgh poetry conference, the utterly chaotic Cardiff poetry conference (called the Commonwealth Poetry Conference and attended by a chorus of bewildered Commonwealth delegates), the Better Books Writers' Nights, Strip Readings at the ICA organized by Eric Mottram and Bill Butler—the potsmoke eddied and the wine flowed free. The high point of these activities was Allen Ginsberg's visit to London during his grand tour of 1965 which drew a line of contact from India, through Greece, Yugoslavia, Czechoslovakia, Poland, to London, back to Frisco, and gave London a direct taste of something new, disturbing and intoxicating. At the huge Albert Hall reading organized and presented in six hectic days by John Esam and Dan Richter, not only were Trocchi, Corso, Ferlinghetti, Horovitz, Brown, Hawkins, Richter, McGrath, Lacey, Esam, MacBeth, Logue, Hollo, Jandl and Fainlight (the real star of the show), performing together but all our separate audiences had come to one place at the same time, to witness an atmosphere of pot, impromptu solo acid dances, of incredible barbaric colour, of face and body painting, of flowers and flowers and flowers, of a common dreaminess in which all was permissive and benign. It was also an occasion when two important poems were read which laid the ghost of our previous sickness. Ginsberg's 'The Change' and Fainlight's 'Spider' meet the projected spectres of torment face-to-face– 'Shit! Intestines boiling in sand fire/burned yellow brain cold sweat/earth unbalanced vomit thru/tears, snot ganglia buzzing/ the Electric Snake rising hypnotic/shuffling metal eyed coils/ whirling rings within wheels/from asshole up the spine/Acid in the throat the chest/a knot trembling Swallow back/the black furry ball of the great Fear'[1]–'I WANT TO VOMIT UP A SPIDER'[2]–and disarm them with sheer love–'I am that man trembling to die/in vomit and trance…Come sweetly/now back to my Self as I was'[1]–'Flowers where I still lie amidst my slime…The lovely shame of knowing myself deep in my heart an adorable young female spider. (It is the point where you start thinking of the hair as fur that it no longer seems so sinister).'[2]

There was a frisson for us all to savour as there had been at the first Aldermaston, and the Underground was suddenly there on the surface, in open ground with a following of thousands.

It seems fastidious to pretend that the overriding agent which produced this new bizarrity, the new relaxation and colourful contrast to previous earnest tight-lipped attitudes, was not Lysergic Acid.

After the Albert Hall I wrote to Klaus Lea crying: 'London is in flames. The spirit of William Blake walks on the water of Thames. sigma has exploded into a giant rose. Come and drink the dew.'

Weissner wrote me, transported by the effect Ginsberg's tour, the crusades of the Living Theatre and the Ornette Coleman group were having throughout Europe.

After the sick capitulation of CND it did look as though we were once again winning. The Philadelphia Foundation had

[1] ALLEN GINSBERG: 'The Change'. Writers Forum Poets No. 5, also in *The New Writing in the U.S.A.* Penguin.

[2] HARRY FAINLIGHT: 'The Spider'. *Fuck You* Magazine ed. Ed Sanders, and 'Wholly Communion'. Lorrimer Films.

procured Kingsley Hall for their community of regenerative madness. Leary had set up and established the Alte House at Millbrook. We were all suddenly in touch with one another, thrown out by the termination of our loneliness.

In London we tended quickly to sidestep, duck, retire into our own affairs until we could get our bearings. What we had striven for seemed to be happening now without us. It was against this tendency that Criton 'went mad'.

Things seemed to slacken off. In the summer of 1966, after making a hilarious speech in Trafalgar Square, I wrote to CND advocating a new policy, with some suggestions for the next Trafalgar Square rally. Peggy Duff didn't exactly embrace my suggestions but she passed them on to *Peace News* who published them:

'If there is one mistaken concept that has undermined the effectiveness of anti-bomb movements in Britain it is that man is primarily a socially oriented political animal: he is certainly this but not primarily. Man is a welter of fears, urges, needs, aspirations, appetites, and emotions, on which his political rationale forms a mere crust, and a pretty thin crust at that.

'Thus to speak to the common sense and the conscience of the public, as the anti-bomb movement has done, might work were it not for the fact that the whole movement is pitted against an establishment which threw away the pathetic fallacy of honour years ago, and now knows how to communicate with deadly efficiency to the *total human being* by all the subliminal methods of publicity and propaganda.

'I agree with all who say that this *should* not be the case and with all who say this *should* not invalidate the appeal to honour, the conscience, the political crust on the psychic cesspool; but it *is* the case and it means that propaganda of the CND type is outflanked from the beginning. No good for a man to go home upright with righteous facts when the social soporifics of muzack and politically tailored TV are already infiltrating his bloodstream before he gets through the front door.

'The automatic extension of this naïvety, or perhaps the root of this naïvety, is the idea that governments are in any way susceptible to direct political appeal by any party which is not in power over them. It is a fact of political power that

184

the big fishes ignore the little fishes unless the little fishes either get bigger or grow teeth.

'Neither CND, the Committee of 100, nor the anarchist movement has as much money or as many guns or even as many people as the government. Also, lamentably, no anti-bomb organization seems to have as much stamina or organizational power as even the lower ranks of the civil service.

'We can, however, make ourselves effective by changing our tactics. We can pursue a course which, unlike civil disobedience and strike action, we have sufficient numbers to carry effectively. This course should employ the subliminally communicative techniques of heavy advertising. It should speak to the *whole* human being in such a way as to tint his very consciousness before he's even had time to "make up his mind".

'If this campaign were quick enough and widespread enough it could transform the mental climate of our society as rapidly and as thoroughly as that climate has been recently transformed by the publicity behind pop music.

'I would advocate, then, that all posters become stickers (that, in fact, the whole of this campaign stays outside the pale of civic control as much as possible) and that stickers *do not put all the right arguments in a right and honourable way*. Photos of bonny babies should be coupled with photos of mutated children with the caption "In Only Five Years Time". On a more positive plane the "Make Love Not War" badge could be the beginning of a more sophisticated and audacious series of pacifist erotica.

'I would also advocate that pop groups (not folk groups) be approached to flavour the hysteria which is their stock-in-trade with reference to the sweetness of life and the imminence of total death.

'Local groups I would advise to conduct public events like, for instance, this: ambulance speeds into public place. Pregnant woman is unloaded and baby is delivered while people in bureaucratic uniforms stand around loudly taking statistics. Or: a soldier in blood-sodden uniform falls into a tube train. A priest gets in the other side. Man writhes and whimpers on the floor. Priest prevents anyone from leaping to his assistance. At the next station both priest and soldier hand out Vietnam news clippings and get off the train.

'I intend to provide a pamphlet of suggestions for events such as these, but it is really best if groups devise their own. NB: the idea of such an event is implicit in the action. The uneasiness created is more important than the communication of hard propaganda. These are not stunts whose only purpose is to attract public attention; they are ends in themselves. Each event, poster, whatever, should be a little seed from which the following flowers should spread like a rash: identification with other people, a sense of the common condition of humanity, disgust and alarm at the political situation, a love of the life principle and each other, a sense of everyone's responsibility for everyone else's wrong, above all the direct awareness of flesh and spirit, a proper and fully realized sense of self.

'And ultimately, of course, a dance and a music to celebrate these qualities.'[1]

I need not have bothered. Within a month everything I suggested so desperately was clearly happening. The Provos had erupted in Holland, giving a pattern for the Berlin Commune I, the New York anarchists and the New Orleans Copkillers with their recruiting station happenings. The Beatles made *Revolver* with all that it implied regarding their change of attitude (LSD again), and Timothy Leary, having been arrested on a pot charge, gained access to every conceivable publicity organ and spread the word at colossal speed. The badge movement spread, the sticker movement spread, the poster movement spread. The International Times opened its office under Miles's new Indica shop. Miles, whose magazine *Long Hair* had been a fine anthology of the talents around the Albert Hall reading, was the first to feel the benefit of the new favour shown by pop stars Marianne Faithful, Paul McCartney, Mick Jagger. Revolt had never rubbed shoulders with wealth before.

John Wilcock edited his *East Village Other* in New York and went on to the *Los Angeles Free Press*. Duplicated mags were outdistanced by the proliferation of Underground news-

[1] From *Peace News*, 2 September 1966.

papers and art was outdistanced by acid. The psychedelic movement was under way.

As is now common knowledge, Drs Leary, Alpert and Metzner had been sacked from their Harvard sinecures for exploring the possibilities of hallucinogenic drugs in breaking the deadlock of our destructive sickness, our loss of wonderment. After brief periods in Mexico and New York (where Burroughs, I'm told, dismissed them as 'metaphysical slop-buckets') they acquired the Alte House at Millbrook and started their week-end sessions at a stratospheric fee. Since Harvard they hadn't failed to produce the *Psychedelic Review*, a learned and decorous little magazine that contrasted radically with the scruffy mimeos of the Underground and the extravagant neo-art nouveau of the Underground newspapers. From Alte House they corresponded with Trocchi and Laing (Laing visited Alte House in 1964 and was impressed) and produced a pamphlet which Trocchi distributed as part of the sigma portfolio:

'Castalia Foundation
EXPERIENTIAL WORKSHOPS'

BACKGROUND

In each generation a few men stumble upon the riddle of consciousness and its solution; they discover, once again, that beyond the ordinary world of microscopic, tangible, material things, there are endless levels of energy transformations accessible to consciousness. They learn again the age-old lesson taught by mystics and philosophers of East and West: that most of mankind is sleepwalking, moving somnambulistically through a world of rote perceptions. They learn that it is possible to 'come to', to awake, to be liberated from the prison of illusory perceptions and conflicting emotions. As many internal explorers of the past, they become dedicated to the process of consciousness expansion, to the ideal of maximum awareness and internal freedom.

The first step is the realization that there is more: that man's brain, his 13-billion-celled computer, is capable of limitless new dimensions of awareness and knowledge. In short that man does not use his head.

The second step is the realization that you have to go out of your mind to use your head; that you have to pass beyond everything you have learned in order to become acquainted with the new areas of consciousness. Ignorance of this fact is the veil which shuts man within the narrow confines of his acquired, artifactual concepts of 'reality', and prevents him from coming to know his own true nature.

The third step (once the first two realizations have taken place) is the practical theoretical. How can consciousness be expanded? What is the range of possibilities outside our current verbal-cognitive models of experience? What light do the new insights shed on our view of man and his place in the universe? And, perhaps most important, how can the new levels of awareness be maintained?

For those concerned with the 'third step' questions, a series of weekend workshops in consciousness expansion have been instituted by the Castalia Foundation, a non-profit corporation.

STAFF

These educational experiences are designed and guided by former members and associates of the Harvard-IFIF psychedelic research project. The permanent staff consists of Timothy Leary, Ph.D., psychologist and former lecturer at Harvard University; Richard Alpert, Ph.D., psychologist and former assistant professor at Harvard University, and Ralph Metzner, Ph.D., psychopharmacologist and former research fellow at Harvard University, presently editor of the Psychedelic Review. These three are co-authors of The Psychedelic Experience: A Manual Based on the Tibetan Book of the Dead (University Books 1964).

Each weekend this staff will be joined by one or more of a group of about fifty professionals who specialize in some aspects of the theory and practice of consciousness expansion. Some of this group are scientists, scholars, religious leaders and creative artists who, since 1960, have been exploring the effects of psychedelic (mind-manifesting) chemicals such as LSD, mescaline and psilocybin. In the course of this research, this group has studied the psychological effects of these substances and their applications in therapy and rehabilitation, the study of mysticism, creativity and communication. A number of transcendental communities patterned after Aldous Huxley's visionary 'Island' have been set up, in part to act as psychedelic training centres and in part to apply the insights of expanded awareness on a day to day basis. The practical work of the group has been very controversial—two of the members (Drs Leary and Alpert) were dismissed from their posts at Harvard University and the psychedelic training centre in Mexico was closed by the Mexican government.

PROGRAM

In the course of the research with psychedelic drugs certain broader implications and applications become apparent. In the first place it was clear that drugs are only one way of altering consciousness and that many 'spiritual' 'schools', particularly the Hindu and Buddhist yogic traditions, have developed a sophisticated repertoire of non-chemical means of transcendence—meditation, visualization, breathing, movement, sensory withdrawal. Second, many techniques have been developed or rediscovered in recent years in the West, techniques for reducing some of the barriers to increased awareness—Gestalt therapy, T-groups, Gurdjieff's training in self-awareness, dance, diet, and psycho-drama, to mention only a few. Thirdly, the experiences of expanded consciousness shed much light on our understanding of religion, mythology, art, philosophy, and psychology. And fourth, they have profound implications in our thinking about social forms and institutions (what might be called the politics and architecture of ecstasy).

To communicate and explore these ideas and techniques is the purpose of the weekend workshops. The findings and methods of Eastern philosophy and Western science will be drawn upon to expand our awareness of participants. Specialists in the various areas mentioned above will from time to time join the regular staff, and contribute their own theories and techniques. Each weekend will be balanced between verbal-cognitive communication and direct, metaverbal experience.

Because of the complicated current legal situation in the

United States, psychedelic drugs will not be used in these workshops.

Every effort will be made to create transcendent experiences through non-chemical means. The experience of the staff-members, the setting of the house and surrounding country-side and the programmed activities should help each participant to make a step in the direction of greater self-awareness, to expand his consciousness and to move closer to that unitive vision which liberates and enlightens.'

The thing which recommends acid above all things is its unparallelled spreading power. Cutup, the dislocation of definition, the mounting figures of psychosis and breakdown, sick culture, had all gone some way towards creating a public delirium in which dislocation was dislocated, destruction destroyed. The virus had already begun, as I hope I've made clear. But once Lysergic Acid was launched as something other than mere pleasure, as a ready window on the Zen eternal, as a short cut back to the organic life, religion and wonderment, as an open road to Laing's lost self, it left art and Timothy Leary standing and took protest and pop with it.

The sit-ins, riots and marches at Berkeley failed. All they produced was added legislation from Governor Reagan, alterations in the staff so that even the old permissive leftish regime of the University was disrupted, police brutality and the continued war in Vietnam, a war conducted with senseless weapons like napalm and Lazy Dog bombs, which make Leary's catchphrase 'Turn on, tune in, drop out' almost the only alternative to the previous 'ban the bomb'.

'Dropping out' means merely dissociating yourself from your society—disaffiliation. The artists dropped out at the end of the eighteenth century voluntarily. The teds, rockers and mods *were dropped* out of society as surely as the pint-sized bomb was dropped out of the plane over Hiroshima in 1945. Timothy Leary was as ignorant of the process as most academics until he *was dropped* out of Harvard (that he was only able to convert this process to praxis by turning on and tuning in, chemically, is symptomatic of the fallacy behind his dogma). When CND failed British protesters dropped out into sickness.

When the Berkeley peace movement failed Berkeley protesters, followed by other American liberals, dropped out into LSD.

The most able defence of the drop-out, and the most intelligent analysis of it, came, not improperly, from Allen Ginsberg in his address delivered at the Arlington Street Church in Boston in the November of 1966: 'What can the young do with themselves faced with the American version of the planet? The most sensitive and among the "best minds" do drop out. They wander over the body of the nation looking into the faces of their elders, they wear long Adamic hair and form Keristan communities in the slums, they pilgrimage to Big Sur and live naked in the forests seeking natural vision and meditation, they dwell in the Lower East Side as if it were an hermetic forest. And they assemble, thousands together as they have done this year in Golden Gate Park San Francisco or Thompkins Park in New York to manifest their peaceableness in demonstrations of Fantasy that transcend protest against—or for—the hostilities of Vietnam. Young men and women in speckled clothes, minstrel's garb, jester's robes, carrying balloons, signs "President Johnson we are praying for you", gathered chanting Hindu and Buddhist mantras to calm their fellow citizens who are otherwise entrapped in a planetary bar-room brawl.

'But there has been no recognition of this insight on the part of the fathers and the teachers of these young. What's lacking in the great institutions of learning? The specific wisdom discipline that the young propose: search into inner space...

'...Likely an enlarged family unit will emerge for many citizens; possibly, as the Zen Buddhist anarchist anthropologist Gary Snyder observed, with matrilineal descent as courtesy to those dakinis whose shaddhana or holy path is the sexual liberation and the teaching of Dharma to many frightened males (including myself) at once. Children may be held in common, with the orgy an acceptable community sacrament—one that brings all people closer together. Certainly one might seduce the Birch Society to partake in naked orgy, and the police with their wives, together with Leroi Jones the brilliantly angry poet. America's political need is orgies in the parks, on Boston Common and in the Public Gardens, with naked bacchantes in our national forests.

'I am not proposing idealistic fancies, I am acknowledging what is already happening among the young in fact and fantasy, and proposing official blessing for these breakthroughs of community spirit. Among the young we find a new breed of White Indians in California communing with illuminated desert redskins; we find our teenagers dancing Nigerian Yoruba dances and entering trance states to the electric vibration of the Beatles who have borrowed shamanism from Afric sources. We find communal religious use of ganja, the hemp sacred to Mahadev (Great Lord) Shiva. There's now heard the spread of mantra chanting in private and such public manifestations as peace marches, and soon we will have Mantra Rock over the airwaves. All the available traditions of U.S. Indian vision-quest, peyote ritual, mask dancing, Oriental pranayama, east Indian ear music are becoming available to the U.S. unconscious through the spiritual search of the young...

'...What satisfaction is now possible for the young? Only the satisfaction of their Desire—love, the body, and orgy: the satisfaction of a peaceful natural community where they can circulate and explore Persons, cities, and the nature of the planet—the satisfaction of encouraged self-awareness, and the satiety and cessation of desire, anger, grasping, craving...

'I am in effect setting up moral codes and standards which include drugs, orgy, music and primitive magic as worship rituals—educational tools which are supposedly contrary to our cultural mores; and I am proposing these standards to you respectable ministers, once and for all, that you endorse publically the private desire and knowledge of mankind in America, so to inspire the young...'[1]

No one pointed out to Ginsberg that the quick and only way to that peace beyond 'desire, anger, grasping, craving', is to cut your throat, that anyone who has no appetite for stress has no appetite for life on human terms, desires merely life on cosmic terms, desires death.

Acid advertises its usage more quickly than other drugs.

[1] ALLEN GINSBERG, from *International Times*, no. 6, January 1967.

It takes a quick and sophisticated eye to detect the over-confident speech and movement of heroin and methedrine users. It takes an experienced eye to identify the benign dreaminess of potsmokers or the blinks and grinding teeth of amphetamine and cocaine users. But LSD is a drug of *visual* dreams and *visual* experiences and advertises itself immediately in the re-implementation of the visual aesthetic sense of users. This has been apparent in the mescalin culture of the desert Indians. It quickly became apparent in Haight-Ashbury, the run-down area of San Francisco into which the failed protesters moved and constituted at least the outward impression of an alternative society, tribal, religious, organic and pseudo-pastoral. Accounts vary: 'As soon as I knocked, a young bushy-haired blonde cat with a fullback's shoulders answered and invited me in. On the phonograph was the Beatles singing "Eleanor Rigby", in the air was the happy odor of pot, and so I stretched out my alto sax case, my tambourine and movie camera into the corner and laid out on the floor to relax and dig. I looked around this two and a half room pad, there were three cats in the music bedroom and about four or five more in the kitchen. All these cats were in their early twenties or late (18 or 19) teens. I was immediately struck by this one cat in bed. He or she looked just like my ex-wife, honey-red blonde hair in a medium page boy, big blue eyes that seemed to solefully twitch or stare...'[1]

'Cindy's entire picture of what she'd find here (L.A.) had been conveyed to her via the national magazines, an occasional television show, two copies of the LA Free Press which had been smuggled into her town by a friend.

She was broke when she arrived here. Now, after three weeks, her financial situation remains the same. Her stay here has been a most unpleasant one.

The first cat who took her home to "get cleaned up and spend the night under fresh sheets" turned her on to speed and acid and wouldn't let her out of his locked apartment for three days. It was a miserable first trip complete with sadistic overtones and his own acid-stimulated personality hangups.

He finally dropped her off in a desolate area near Malibu.

[1] ISRAEL HALPERN, from *Grist*, ed. John Fowler.

He kept her suitcase with all her pitiful belongings. No 17-year old runaway could go to the police.

She walked most of the following night and finally fell asleep on the beach.

I met her a few days later.

She told me she had already had to turn two tricks (of her own volition). The Johns were motorists who picked her up late at night.

She still had no place to stay and was considering a new hitch-hike journey to the Haight in search of her girlfriend who is a year younger than she...

...When she arrived here, she was just another wide-eyed, childishly-attractive runaway chick in search of Hippy Heaven.

Today the trippy abandonment of youth and the magic which should have been part of her scene are buried beneath a calloused, disillusioned blanket of fear and distrust.

Too few of the Cindys now in California are making it to the Love-Ins and savouring the truly incredible experiences which the hippy scene offers.

They are the lost and innocent who are such an easy prey for those who only pretend to offer care and aid.

In San Francisco they are beginning to call such blind followers of the Psychedelic Revolution "Uncle Tim's Children".'[1]

'Tune in, turn on, drop dead. Are you aware that Haight Street is just as bad as the squares say it is? Have you heard of the killings we've had on Haight Street? Have you seen dozens of hippies watch passively while some burly square beats another hippy to a psychedelic red pulp? Have you walked down Haight Street at dawn and talked with the survivors?... The Street reeks of human agony, despair and death, death, death.'[2] Which is what Allen Ginsberg had always been talking about anyway, according to Ferlinghetti's poem.

The effect of LSD is the dissolution of the self into other dissolved identities. Inanimate things become animate. Existence heaves in a great all inclusive movement drawing in the self. The aesthetic then is one of indefinability and movement, images and lettering swollen to the limit of discern-

[1] ELLIOT MINTZ, from *Open City*, no. 15, August 1967.

[2] From the Boston *Avatar*.

ability, swooping arabesques eradicating all possibility of stable geometric images and nuances. In a culture like that of the plains Indians the animated arts—improvised music, aural poetry, improvised dance, informal ritual, sex, clothes, jewellery and cosmetics—are the channels of expression whilst the inanimate arts of sculpture, architecture and civic design are well-nigh impossible. The significant difference between the Haight-Ashbury culture and the Indian culture (which it oh-so-consciously imitates) is that Indians balanced and supported their mobility with portable skills like hunting, riding and fortitude, whilst the West Coast hippies were utterly parasitic, not other, not alternative, not truly a community, in that their whole self-maintenance relied on the excess material in the overmaterialistic culture they purported to despise—the unoccupied house, the excess of supermarket foods, the clothes jettisoned before being worn out. This same paradox is continually present in Leary's public statements. In one breath he contemptuously consigns the 'mineral culture' (technological civilization) under the ground, into the subways, giant bomb shelters, underground nuclear testing pads, secret factories. He says it will become feasible to banish the 'mineral culture' if everyone drops out and forms a majority of nature-orientated visionaries, a 'vegetable culture'. Then with the next breath he says that the economic self-sufficiency of such a culture is not a consideration because dropouts are by definition a minority and will always have a majority to feed off.

In Haight-Ashbury the seemingly oddly-matched elements of spirituality and debauch combined in the freak-out. The first freak-outs were forty-eight-hour events using all the techniques of sense distortion—lights and sounds pushed to the point of pain and coupled with music by groups like the Jefferson Airplane and the Grateful Dead. The freak-outs were heralded by week-end parties held at the country residence of the writer Ken Kesey. Kesey was the centre of a crowd of dancer-bacchantes called the Merry Pranksters. Close associates of Kesey at that time were Chet Helms and Emmet Grogan. Leary had transformed the Castalia Foundation into the League for Spiritual Discovery which he defined as a church. He followed this step with the instructions to his followers to form their own churches according to their tastes. Helms was quick to see that there was no difference between a freak-out and a church in which all members 'did their own things'. His 'Family Dog' was the first monastery of this anarchic calling, and being the religious articulation of an animated culture, was not a static community but nomadic. Helms and his priests—dancers, painters, musicians, poets, electricians (for the lights—from this time on pop groups began to employ electricians as creative members of the company), lived and travelled in a bus. They were finally doing little new. The early Wesleyans and Quakers had lived in nomadic tribes, sexually interconnected in this way, spreading their word by contrived hysteria. The big jazz orchestras of the thirties and forties had taken their Dionysian package-shows across the American plains and lived in a bus while they did it. The Living Theatre had done from necessity what Family Dog attempted from choice. Family Dog was a finger-popping Jesus Christ road-show.

Keysey and Grogan were alive to the contradictions inherent in living parasitically off the society they opposed. Largely guided by the techniques of self-sufficiency Gary Snyder had developed through years of Buddhist disciplines, they initiated the Digger movement named after one of the 17th century religious dissident communities the hippies so resembled. The Diggers' preoccupation is not metaphysical but economic. They took steps first to ensure that the Haight community were sufficiently well-fed to maintain themselves as a breakaway culture by starting a farming community from which fresh vegetables, for a while anyway, were driven every day into Haight and given away. The Diggers' free clothing shop, run on a kind of jumble-sale principle, provided the raw material for the extravagant hippie tribal dress. The story goes like this:

SQUARE CUSTOMER: 'How much is this?'
DIGGER: 'What d'you think it's worth?'
CUSTOMER: 'Two dollars.'
DIGGER: 'That's the price—two dollars.'

CUSTOMER: 'Here you are.'

DIGGER: 'Thank you ma'am. HEY, ANYBODY WANT TWO
DOLLARS?'

The Diggers work in fairly close conjunction with the San
Francisco health authorities and ensure that hippies physically
affected by privation or excess are properly attended to in
city clinics.

Their other preoccupation is the dissolution of the concept
of property. Another story tells how Grogan, passing through
New York, performed a public burning of dollar bills and the
dollar dropped six points on the stock exchange.

The Digger/Merry Pranksters bus, recently prepared for a
gospel-spreading tour of Europe, is fitted with earphones and
mikes in the seats so that evangelists might cultivate a closer and
more perfect rapport. It also carries its own acid producing equipment although this, in San Francisco, involves increasing risk.
The Mafia cut off the arm of a hippie pusher some months ago.

The acid culture, chanting its slogans of 'Turn on, tune in,
drop out' and 'Do your own thing', spread throughout the
western world at a brisk rate. Throughout 1967 the spread was
marked by the appearance of scores of psychedelic newspapers,
mixed-media pop clubs, big bright unreadable posters and
'head shops' dealing in badges, beads, prayer wheels, joss
sticks and all the paraphernalia of pop-buddhism.

The typical newspaper involves bright, subtly discordant
colours like those on the posters, neo-art nouveau drawings,
viciously aggressive cartoons, and local drug and pop gossip.
The best of them, however, include coverage of avant-garde
activities in all the arts, articles and interviews from Alpert,
Ginsberg, Zappa, McCartney, Laing, Fiedler, Leary, Snyder,
Watts, and other leading figures. The Underground Press
Syndicate is made up of *Art and Artists* (art glossy—England),
Avatar (Cambridge, Mass.), *Berkeley Barb* (Berkeley, Calif.),
Canadian Free Press (Ottawa), *Connections* (Madison, Wis.),
Crocodile (Gainsville, Fla.), *Communication Company* (N.Y.
and S.F.), *The Eagle* (Washington), the *East Village Other*
(N.Y.), *The Fifth Estate* (Detroit), *Graffiti* (Phil.), *Guerilla*
(Detroit), *Helix* (Seattle), the *Illustrated Paper* (Calif.), the
International Times (London), *Inner Space* (N.Y.) the *Los*

197

Angeles Free Press, *Other Scenes* (all over the world), the *Paper* (Michigan), *Peace Brain* (Chicago), *Peace News* (London), *Punch* (Mass.), *Promethean* (N.Y.), *Modern Utopia* (Mass.), *Maverick Press* (S.F.), *Notes From Underground* (Dallas), *The Rag* (Austin), *Seer* (Oregon), *Sounds on Campus* (N.Y.), *Spokane's Natural* (Washington State), *Sanity* (Montreal), *Satyrday* (Toronto), *San Francisco Oracle*, *Oracle Southern California*.

The inclusion of *Peace News* indicates the remaining pacifist concern of the whole movement. *Open City* is probably the best of the papers to date. Coming from Los Angeles, it carries regular features by Bukowski and a reasonable proportion of writing besides psychedelic chat. It reflects the intelligence of John Wilcock who can be called the initiator of the whole newspaper movement being an early editor of *East Village Other* and *Los Angeles Free Press*. Wilcock now distributes his own newsletter, *Other Scenes*, from wherever he happens to be on his journalistic round. The *Real Free Press of Amsterdam* is the sigma newspaper, colours, drawings by R. O. Stoop and good, witty pornography.

The *International Times*, sponsored by Jim Haynes and Miles, edited by Tom McGrath and John Hopkins, grew out of the ill-fated London Free School. The free university movement, well established in the United States and the backbone from which the strength of the Underground must ultimately spring, consists largely of voluntary week-end schools at which radical academics can meet their non-academic counterparts and pool their ideas. Joe Berke, a New York psychiatrist who had conducted a free coffee bar clinic, appeared at the Kingsley Hall in London as soon as the Philadelphia Foundation took over in 1965. Immediately he wanted to start the same activities there as had been taking place in the Free University of New York. Unfortunately he hadn't accounted for the yawning gaps existing between the English Underground, the English left-wing liberals, and his 'professionally' defensive colleagues in the Philadelphia Foundation, who refused to allow him to use Kingsley Hall for his week-end schools. The London Free School moved, then, to a disused cellar in Notting Hill Gate where John

Hopkins and Rhaunie Lasslet struggled, in opposite directions, to make it into a kind of local spontaneous Centre 42. Inevitably the voice of Michael De Freitas, since become notorious under his Mohammedan name Michael Abdul Malik, made itself heard in the Free School. The exciting musician Dave Tomlin was also around. Harry Fainlight was an eminence grise at Hopkins' shoulder.

Ultimately the Free School did nothing constructive but put out a local Underground newsletter and organize the two Notting Hill Gate Festivals, which were, admittedly, models of exactly how the arts should operate —festive, friendly, audacious, a little mad and all taking place on demolition sites, in the streets, and in a magnificently institutional church hall in Powis Gardens.

Hopkins however, nudged along by Fainlight, had a whiff of the psychedelic movement and knew more clearly what he was after, a quality and an atmosphere unobtainable in the Free School as it stood. Nevertheless he launched the Pink Floyd, the first English psychedelic pop-group, complete with lights and blitzing volume, at the same church hall where the festival activities had taken place.

In early 1967 he shifted to the old Shamrock Club in the Tottenham Court Road and opened Unidentified Flying Object —UFO —which was the scene of the wildest regular public events London has yet experienced. Aided now by Jack Moore, Jim Haynes and Mark Boyle (making brilliant use of light and colour techniques) Hopkins, by now affectionately known as Hoppy, introduced all the adventurous electronic pop groups: the Floyd, The Move, The Soft Machine, The Social Deviants; The Sun Trolley, Arthur Brown. The Beatles had doubled the scope of pop music with *Revolver*. It was amongst these groups inspired by the Beatles' experiments that pop music began to be more than merely an amusement. They played with sound in both an abstract and an expressionistic way. They featured lyrics which were sincere, intelligent and witty. The Incredible String Band, operating mid-way between folk and psychedelic pop, have probably reached the highest level yet achieved by contemporary popular music. They also were introduced to the London public at

UFO. A number of inventive artists staged happenings at UFO. The Exploding Galaxy, a particularly Goonish dance-troupe run by David Medalla (who had previously been active at Signals, the London centre of kinetic art) made its debut there. The People Show, a theatre group who combine techniques from music hall, happening, straight drama, cabaret, funhouse and children's party, sometimes ventured out of their own domain in Better Books Basement to perform at UFO. All this juxtaposed with underground movies, old silent comedies and Mark Boyle's perpetually changing lights created an atmosphere in which young people could relax quietly or create frenetically. If drugs are to be taken into account in the assessment of UFO it was perfectly obvious that LSD and pot created an atmosphere of harmony and inventiveness, whereas amphetamine and alcohol, at the old mod clubs, created an atmosphere of sourness, scepticism, alienation and aggression. The atmosphere spread to the Electric Garden (now renamed Middle Earth) where it continues.*

From UFO the fad for freakouts on a San Francisco scale spread through 1967—UFO held freakouts at Wesker's Roundhouse and the Alexandra Palace and commercial promoters picked up the habit and put them on throughout the country. The national press assisted splendidly, particularly the *People* and the *News of the World*, bandying around the Castalia Foundation's term 'psychedelic' like any popularized psychoanalytic phrase, talking about 'flower power' and drug-crazed youths with that menopausal tone of total scandal that is guaranteed to bring the English clustering like flies to the subject as participants or sight-seers. Nine months after the first gatherings in Haight-Ashbury mill-girls and office workers were wandering down the Brighton and Blackpool seafronts, jangling their souvenir prayer-belts, trailing their Paisley bedspreads, brandishing daffodils and trying to look tripped out. The Beatles had gone 'flower-power' and it was up to the kids to do their best to follow. One of the richer ironic sights in the summer of 1967 was the in-group Underground pop singers and drop-outs turning away in disgust from the widespread success of their ideas, seeing their much

* Middle Earth is now closed.

valued exclusiveness evaporating, realizing, perhaps, that when their ideas were as widespread as that they could turn away altogether, their function over. Like Marshall McLuhan, Timothy Leary and Brian Epstein, they had been outdistanced by LSD and the Beatles. When—was it the Sun Trolley?—refused to play to an influx of North London mods at the Alley Pally it was rather like Peggy Duff and the Aldermaston ravers, a fastidious: 'If I've got to succeed that way I'd jolly-well rather fail'.

Centres of the whole English movement throughout were Better Books and Miles' Indica shops, the first one with art gallery in Mason's Yard and the second one over the *International Times* office in Southampton Row. Jim Haynes, disappointed with the way things had gone both at the Traverse and the Jeanetta Cochrane Theatres opened his Arts Laboratory in Covent Garden with an exhibition of artwork by the Exploding Galaxy, a light environment by Roland Miller and the People Show.

The police, with strong indications of direct press liaison, became violently alarmed at the spread of LSD and pot. They had dealt with the far more sinister mod amphetamine craze comparatively calmly. The truth is, I suspect, that the police are wiser than the law or the exact terms of their employment. Existentially they go far beyond their official role of uniformed civil servant and have become the guardians of a definite way of life with its established scale of values not always explicit in the law. They realized that amphetamine, although quickly damaging to the brain and productive of incalculable licentiousness and violence like the mods and rockers riots, generates exactly those situations of power, isolation and combat with which the police can come to terms. (It is perhaps interesting to note that during the Suez crisis Anthony Eden was taking benzedrine.[1]) Similarly the American police are far more warmly inclined to Hell's Angels than to Peace Marchers or hippies. Any copper can understand weapons, fists, rape and conflicting loyalties.

[1] 'Already in July 1956, Eden was taking many pills. When the crisis came he told an adviser that he was practically living on benzedrine.' HUGH THOMAS in *The Suez Affair*, Weidenfeld & Nicolson.

But when the sexes merge, when reserve and privacy are dissolved, when anchorages of loyalty, marriage, country, the church, money, the military dead, work, property, rank, monogamous love are meaningless to a growing section of the community this is something infinitely more sinister than violence, something outside the range of police understanding. They panic.

They attempt to make Brian Jones and Mick Jagger restrictive examples and make them martyr-heroes. They arrest a boy for blowing bubbles in Trafalgar Square. They throw the Exploding Galaxy out of St James' Park for dancing. They harass all Underground pop groups. They send the narcotics squad to look for pornographic literature in the ash-trays of the *International Times* office, experts who confiscate the complete (and irrelevant) files of the paper, works by myself and Burroughs from Indica Bookshop upstairs, and leave untouched obvious 'heads' among the customers and violently titillatory works on which an obscenity charge could possibly have been framed. They arrest Ed Sanders only to be confused by the differentiation between pornography and art. Could it have been that W. H. Auden was prepared to defend his own pirated gobble poem? They arrest Jim Lowell of the Asphodel Bookshop for his association with the Cleveland poets Levy and Wagner. They raid the *Los Angeles Free Press*. They arrest Suzy Creamcheese and allow her parents to incarcerate her in a madhouse. They arrest and imprison John Hopkins and turn *him* into a martyr-hero. They do the same to Robert Fraser, the only really adventurous art dealer in London. They confiscate the Dine-Paolozzi prick pictures and charge Fraser with *vagrancy* for showing them. They arrest sigma artists for drawing on the pavement and they arrest John Latham for protesting about it. They do their best to prevent the showing of Yoko Ono's arsehole film. They arrest Bill Wantling for exceeding his prescription of cough medicine. They arrest Leslie Fiedler on a comic drug charge. They begin to imprison people not for taking drugs but for permitting other people to take them. They charge Dave Cunliffe with publishing obscenity for gain. In Greece, traditionally unhypocritical, they ban beards. In India, land of the guiltless, they imprison

Malay Roy Choudhury for writing rude poems…and so hilariously on, rewardingly responding to our little prods and turning themselves into a laughing stock to the entire younger generation. Meanwhile the Mafia, the strip shows, the blue films, the bedrock dirty picture shops, proliferate unchecked. Perhaps they pay protection money, but far more probably they subscribe to a hole-in-the-corner, guilt-ridden attitude to sex which is more acceptable to the society the police are at pains to preserve. Someone who steals money is practically a bluebottle's blood-brother compared to someone who burns it. The fuzz can and will get much more vicious.

It's two years now since the Underground surfaced with the Albert Hall reading and Tim Leary's arrest, two years since it spread beyond the in-groups and the minority-interest bookshops and jazz clubs. In that dazzling short time, jet-propelled by the spread of soft drugs (so-called 'so-called soft' by the squares) the genuine alarm of the police can be taken as a general barometer reading of Underground virility.

After the *International Times* raid there were a number of pirate broadsheets, anarchic emergency issues produced under the trade name, which bridged the gap between the resignation of the first editor, Tom McGrath, and the appointment of the present editor, Bill Levy. These pirate issues, whilst leaving a lot to be desired in terms of constructive art work and journalism, are valuable documents in that they reflect accurately the strength and weakness of the Underground. They are vital, audacious, reckless insofar as they represent an extreme view adopted in a broad popular way, and they have a curious brave spirit in that their very function was to keep the flag perilously flying until things could get organized again.

They are also inept, irregular, stretch thin material to fill too large a space, are badly written, even badly spelled, reflect the minds of searching, well-meaning, even desperate youngsters who are nevertheless ignorant of anything but the trendy frissons of the subculture and are therefore incapable of contributing original thought, merely capable of repeating tribal attitudes. Their chief weakness however is a weakness that becomes increasingly obvious as the winter draws on, with Better Books closed, UFO closed, Haight-Ashbury having conducted its own funeral, Hoppy still in jail, McGrath disappeared, Trocchi silent, Burroughs hibernating, the Beatles absorbed in their navels, the novelty of the first trips wearing off.

The weakness is a kind of fatigue of communication and constructive action, a pursuit of inner spaces which has allowed outer densities to stagnate. A reaching out for the stars that failed because the technology was not available within the inner self—Eric Clapton of The Cream plays far less ably than Charley Christian did thirty years ago and yet attempts so much more; the Exploding Galaxy expand the whole concept of theatre and yet lack a single exciting actor, comedian or dancer. Arthur Brown is full of bright ideas and the sanest madness but lacks the timing of even Lord Sutch. None of the wandering poets seems to be a Ginsberg. Established artists lean heavily on their past masterpieces. What young talent there is, in the Westbrook, McGregor, Mel Davies, Osborne jazz bands, in the People Show, in Mark Boyle's dance-and-light shows, in American hardmouth poetry and funk art, among the Archigram designers, among the students with Corny Cardew at Watford, in the Incredible String Band, the Mothers, the Fugs and the Beatles, seems caught in a temporary hiatus.

It's as if the praxes of art were involved, to their detriment, in the processes of social dissolution. The nature of the revolution to which they belong necessitates a change in direction before art can reassert itself as a root force.

Tom McGrath wrote before leaving the paper he had so capably launched: 'Here are some thoughts I have arrived at in the last few hectic days since IT was busted.

'1. It is essentially an inner-directed movement. Those who are involved in it share a common viewpoint—a new way of looking at things—rather than a credo, dogma or ideology. This can never be suppressed by force or Law: you cannot imprison consciousness. No matter how many raids and arrests the police make on whatever pretence—there can be no final bust because the revolution has taken place WITHIN THE MINDS of the young.

'2. It is impossible to define this new attitude: you either have it or you don't. But you can notate some of its manifestations:

'(A) Permissiveness—the individual should be free from hindrance by external Law or internal guilt in his pursuit of pleasure so long as he does not impinge on others. The conflict between the importance of the individual's right to pleasure (orgasm) and his responsibilities towards other human beings may become the ultimate human social problem. The search for pleasure/orgasm covers every field of human activity from sex, art and inner space, to architecture, the abolition of money, outer space and beyond.

'(B) Post/anti-political—this is not a movement of protest but one of celebration. Although it is futuristic, looking towards the leisure of a computer culture the new man of the space age…those involved in the "new thing" are having a good time now. And they are succeeding. This gives rise to envy and creates enemies. Favourite put-down words against the new movement are "frivolous" and "irresponsible." The "pleasure now" attitude ensures, however, that whatever happens, this is one revolutionary movement that must win one way or nothing. If our ideas are quashed in the future, at least we can look back on the ball-up we had now.

'3. Even to call it a new "movement" is to create a false impression. This new thing is just people coming together and grooving. If you don't know what grooving means then you haven't yet understood what is going on. There are no leaders: each individual follows his inner voice in the most honest way possible—"Does this look like something I will enjoy getting involved in?" "Yes." "Crazy." But there are influences ranging from the Beatles to William Burroughs. Leaders of comparable movements in the States don't have much of an influence here despite so many sneers to the contrary. Most of the people I have come into contact with in England are suspicious of Leary's "Turn on, tune in, drop out" slogan, for example. Despite A. J. Ayer and all that, Britain has come up with a new spiritual movement. But it has one clear distinguishing typically British feature—its common sense practicality.

'4. The new movement is essentially optimistic. It has a

happy view of man and his potential, based mainly on his creativity. This is a post-existential movement, bringing an end to years of tough and painful despair. That optimism has been reborn in the face of the H-bomb, Vietnam, poverty, hunger, etc., is so surprising it is almost a miracle. Again, the optimism is tinged with commonsense. The big world problems that concerned CND and the Committee of 100 at their zenith have not been forgotten. The new approach is to make positive changes wherever you are, right in front of your nose. The weapons are love and creativity—wild new clothes, fashions, strange new music sounds. The new movement is numerically weaker than CND at its strongest, but its members seem to have an instinctive understanding of McLuhan-style media theory: they know how to use the media to strongest advantage. In an instant-communication age, any act anywhere can be given world-wide significance if your communication link-up is efficient enough. This is one aspect of what IT and the Underground Press Syndicate is all about.

'5. The new movement is slowly, carelessly, constructing an alternative society. It is international, inter-racial, equisexual, with ease. It operates on different conceptions of time and space. The world of the future may have no clocks.'[1]

[1] TOM MCGRATH, from *International Times*, no. 10, 13 March 1967.

III

April 1st, 1966: the night of Criton's happening. The Phila-delphia Foundation have whipped round Better Books and Indica posting up denials of Criton's invitation. Criton has already told me that he won't be there. Bruce Lacey, who called to rig up the loudspeakers, was turned away. I get off the tube at Bromley, have never walked so high on the liquid of the evening. I walk to the Kingsley Hall—the Gandhi sign, blue and white, on the wall. I knock and there's no reply.

I go to drink in the little pub around the corner. Every time I go I put a new analysis on the relationship between the three or four family-members who serve in the three bars. I drink enough to let the evening run through my mouth with its slow patterns of events.

Then I knock at Kingsley Hall again. There is still no answer. My mind and system is a sea of coloured shocks, a tearing glad-ness underneath the implicit irony of the dead-end events.

I walk round the estate where Criton circulated his invitations. A little girl hauls up her skirt and shows me her wet, grey knickers. I pull a face at her. 'Fuck off, you', she husks. I give her sixpence. 'Fuck off', she says.

One more knock on the Kingsley Hall. A voice above—dark, pale American girl, John Keys' bird (John Keys left in anger—Gave me a savage poem to Ronnie Laing for the Mag) leans over the balustrade above, 'Do you want to come in?'

'Yes' I say. I feel that from now on the absent Criton and the gods control events. Again I'm merely a witness, floating.

The big common room upstairs is untidy. In the dining room is a half-finished mural, improving, says the girl, as the artist becomes happier with her mind. Flicker of anger—she's got a good long way to go. There is embroidery in one of the rooms, terrible embroidery, a veritable Rechabites' tablecloth, apocalyptic sun and all.

Evening lies dying on the remaining furniture in the recreation room, billiard table, upright piano, chairs—The walls are partly painted, no completion anywhere. The furniture, remaining from the time when the Hall was a community centre, is like a glimpse of a homely familiar domestic life left littered in the rain.

I wander aimlessly round, tinkle at the piano. The girl makes coffee. There is too much washing-up.

I am worried about the washing-up. 'Shall I do it?'

She stayed when John left. With John?—oh—for years. What she wanted—you know when you find it. A sense of belonging and possibility.

David (I think it was David) joins us from his room. He sits in a kitchen chair, periodically permitting his whole body to be caught up in paroxysms, small broken orgastic spasms of movement. During these violent little climaxes his face remains impassive and unhappy. His static dances come sailing down the evening to me and twist into smoother curves in my dream. They signal sarcastic attitudes about the situation—the situation always, the perpetual situation.

I start vaguely to wash up. The girl is sad. She disappears a while. I wander lamely about the common room. I remember my coffee in the kitchen, go and finish it. Images from that berserk week-end at Brazier's Park swell and wane in my imagination.

The girl comes back. She talks a little of New York. No, she hasn't been to the pub round the corner. No she hasn't been into London. No, she doesn't want to. Inner space. Crazy.

David twists his way in from the kitchen. He picks up a billiard cue. I want to say 'Forget it David. Don't do this mad bit any more. It's all a load of shit.' He starts a burlesque game of billiards. I pick up a cue. We swing around, cues skidding across the baize, balls thumping across the floor. The girl smiles sadly.

David gets excited, starts breathing heavily, panting, grunting; his eye lights up, he wants to play, he wants to force his play through the compulsive piss-take of my own ebullience which it now is. He might break back into touch with bloodshed. So I cool it.

He slumps back into isolation and stands, listlessly holding the cue, looking into the corner, waiting for the next ceremonial twitch to hit him.

Whistle from outside. Dick Wilcocks and his lovely bird, Jenny. There are times when beautiful women come like food to the starving. Not to hold or make love to or talk to, but just to be there with their lovely hair and breasts, with their peaceful flesh.

I run down the stairs to let them in.

'Where's Criton?' says Dick. 'What the hell is this anyway? Where's the happening?'

'This is it.'

'What?'

'Nothing. As Criton intended.' Nothing but ourselves, that is, our secrets, our potentials, our absences.

Criton had come to the Hall the previous Sunday afternoon, a final effort to get the doctors to climb down, the poets to co-operate, the 'patients' to open themselves. He came with Keith and Heather Musgrove. Keith wrote me: 'Criton is by no means mad.'

I tell Dick about this. Jenny has a green paisley dress on.

The girl makes more coffee and we sit around in the dining room. Joe Berke comes in with some friends, other doctors and ex-patients. A beautiful man arrives, invited by Criton. I am stoned, by now. Soaring. I feel in possession of a strange knowledge and a strange impartiality but can that be knowledge when I don't know what it is? David knows. Suddenly he is fixing me with a round baleful chicken's eye. One ring inside another.

And then, suddenly, it's all done. Time to go. Go back to the pub, me and Dick and Jenny.

Dick harangues me about my ambivalence. I don't march. I won't sit on committees. I must draw the scene together. I can do it and I must and I tell him, try to tell him, how the whole predicament draws me away from my wife, cuts across the integrity of my imagination. The night coagulates. Pint after pint. We are embracing on a bomb site. We are shambling through a half-demolished pre-fab. Somebody is crying. Jenny? Dick?

I laugh angrily at the sky. We plead towards each other repeatedly and I hack cruelly through the contact at every last minute—stagger down to the train, laughing.

Dick sends me some drawings after—'See what I scrawled on the way home'—and I publish them in the mag.

Trocchi lived in the hotel where I'd met Burroughs. We talked. A place, a week-end conference, even. Duplicating.

Coffee around the corner on the Queensway in a brash, crowded mod restaurant. He bought me ten Players. I didn't know whether to be charmed, touched or suspicious. Was he really hip enough to pamper the anxious child? Was that the part I wanted to play?

The next time I had the new copies of *Invisible Insurrection* duplicated for him. Bob and Jennifer Cobbing were with me. Lyn Trocchi came in while we talked. She had the child, Mark, with her. She leaned against the wall by the door in her black leather and looked like a young Susan Hayward.

The third time Alex and I sat in a pub near Marble Arch. He drank rum and coke and I drank beer. 'Let's get this clear,' he said. 'What this is all about is the complete rejection of *everything* outside that door.' The letter of his meaning indicated that society was to be rejected, fine, but it flashed through my mind then that the door represented the seven holes in Alexander's skull and therefore all but self was to be rejected, perhaps the only way that such a self could live.

Later, in his room, I said, testing something that was worrying me—'I want to work for sigma as an artist. Let's have *that* quite clear.'

'After a while it wouldn't make any difference.'

'Well' I said, 'let's get it launched and see.'

'D'accord,' purred Alex. He took a fix. Watching somebody fix is like watching them masturbate.

I was in a hurry. There were two organizations Alex knew of, a group of mad doctors at Millbrook centred around a man called Leary (who, after their expulsion from Mexico, had advertised in London papers as a group of schizophrenics who wished to set up shop in Britain) and a group of mad doctors in Finchley centred around a man called Laing. Alex wanted to contact them both. One thing uppermost in his mind was his safety. Doctors meant protection. 'I hate doing anything outside the law,' he said.

Mark Trocchi ran in. He'd run away from his mother in Queensway and come to Dad. Alex embraced him and looked worried. Lyn came in. 'Oh so he's here,' she said. She seemed curiously unconcerned.

I wrote to Brazier's Park in Oxfordshire. Would it be possible to run a week-end conference there? We made a date to see Ronnie Laing. Alex and Lyn went to dinner.

I went to a pub where a bunch of the lads were playing— Gas Griffiths, Johnny Fry, Ken Kennedy. I sat in, blew some crude showy horn. Feeling on top of the world I showed up on Ronnie Laing's doorstep with a bruised lip. I talked to Lyn and Mrs Laing. Beautiful women again. Mrs Laing was a husky, ironic redhead. Alex fixed somewhere. Ronnie prepared the front room. Shortly Beba Lavrin (late of Centre 42—background of left-wing fund-raising and bad art), David Cooper, Aaron Esterson, Sally Gooch and her poet husband arrived.

Everybody but the wives went upstairs to talk in Ronnie's office. We filed in and sat in a ring, most of us on the floor. The old conflicting divisions—ban-the-bomb politics and eastern metaphysics. Some wanted to talk mind. Beba, a little militant, wanted to talk money. Ultimately Mrs Laing, proclaiming that we all had the manners of pigs, summoned us downstairs. Another familiar hangup—business or pleasure, yes there is a difference, always a difference.

Downstairs a new start. Alex moaned. Mrs Laing took him aside. Alex stopped moaning. Ronnie played a Billie Holliday record to cool our minds. Beba fidgeted and Mrs Laing, bless her, took the piss out of Beba's Hungarian accent.

Ronnie introduced the Philadelphia Foundation. Beba and I sat, a little amazed at his 'deep speech' bit. The Glasgow hardman's accent, wreathed face, his 'ah'm-fucken-taillin'-ye' expression (remembered from God knows how many lance-jacks in the Royal Scots Greys) dressed in a Presbyterian resonance and a junky's speed. He finished, bringing his hands up close to his face, as though holding the 'No Theng' (Noh thing? Refusal thing?) and said 'The only way—the only way we can define our aim is as this: to reveal the greater glory of God'.

Beba—bewilderment, after years of business-like, fast-moving committee work with Arnold Wesker and chums.

Alex—patiently absorbing the sinister monosyllable into his evil atheistic soul and smothering it.

I—suddenly interested.

Mrs Laing—loyally suppressing her giggles.

Alex did a little seductive purring and name-dropping—Bill Burroughs, Francis Bacon. Good old Alex.

Then a growing fragmentation, talk breaking into groups, half a dozen different conversations. I thought Esterson looked as though he had been in a concentration camp—a sort of lucid bestiality about him that put him, somehow, in that setting. I asked him if he'd ever been in a concentration camp. 'No' he said. I told Cooper I felt that I should have been in one, that this would have been tantamount to suffering the century. 'To suffer society is enough', said Cooper. 'Society is a concentration camp.' Christ what a nut.

I was still in a hurry. No sidetracks. I could perhaps kick this introspective shambles into a body that would take up where the Committee of 100 had failed. I was wrong. I needed a reputation for that. Professional rank was, finally, fairly rigid.

But time and the wailing clarinettes of the whiskey indicated I should leave, and I'd promised Beba some concrete decision. I willed down the alcohol. 'How would it be if I fixed a week-end conference in the country? Would you all come?'

'Yes,' said Ronnie loudly.

'I'll do it then,' I said. In fact, I already had.

Nevertheless I had to persuade the people at Brazier's Park to accept a series of afterthoughts and additions amongst the guests and act as a go-between for two grotesquely different groups.

The community at Brazier's Park, a little colony of quiet, self-sufficient middle-class intellectuals, totally square with heavy overtones of Quakerism and Fabianism, was anxious to extend every kindness and expected, in return, good manners and an observation of the minimal regulations they imposed.

The group I represented was turned into the examination of their own minds, partly driven there by their fear and hatred of anything outside their own minds, with an angry contempt for most ordinary conventions and all regulations, with no intention of playing guest to the Brazier's Park host, merely wanting to pay their way for a place where they could go a little madder than they already were. I put down twenty-one quid as a deposit, and on that sunny Friday, got off school early and made my way to Reading. At Reading I missed the bus so started out on the Oxford Road. An old man gave me a lift; courteous, kindly, at peace with himself, he seemed the embodiment of all that was good about the way of life we were out to destroy.

He put me down on a high road where cornfields lay around like sumptuous mothers, apple green and gold, russet, bread-white, toasted brown, on all sides. The breeze stirred the wildflowers in the shallow hedges.

'Brazier's Park is down there,' said the driver, pointing to a lane. He drove off and I walked down the gentle side of the swell towards a family of trees, mossy, sooty-black and green, clustered in the hollow. I could see the little minarets of Brazier's Park above the trees. I felt exhilarated, moved by the shimmering cleanliness of the summer and the light.

Rounding the curve of Brazier's Park drive, I saw a group standing in the porch, recognized Esterson. I waved but nobody waved back. I laughed aloud for contempt and waved again.

'Hello,' I said. Esterson nodded his reply, introduced me to others in the group. 'Nice evening,' I said. It was such an understatement of my obvious exhilaration I must have sounded grotesque. It was a beautiful place and a beautiful summer and we were going to stop the squares scorching it to death (what, sixty miles from London? Outside the blast of 100 megatons—just fires and roast flesh and heavy fallout).

Opposite the porch was a high elm sodden with light, luminous and liquid masses of foliage clotted sumptuously to a regal altitude. Esterson said, 'I wonder if you could guess the height of that tree'. I knew immediately that we were in for trouble. Their eyes were closed.

I was eager to begin, to meet, to talk. Was Alex here? Where was the clueless nit? Wandering round the Oxonian downs with a dropper up his nose? I talked to the hosts. They were anxious to give out with a formal welcome at dinner. Yes, we had all been asked to be there for dinner. But dinner came and went and still no formal announcement. That would have to wait till after dinner. Tom McGrath showed with wife and baby. Cooper and I went to meet Laing and look for Alex (visions of him put down facing in the wrong direction by a bus conductor and wandering off to the south). Cooper whipped along the lanes in his flash car. We met Ronnie. He was with Clancy Sigal and Joe. We chased round the lanes looking for a pub. In the pub I said to Sigal 'I can't see you'. 'Oh sorry,' he said. He lifted his shades.

Joe rode back with Cooper and I. A Hungarian brain surgeon with huge maudlin eyes and a big Jewish yearning in him, Joe talked about the play he was writing. 'This is Kafka' he said, indicating the bleeding landscape. I thought, 'For these cats everything is Kafka'. I said 'You should have seen the sun earlier this evening—like a bloody great fried egg'. So Joe smiled and that looked a bit more promising.

Half the people had been in to dinner. There were two times suggested to meet after dinner. Alex arrived, nerve-wracked from Jim's driving, wanted to leave this evening informal until morning. Joe and Ronnie wanted to go on the piss. The hosts wanted to give their welcome and outline their regulations. I was beginning to stretch between appeasement of the hosts, excitement at the people, excitement at the place, and a powerful unassuaged thirst of my own.

By ten-thirty we were assembled—wanderers back from the pub but Alex in his room. The Philadelphia representatives were a little sceptical about the whole project. What the hell was sigma anyway? I started to try to tell them. Tom sloped off to get Alex. Alex, irritable, came down. For all his inadequacy and megalomania there was something warming about him and his wife—there always is—a warming virile whiff of sheer jazz about them.

Confrontation between Bob Cobbing and Alex. Alex sitting cross-legged on the floor painting a piece of driftwood in Cryla colour.

Cobbing: 'Where is the money coming from?'

Trocchi: 'The money is *no problem*.'

Cobbing: 'Where is it then?'

Trocchi: 'I've *got* the fucking money.'

Cobbing: 'How much?'

Trocchi hurled his driftwood at Cobbing, Cobbing grinned.

Trocchi: 'Have I got to sit here all night looking at your fucking ugly face?'

Play this man right like an instrument, I thought, and you'll get a good song. Thinking vaguely that the Philadelphia Trust must be trusted with something, I said 'It's okay Bob. There *is* money.'

At this point the host, Mrs Faithful, came in to deliver her official welcome. She had waited patiently since dinner four hours ago. 'I don't want to listen to any administrative details,' growled Alex.

Later we fixed a meeting for ten in the morning and broke up. Sigal, McGrath and I talked. 'You're awful hung up on art,' said Sigal.

John Latham had a pint of whiskey. He shared it. Joe crooned Hungarian Yiddish lullabies to Beba Lavrin.

In the morning Alex overdosed. I began to get the pattern of his habit. It was, basically, a kind of worrying towards self-perfection. Thus he had lasted longer than most. He came down to the meeting late. By the time he came down Ronnie, Joe and Beba had gone off on the piss again. Another pattern. These people *dreaded* meeting one another. Deeply they *dreaded* it.

So through most of the morning session Tom McGrath and I talked about an art centre and nobody dug the idea too much.

We had lunch. Ronnie, Joe and Beba were back, picnicking with wine and garlic sausage on the terrace. 'My obligations do not go so far as to have to eat their fuck-awful food,' said Ronnie and hurled a stone out into the park.

The picnic got wilder and drunker. Wine got into people like the sun got into the butter. The picnic table became an image of the whole meeting. Discordant, messy, runny, sticky and finally abandoned.

I began, doggedly, to make mere meeting times my business. That final abandonment was not going to happen if I could help it. Graham Howe had already left in disgust.

In the afternoon Ronnie sat in a centre chair, magnificently slewed, with a litre of wine at his foot. 'I want everyone in this room who is not prepared to be a fucken *general* in this campaign to walk out of that door now.'

The discussion started circling. Joe asked, '*What* is this sickness in society you refer to?'

Everybody sounded off abstractedly. Joe kept asking. I said 'Ronnie, will you for Christ's sake give Joe some definition of the social sickness so that we can move on?'

Sigal said 'Jeff, you're beginning to bug me.'

That was it. I crumpled into a chair with the wine and held back angry tears. There is a movie somewhere of my beergut rising and falling on that occasion, tumultuous with suppressed wrath and frustration.

'Why put down Jeff and not Joe?' asked Tom.

'Because Joe seems to have a little more behind his asking,' said Sigal.

Laing pointed at McGrath. '*You* are an innocent man,' he accused. John Latham burned a Skoob Tower.

In the evening there was a hurtling drive to Oxford. Beba Lavrin's teenage son, who suffered with a violent nervous twitch, sat in the front of the car. As we crashed the traffic lights or hurtled towards slowing vehicles Jim, driving, threw his left arm across the boy's chest. And a hell of a lot of good that would have done had it come to the crunch.

At dinner I sat by Joe and the boy. Joe, well-plastered by now, talked to the boy about his twitch, then screamed 'For Christ's sake stop it!' The boy froze. Joe turned to me with an expression of dreamy benignity: 'I'm winning,' he said.

The bill for dinner came to a hundred pounds. Somehow Ronnie paid it.

One of Cooper's patients drove me back to the Park. I had to get petrol for him on the way—conned a passing motorist into driving me to a garage and back with the can. A mile from the Park we ran dry again. Joan, Sid, the driver and I piled out and pushed the car home.

In the house everybody was stoned. Alex and Ronnie squatted cross-legged on the floor, forehead to forehead, eyes closed. Sigal had some jazz records. I listened for a while—Joe Turner—then turned in.

A smell woke me up. On the stairs it was stronger, a cheap scented chemical kind of smell. I expected chaos in the lounge and vaguely intended clearing it up. That at least I could do for the Faithfuls (who, I later discovered, had sat up all that Saturday night with a gun.) I opened the lounge door. John Latham met me with a steady staring eye. There's something about Latham at such moments that is mad beyond madness. A staring immovable shocked and shocking inner violence. Latham had taken a book (an irreplaceable book belonging to a pleasant little Chinese friend of Alex's) stuck it to the wall with Polyfilla, and shot black Aerosol all over book and wall in a big explosion of night. That was the smell. Otherwise the room was tidy.

Until breakfast-time John reassured me that the Faithfuls had given him permission to do a mural. Later it caused serious mental distress to aged community members. That Sunday morning it stood, overlooking the talk, a stark, beautiful, violent emblem to pure action, the most graphic condemnation possible of our evasive ineffectual waffle.

So that Sunday morning Cooper and Laing spoke well. Calm after the party, relaxed, knowing us now and we knowing him, Laing enacted a catatonic ceremonial, summarily describing its magical function. 'It's a question,' he said, 'of coming down from the surface of things, from the surface of yourself, down to the core of all things, to the central sphere of being of which all things are emanations.'

At mid-day we fled from one another with colossal relief.

April 3, 1966: 'It was worth it,' I say to Criton. 'No bastard came but Wilcocks and his bird, oh, and some friend of yours, but there was something going on.'

Criton nods. He seems pleased and calmer. We go to the pub. Criton talks about his sexuality, his hangups. I talk about mine.

I am seeing more clearly now what Criton is about. Criton has listened and learned well. For three years he, finally a Christian idealist, has been buffeted between the ideas of me, Keith, Burroughs, Laing, striving selflessly and giving his best in despera-

tion. He has, in doing this, countenanced obscenity and extravagance repellent to his very nature. He has seen his ideas mangled in meetings, swamped in exhibitions, cut-up with everybody else's in My Own Mag, *and ignored at Kingsley Hall. Through this he has given no time to sex or pleasure, merely to his most honourable commitment. And this would be fine were everything going well. Now, a year after the sTigma, nine months after the Albert Hall, six months after the abortive display of his own environment-scheme, he finds the very people who drowned out his ideas scattered into something he doesn't understand. sigma dissolving in seas of junk, Keith and Heather, Dave Trace, many of the sTigma team, dispersed in disappointment and general scepticism, Laing and I wasting our energies in domestic difficulties, John still in the madhouse and nobody seemingly giving a shit, an American poet living merrily in Criton's back room with the wife of one of Cooper's patients, the Free School of London broadening its aims out of all reach of its ever being a university, the Philadelphia Foundation trying to tap the common soul of man through the barrier of professional status and the locked doors of the Kingsley Hall. It is the time of my oft-quoted editorial in* My Own Mag, *the time of the doldrums between Ginsberg's world tour and Turn On, Tune In, Drop Out.*

'...let us, to quote Sartre, "get on with it." Clearly one of the ways we can get on with it is first of all to take steps to ensure that human beings remain in existence at all. After trying to stir various bunches of people into concerted action I am coming to the conclusion that possibly the most hot-blooded insurrectionists hold their role of "oposition to a thoroughly secure establishment" as more important than the overthrow of that establishment. After all, the salaries for steppenwolves are quite high in some quarters.

'Up to this point subversion has been the aim of this magazine. Subversion is revolution by infiltration rather than confrontation. I give here a list of individuals, institutions, organizations, magazines which seem to me to be concerned with subversion rather than literature, art, pornography, underground movies, heroin or other quaint rural handicrafts. I can envisage clashes between materialists and romantics, communists and anarchists, atheists and mystics. Nevertheless we all share the clear certainty that the

present situation is suicidal. The only real obstructions, as I see it, are the ones so common amongst ourselves—solipsism, professional jealousy and junk. WITH CO-OPERATION WE COULD ALL ACTUALLY WIN. DO WE REALLY WANT TO WIN?'

So Criton is angry rather than mad—He is saying 'Right, I'll go into my mind, perform the Laingian strategy of psychosis better than any. I'll rattle out all your secrets passing through my consciousness and cut them in with your poems and letters, like in My Own Mag, I'll peel the foreskin off your privacy more ruthlessly than Bruce, or Burroughs, or Nuttall for that matter, and in doing so I'll shatter your individual meanderings and force you back into the collective purpose, bring you back from girl friends, junk, neuroses, back to our declared aims.

And sitting in the pub (Criton having told me he has left his job in a Lord-will-provide kind of voice, wearing this solemnity like a sort of self-woven robe) I talk about sex-need, about being in love, about helplessness in the face of these things and he comes back with—'One can have a good fuck without even touching the other person'—and I say 'Yes' but begin, just begin to know that Criton has no capability or vulnerability towards the ecstatic hungers riding Alex, Ronnie, me, Keith, John Keys, that Criton is not the stuff whose principles are decapitated by a whiff of the subtler wines, the dream, the sweet cunt of fast blood and heady music. And Criton is, of course, right, no doubt about it. And I agree with Criton. No doubt about that.

But I am of the other kind, the fallible kind and, right or wrong, I'm not sorry. Not sorry either for Criton, with his stern purpose and his desolate integrity.

So, walking away, I begin to get an anger, a tiny trickling anger, not yet fully identified, for while Criton is right and rightly cuts clean through our sick preoccupations, Criton doesn't know the worth of what he's cutting, doesn't know the price of principle to a sensual man.

Criton circulates his delirium in letters, streams of consciousness rattled down and mailed to all the people swimming in the stream, drawing patterns of relationships, some real, some imagined, like a spiderweb to trap us all. Some of them arrived before his visit, mixed up with the Clifton de Berry letters from Dan Georgakas. Ronnie sticks them all on the notice board at Kingsley Hall.

'*And if I tell Joe Berke on the telephone that this is Criton (still) and he echoes me back saying…rather surprised…'O, Criton… I thought…YOU WERE…and I reply…I AMM all the same' and he laughs a little as I myself a little desperate at the situation which is becom…ing f…u…n…n…y when I losee the vo…I would say…at a…guess that he is far from BEING with it YET! and he can take as much dope as the fury demands …TO PROVE THE OPPOSITE! Wouldn't YOU ronnie think the same! my first…dis…ciple, Who! denied me first also!*

'*And tell…the DUMB FISH…that his silence though still… of…some value…is a sponge that has very few secrets to tell me at the moment…he's been afraid as I expect(ed) to REACH ME NAKED AND SMILING! AT ONCE.*

'*BE OPEN I said which means that when the doors are open for everybody and nobody is chucked out without…the (dictator's!) …NOBODY'S Request…not even the baffled neighbours who are still HARD AT guessing what the hell's GOING ON IN THERE! So let them in—right into your bedroom while you copulate …with anybody you like and tell them: "IT'S ALL PART OF THE TREATMENT!"*

'*…perhaps THE VOICE could reach through Keith-Heather-Criton-David-John etc…MY REAL EARS it was found preferable to…lock the main door…While…somebody was doing something to somebody ELSE! "Keep that door locked" grinned Heather's authority or something… "OK.OK," said the little arsehole who was earlier hunting for hashish or… something… terrified that…THE QUEENS…had arrived to chase his own arsehole…"I've seen him push the woman down the stairs"…"which is inaccurate" correct Keith and Heather "Therefore I've seen NOTHING" he said…little? knowing that I WAS THERE shaking a criton-chicken and for that MOMENT truly WRINGING Christ's Ghost for the pleasantly surprised policemen…smiling at us all…holding M.E. bleeding between them…'*

Another batch of duplicating comes through the post for me to do and I realize I've had enough. I try to articulate my alienation from Criton. I write, to begin with frankly and kindly:

'*Dear Criton*
Wd have gone further (could have gone along even further) had it not been for the growing certainty that your cosmic plan-chette is totally insensitive or antipathetic to a whole area of existence...' but going on to a flat and frightened brutality: 'gleefully annihilating in clouds of empty clemency the very thing you haven't got and never will have until you come out of your godawful disinfected mental bath room...'

On the morning of Good Friday, dig that, Good Friday, a phone call. Criton's flat-mate, the little Chinaman: 'Criton's had an accident, Can you come?'

'I'm glad we had it,' said Ronnie over the phone.

Through that summer of 1964 we turned our possibilities over between use like enigmatic stones. Alex and Lyn moved back together. Lyn had kicked her habit successfully. Their flat was a three-room place near Westbourne Grove. The discarded cars rusted away in the street.

I spent long sunny afternoons sitting on the balcony playing with little Mark, sitting in the pub talking to Lyn. Our intentions and schedules submerged into a warm ambience, compounded of Lyn's gentle slatternly beauty, the soft purr of Alex's voice, an ambience of tenderness, intelligence, total licence and crackling undercurrents of a kind of sad cruelty.

Alex rigged up his study like an office. People passing through London dropped in, Jack Michelin, Gregory Corso, Bob Creeley, Ian Sommerville. Posters went up on the walls, statements of policy, plans of action. I drew up a plan for a sigma poster magazine and found a cheap printer at Hertford who'd print it like a wrestling poster. Alex didn't like it. He drew up his own mock-up and passed it on to Sankey at Villiers Press.

I duplicated the sigma portfolio and Alex and I went up to the unofficial poetry conference at the Traverse with something to sell. Jim Haynes' vast Edinburgh flat was like a Bedouin encampment. Actors, poets, folk-singers, dancers came in, dossed down and passed on. A man from Millbrook showed up —actual tangible proof of the psychedelic movement.

The dream was strengthening. My best things I said to myself—auto-responses to passing remarks and half-memories. A little man called Jack Moore held my hand in the Traverse Bar. I caught my nose in the door of a telephone kiosk on the Royal Mile and a fat man called Adrian Henri released me. Chinese lunch with Alan and his bird. Ferocious embrace from Roddy Carmichael. George Lawson like a wren. George MacBeth like a predatory spider. Martin Seymour-Smith and I and two vacant American girls. The Corries late night at the Traverse reminding me of Dennis Winnie and Dennis Winnie dying. Looking for Bill McArthur and selling the Festival Special Mag. Sunday morning sunshine waking the beatniks dossed out in rows in the castle gardens.

Phil Cohen found the Kingsley Hall. What was the Kingsley Hall? A beautiful hall, says Cohen, what you might call Bypass Ecclesiastical. Who's running it? Oh some trust, some collection of social workers, working more or less under David Sheppard (who was, at that time, unsullied by *Last Exit To Brooklyn*).—Gandhi slept there—Social centre in the East End. What are they doing with it? Absolutely fuck all.

The exhibition. Yes, the exhibition. I went to see the Kingsley Hall. Latham had his Skoob Box, a strange dark environment, in the basement. Cohen was dossing in the organ room. The Philadelphia Trust wanted it for their community. Cohen wanted it for a youth recreation centre. I wanted it for Criton and me, to house our exhibition. I contacted Criton and called a meeting. John Latham, Bruce Lacey, Islwyn Watkins, Criton, Dave Trace, Phil Cohen, Keith and Heather Musgrove, came.

Meanwhile I learned something more of Alex and the price of his self-perfection—how each step towards his own apotheosis cost him dearer in terms of need—a veritable Faustian progress with the Devil upping the price all the time, so that each project that his aspiring sensibility conducted him towards, each ideal, each aim, each plan too huge and too audacious for unstimulated minds, carried with it its sad reverse of negatives. Each gesture of self-realization carried an aspect of snide self-gratification. The funds poured in. But the funds also poured out. In September Tonk sent me ten bob from Liverpool with the note, 'Is this any good for sigma?' I sent it back by return.

Good Friday, April 1966. Criton's curtains are, as ever, drawn. 'He fell in the kitchen and cut his head,' says the Chinaman. 'He says he's paralysed.'

Criton lies on a mattress on the floor of his half-dark studio. The mattress is made up neatly with clean sheets and he lies neatly on his back. Even the cut on his forehead is bleeding neatly in a single decorous track.

The rest of the room is disturbing. It is in a strange disorder—not the usual squalor of an artist's studio but an almost compulsive plethora of stuff. The duplicating job I refused has now been done and the stacks of paper are all across the bed. Constructions, drawings, clothes, gear everywhere, not dropped or left, but placed. The effect is rather like that of a kleptomaniac's uncovered magpie hoard.

'Sit down,' says Criton.

I sit.

'Have you paper and a pen?'

I say 'Yes'.

'Over there', says Criton, 'are the pamphlets. I want them sent to the following people—The Queen, the Prime Minister—'

'Oh-oh' I think. 'The real thing.' Criton's little excursion into the subliminal has turned into schizophrenia.

'I think you're mad,' I say.

Quotations run off Criton's tongue—things I have said throughout our relationship—whole conversations remembered word perfect but translated into persecutionary terms and juxtaposed now as evidence of my imposition. Perhaps I have imposed on Criton but this is the first, honestly the first, I know of it.

'Perhaps you'd better ring your wife. You're going to be here for some time.'

'No I'm not,' I say. *'I'm going home for my dinner.'*

Criton is out of bed like a shot. Coldly angry, he walks about the room moving things. I ask him for the telephone number of his doctor. Then I bid him goodbye. Outside in the hall I tell the Chinaman that Criton is mad and give him the doctor's telephone number. I go up the road in the bright Easter sunshine. I ring the doctor and tell his secretary that Criton is mad, that he believes he is Christ, that it's Easter, so for Christ's sake get a move on. The doctor is on Easter vacation, she says, but she'll do what she can.

I ring round the Philadelphia Trust trying to get some response. Kingsley Hall residents are so pissed off with Criton by now they don't want to know. Joe Berke is sympathetic, asks me to ring back and tell him what happens. We make a date to meet in the Porcupine on Easter Monday. David Cooper says *'Well, we all think we're Jesus, don't we, Jeff?'*

The Kingsley Hall went, of course, finally, to the Philadelphia Trust. By now we had another place—Better Books basement. Tony Godwin had opened the new paperback shop with Bill Butler as manager in November 1964. I wrote to Tony Godwin. Fine, he said and we went to work. We did a happening with Charles Marowitz and Ken Dewey and then proceeded to build the sTigma in early 1965. Criton had made a plan and a model. Bruce and I had disliked the arty look of it but we adopted the main ground plan. We apportioned off the parts. Latham, the entrance; me, the passage; Watkins, the darkened passage; Lacey, the polythene maze and the dentist's chair; Trace, the café; me, the living room; Keith and Heather, the cylinder and the tunnel; Criton, the remainder.

Criton and I started just after Christmas. It was the first time I'd actually, physically worked with Criton. It was murder, two different speeds and both of us incapable of working outside those speeds, me like a bull in a chinashop, Criton like a cabinet maker. Cohen came down to help, saw that it was real, really taking place, not just being planned, and went away again. We put up a steel framework. After Christmas Keith came and knocked it down.

Through January Keith was out of work. He spent every

day down in the basement hurling his considerable energy against the concrete and the crumbling walls. By February, almost single-handed Keith had put up a new framework. We went to work.

I tried to fix it for everybody to get together on Saturdays and talk about progress. Criton was almost desperate to get a monastic thing going. He rang me up and suggested we all get sleeping bags and live in the basement. This was first impressive, then a touch alarming, and finally made me angry, a quick unpleasant impatience with the other man who dogs my footsteps and calls on me to dog his. I could hear over the phone that Criton was angry also. Wasn't our cause the most sacred possible? Wasn't it a cause demanding our total commitment? I told Criton bluntly that I had other sacred commitments and that the rest of the gang wouldn't play either.

As Saturdays passed it became obvious that we were once again avoiding one another. Everyone in the team seemed to be hiding behind a separate stance and a separate concept of what the exhibition stood for.

For Keith and Heather it was a bunch of friends doing the thing primarily for fun, a kind of practical joke, cocking a snook at the squares. For John Latham it was another gesture against the printed word. For Bruce it was one more item in a confused frantic programme all more or less devoted to his socialist obsessions. For Nick and Dave it was the art game—form. For Criton it was sacred dedication. For me it was anger, ebullient sarcasm and a public for my art work at last. For Criton and I it was intensely serious, a last chance. For the others, only partly so.

I tended to find myself spokesman for the group and explained the show as best I could according to the original ideals of Currel-Brown's letter. It was propagandist rather than art. Its brutality, its nauseous elements were intended to enforce life and to inspire compassion, an angry diagnosis intended to provoke correction.

Increasingly I realized that only Criton, Bruce and I were thinking in these original terms.

The entrance to the sTigma was through three valve-doorways lined with old copies of the *Economist*. The last you could just squeeze through, but not back, no return. The corridor this led to was lined with hideous bloody heads, photos of war atrocities, Victorian pornographic cards, tangles of stained underwear, sanitary towels, french letters, anatomical diagrams; the passage narrowed into complete darkness—tin, glass, wet bread, plastic, sponge rubber, then a zig-zag corridor of polythene through which you could glimpse your goal, a group of figures. They were gathered around a dentist chair which had itself been turned into a figure, with sponge rubber breasts and a shaven head. On the seat of the chair was a cunt made of a bed pan lined with hair and cod's roe. Detergent bubbles spluttered from between the slabs of roe, which remained spluttering and stinking for four weeks. Then a corridor of television sets led past the window of Dave Trace's sleazy cafe with its festering meal, also left through four weeks, into a replica living room, furnished with choice items of ghastly ornament and with a sideboard drawer containing human toes. The voices of Trocchi, Burroughs, Mike Osborne's alto and the BBC leaked out and intermingled from concealed loudspeakers. After the living room a corridor of old clothes, a red cylinder, knee deep in feathers, a vaginal tunnel of inner tubes scented with Dettol through which the public had to crawl to get out, a womb-room with a plastic abortion nailed to the wall, a plethora of political and religious propaganda and a beaming photograph of David Jacobs.

While we made all this John Moore, a flat-mate of Bill Butler's who worked at Better Books, worked with us. Dick Wilcocks was never far away.

George MacBeth produced a hilarious radio programme about it. T. G. Rosenthal wormed his way through with a BBC cricket-commentary voice. Then he interviewed us.

We said our spiel. I had some uneasiness about the whole show. Its unrelieved obscenity was neither dynamic nor bawdy. It was headachy, oppressive. You came out and the world was dimmer, the reverse of *my* intention.

John had, unknown to me, been going round and round the show all day long. Before the broadcast he had hurled coffee all over the books in the bookshop upstairs. When the interviewer turned the mike to John there were minutes of silence and two bleak hostile responses. Could he describe what the exhibition meant to him? 'No...

Not your way...'

Within a few days John was in the madhouse, the victim and scapegoat it seemed of our collective disease. His eloquent silence was broadcast. Anne Duchene gave the broadcast a rather patronizing review in the *Guardian*. Criton was angry now, coldly and unchangeably angry.

As the sTigma was wrecked, abused, repaired, as the radio and press interviews passed, as we realized by the graffiti that what was hell to puritans was a heaven to sadistic fetishists, as the toes we had reeled from and steeled ourselves to use were drawn on the living room walls in erotic contexts, as it became obvious that someone amongst us was nicking the gate money, as we shifted the little tribes of beatnik squatters out with their droppers and guitars, the sharp angers, jealousies, differences between us flared. At the end of March we tore it down thankfully. We tore it down and let the daylight in and forgot it as best we could. We forgot the plans to reconstruct it on a bus and take it round the provinces. We forgot our plans for shock happenings on London Transport. We left it to John to do our remembering for us.

Easter Saturday 1966. I go to Uxbridge. The Freeman Syndicate, a bunch of energetic young West London anarchists, are running a poetry and jazz session. I am directing a happening with the Mike Westbrook Band. Motor-bikes round the hall, simultaneous films, lights, dark, whistles, Osborne, Griffiths and Surman flipping their sweet lids.

Easter Sunday. The phone rings at regular intervals through the day. Two rings and then stop. Criton signalling. They haven't yet collected him.

Easter Monday. I meet Joe Berke in the Porcupine. We talk about Criton, vision, Louis Wain. He flashes his gammy finger at me as I expected him to. With about four pints under my belt I go down to Trafalgar Square. The same old tremors of anger and frustration. I see John Keys and his bird. They are angry at Criton's interference. Keys compares the numbers with Bayard Rustin's massive civil rights march. We watch Adrian Mitchell's and Mike Kustow's puppet play. I got a meeting together earlier in the year, a lame effort to follow on from the sTigma. Keys remarks that of all the people at that meeting only Mitchell and Kustow have actually done anything. I say 'How about Criton?'

I go to talk to Adrian and Mike. Wilcocks and Foley grab me. Half-slewed, I find myself on the platform facing about five thousand people as the Anarchist speaker. I tell them marching is ineffectual. I tell them for eight years they have marched past the Ministry of Defence without 'leaving so much as a bullet hole' to remember them by. A uniformed dinosaur of some considerable rank takes my name and address.

During the evening I run across Dave Tomlin but wish, now, I hadn't. I was no pleasurable company.

On Tuesday half the Freeman Syndicate and John Moore come to visit. In full view of them all, luxuriating in the sourness of my perversity, I ring Criton's doctor, find that Criton has either not answered the door or turned callers away. I call the welfare authorities. In an hour they ring me back and tell me they called round with the police, that Criton is now in Napsbury madhouse. I break the news to the roomful of people. John out— Criton in; somebody, it seems, has to carry the can.

The sTigma closed at the end of March 1965. Ginsberg arrived in May. Unannounced he wandered into Better Books one day and introduced himself. He offered to read anywhere for no fee. His first reading at Better Books was the first healing wind on a very parched collective mind. The sourness, the negativity in the air before his coming was almost tangible. Was certainly poisonous.

We sat, packed tight, rather self-conscious. Bob Cobbing looked triumphant. I was drunk and insane and in love. Bill Morris was sick in the metal waste-basket noisily.

Ginsberg read and it registered that what had seemed over-messianic, grotesquely self-exposing and self-lacerating in print, was, in fact, a gay thing, the violent images delivered with a mischievous twinkle, an incredible milky gentleness flowing out from this one man into the minds and bodies of the audience. After the reading he sauntered down into the audience—cigarette, hands in pockets, not a prophet, not a great poet any more, just a friendly Yank, said: 'Well, where's the party?'

Two women with flowers on their faces whisked him away. Days later, in Marcus Field's room one floor down from Alex's, a crowd of us sat in a circle. Field, a young and capable Australian, had been doing my job for sigma since we began work on the exhibition, doing it far more efficiently than I. Allen was tired. Was I Nuttall? Did I know that Burroughs was against the flesh? I was surprised that he knew. Did the young people read Blake? Rather in the same way that American reporters thought the Beatles were queer because of their haircuts, so Allen seemed to think that any long-haired British youth was steeped in Proust. The misunderstanding reached a hilarious peak when, stark naked, he encountered Lennon and McCartney (at that time very sharp little mods) at a party and demanded their embraces. It seems to indicate an insight beyond error, that now two years later both the Beatles and their fans would enjoy Proust very much indeed.

It was a new and elevating summer, a long warm time of colours merging, changing, in a slow exploding orgasm of events.

At the Albert Hall reading John Latham and I were to have a battle. We dressed in blue paint and huge Aztec costumes of books which we were to tear off one another. Trocchi forgot to signal our entrance. As we waited in the wings John passed out. There was a fight with one of the British Legion attendants who tried to prevent Cohen and I from using a door as a stretcher to carry John to Sir Malcolm Sargent's dressing-room. It was the same attendant, pulverized by the goodly Anglo-Saxon pouring forth from Jewish lips down in the auditorium, who burst into Sir Malcolm's bathroom, found John and I giggling and washing one another, assumed the worst and staggered away in an advanced state of shock.

The summer was out of control. I behaved, I am told, intolerably at one of John Calder's parties. Most people, I am told, behaved intolerably everywhere. sigma office was crowded with people wearing flowers. Gregory Corso, a pretty girl and I sold newspapers in the Portobello Road. I wrote real poetry at last. In September Allen went home and we all went to Cardiff. At Cardiff Jean-Jacques Lebel, Tom Hudson and I put on a happening. Cardiff School of Art was full of beautiful young people. The Park Hotel was full of local queers affecting disgust at visiting poets. Henri, Patten and McGough floated on a sea of black sullen faces. Patten took the shoes put out for the bootboy and threw them down the lift-shaft. Paolo Leonni, hiding behind a crazy assumed name because of the warrant out for his arrest, ten miles up on LSD, shambled out to the front of the Commonwealth Poetry Conference, respectable delegates turning with a wince from his cracked black shoes, floppy tweed hat, naked, dirty ankles, and delivered the following message to her Majesty the Queen of England.

'To the Queen

(1) That poetry, as an artistic extension of language, is a concrete alternative in the spiritual vacuum of contemporary everyday life.

(2) That every man, woman and child alive is an actual or potential poet.

(3) That the same words used daily to wilfully create ugliness and division can be profitably turned to attain unity and beauty, through poetry.

(4) That we feel the following to be problems in reality not sufficiently or satisfactorily dealt with in the tacitly accepted structure of politics, diplomacy and finance:

(A) Overpopulation.

(B) Depletion of the earth's natural resources to satisfy artificially created cravings.

(C) The understanding and elimination of armed animosity.

(D) The equitable distribution of material necessities.

(E) The perpetration of official interference in the communicative condition of man.

(F) The nature of legality and crime.

(G) The monopolization of temporal and spiritual authority by businessmen through the governments on the one hand and priests through the churches on the other.

(H) The refusal to grant poets their rightful Periclean role in modern democracy.

(I) The newspaper and magazine monopoly over the masses of man's highest symbolic achievement, the written word; delegating the responsibility of ferreting out the relevant truths of existence to anonymous, advertising-supported uncreative writers called journalists.

(J) The legal perpetuation of archaic, quasi-barbaric and intellectually insulting powerheads such as Kings, Queens, etc. —now often masked and protected by either capitalism or its cancer, communism, but certainly and in any case by those who would exalt the fundamental importance of money rather than man.

(K) The blind spread and acceptance of atheistic and dialectical materialism. We do not deny matter, nor does God need verbal solicitors. We envisage, rather, a world in which, perhaps, no one aspect of human or natural form predominates over the others, at their expense.

(L) The potential of the spoken, sung and written word to change the surface and substance of life.

(M) The need to alleviate pain and raise all men to the highest possible level of human health in their minds and bodies.

(N) The need to remove sex, death and drugs, among others, from the taboo status they presently enjoy, not only within the Commonwealth.

(O) That we are bound by and can attain both individual and collective liberation through our first common wealth as poets— the English language.

(P) That national boundaries are as ultimately unnatural as they are commonly and pragmatically a pretence for the power of destructive forces whose operational existence none can deny.

(Q) That love need not remain a banal cliché but is and must be a constantly original and divine verb.

(R) That the reign of usury still standing between man and his desire and need to do a good job must finally come to an end.

(S) That the debate of truth must be continuous and conconsequential in the world of acts, and that survival at all costs is too expensive for the present-day depleted state of man's spiritual fund. It must be transformed into meaningfulness.

(T) In the meantime, which gets meaner all the time, we will continue to think with our hearts in what is seemingly today, unfortunately, a foolish search for wisdom.'[1]

The squares exploded. Paolo, Alex, Marcus Field, Doc Humes, Michael (Abdul Malik) De Freitas, Mike Horovitz, Pete Brown, Brian Patten, Harry Fainlight, Rosemary Tonks, Dan Richter and his wife, Earl Birney, Tom McGrath and I, amongst others whose signatures I can't decipher, signed the statement and sent it duly off to Buckingham Palace. I believe there was no reply.

Tom McGrath sat on the stairs of the Park Hotel for long periods of time. Dan and Jill had a terrible time with their prescriptions. There was a remarkably beautiful dancer.

Back in London the sigma office was raided. Paolo was chased out of England. The party was, for the moment, over, and Criton and I pestered the sleeping revellers. Criton spent much of his time at the Kingsley Hall. He became very close with David (I think it was David), a catatonic resident. The man from Millbrook we had met in Edinburgh the previous summer and Alex passed their time in mutual euphoria. John Moore went into hospital for his second bout. Criton displayed the maquette for his cage. In early 1966, about the same time of year as we'd put up the sTigma in 1965, I started getting cryptic postcards from Europe appointing me president of the Clifton de Berry for World President Campaign. They were interspersed with mangled signallings from Criton. I produced the Clifton de Berry issue of *My Own Mag*. Then I cracked up. Emerging from the crack-up, I discovered that the Clifton de Berry letters came from Dan Georgakas, who had run the Smyrna Press in Italy. Much later, after I'd started the Clifton de Berry strip in *International Times* I discovered that Clifton de Berry was a coloured venerable Wobbly. I changed the title of the strip to 'Seedy Bee'. As for Criton's letters, well, one night I got this phone call…

The duplicating I refused from Criton is eventually distributed. It is an apology, but worded as though from the Philadelphia Trust to the public.

[1] PAOLO LEONNI, published in *Residu*, no. 2, ed. Dan Richter and *International Times*, no. 5.

'TO WHOM IT MAY CONCERN

The Philadelphia Association, founded by Dr R. D. Laing, Dr Aaron Esterson, Dr Joe Berke, Dr Leon Redler, Mr Raimond O'Connor, Mr Sidney Briskin and Miss Joan Cunnold are distributing this communication to Press, Members of the Medical Profession and other individuals in the way of an apology/explanation for a farcical event staged under false pretences by one of their ex-patients. False invitations were distributed, we believe, to various editors, doctors, patients of mental hospitals, the police and other individuals, about an event which was to take place on the first of April 1966, between 7 and 8 p.m. at Kingsley Hall, Powis Road, Bow E.3. Needless to say such an event was not organized by the Philadelphia Association and never took place here. However, to clear any misunderstandings we enclose a statement of apology by the aforementioned patient by the name of: Criton Tomazos

> *6, Elm Court,*
> *Nether Street,*
> *N.3.*

Further, to clarify any other mystifications, we enclose our own telephone number at Kingsley Hall: ADVance 2532 and our patient's telephone number at his present address: FINchley 5149. He is soon to receive treatment under our super vision. Once more: OUR SINCERE APOLOGIES

And then, overleaf:
'MY.OWN.APOLOGY?MY.OWN.APO-LOGY.
      AP...P...APE...O...L.ORGY...ORGY...
                        ORGY...from
NETHER...STREET...NETHERS...TREAT...EAT... EAT...ME...NOT NOW.'

There follows six pages of the choicest psychic stew, pivoted round the intersection point of the name 'Mortimer'. Penelope Mortimer has written an article about Cooper's Villa for the Sunday Times. *Fragments of her journalistic account are cut in with fragments of another article by her about becoming middle-aged. This is tied up with memories of Ruth Mortimer, a patient-resident at Kingsley Hall, who is the centre of the network of identities with which Criton is obsessed:*

'*(Got it my precious Ministers?)*
*One of the best experiences we have is when the whole group
(including Joan Cun-nold-cun) gets into a terrific conflictful...
disintegration and then gradually...pieces itself.* TOGETHER
AGAIN. *Tom* (?)*azos is* MARVELLOUS *! at managing this !
He'll* (HELL) *come in and smash the* WHOLE THING *to
pieces and then* (continued on page 11)*...all that can be seen of
him is his hair and a hand never holding but holding a cigarette.
Mary starves. She comes in and draws a finger through his eye !
Tastes* LOOOOVE...*ly! Roger takes me back to the Art
Room...he is 21...looks like the real young snake he is...wearing
a gilt bracelet he stole from Harry Pincers during...holy communion...and three large, exactly spaced* SAFETY PINS *to
hold his fly together (for Harry will* NEVER LET FLY:
That's why he groans he's SOOOOO RIDICULOUS *all
the time...*NO GUTS...TO LET FLY*). When he...*CAME
he had a GUITAR *now broken! A wrecked* UPRIGHT *piano,
crusty with* PAIN*, stands in the middle of the art room.* THE
NOISE *produced by sweeping your hand, or a stick, over the
exposed strings is said, by* SOME*, to be more satisfactory than
the noises produced by hammering the Keys. Who? John Keys,
the well known...American poet?* (NOTHING THAT I
SAID *! exclaims Helen. I think the sounds I...produce...are
quie...quite...eh,* Hell! SHIT! *I never said such...*A
SOUND*)'*

—And all this interspersed with fragments from Ronnie's book
The Divided Self *together with violent attacks on the hypocrisies
and double-standards afflicting the whole Philadelphia project:*

'*ARE YOU ALL DRUIDS? You downright possessment by
the devil...you utter contempts of the earth that I* CURSE AND
CURSE AND CURSE*...I merely want to know whether we
shall have* THE TRIBUNAL INQUISITON AND
CRUCIFIXION ON THE DOWNS, OR DO. I. HAVE.
TO. DO. IT. HERE?'*

*I take some comfort from this document that I was possibly
only just in time to interrupt Criton's personal Golgotha.*

Criton comes to see me sometimes on Sunday afternoons, sometimes with fellow patients. He is excited about the madhouse. It is all there, he says. No need to look around for deserted country mansions. Just a few crafty adjustments to the administration of the madhouses, turn on the staff a little, and there you are. Every madhouse is already a university of inner space—and (Criton emphasizes this point) a democratic one at that, no special priveleges for doctors and famous artists.

Then Criton is released and I, still wrestling with my problems, hope the whole affair is over. Criton has neatly pinpointed the absurd division between principle and desire. I have invalidated my principles. Criton has tapped out the very sound—the very intercom poetry—which is the unnerving voice of our collective mind and we have denied it as, Criton claims, the doctors at the Kingsley Hall deny their community ideal by increasingly wanting to live away from the community. None of us wants what we advocate. Criton has voiced, tested and discredited the We we are.

One sunny morning in June of 1966 I am walking out in Barnet—twelve months now since the Albert Hall reading, fourteen since the sTigma. The passing postman hands me a letter. My stomache lurches in anticipation on recognizing Criton's handwriting. It's a magazine. A rich and powerful gesture of honesty and complete disgust. It calls itself, the Moving Times, *has a slice of the old sigma wall magazine for a front cover. It names its editors as Trocchi and myself. It is a mock* My Own Mag, *full of cut holes, with a burlesque facsimile of the original* My Own Mag *No. 1 cover, saying 'Rest your shattered face in this you CUNT'. It has been sent to the Director of Public Prosecutions, Scotland Yard, Her Majesty and Prince Philip, Sir Laurence Olivier, 'with the compliments of the editors'.*

There is a long letter to Aaron Esterson: 'First an offer to stay in Kingsley Hall—then a silent withdrawal of the offer because my correspondence-outflow of my inner self—surrounded your half-hearted experiment with unpleasant odours...' Hideously accurate quotes from my conversation.

A second letter to Esterson. This time back on the collage intercom. People's problems recounted under the wrong person's name: 'Mr X. has risked his "sanity" before reaching a viable compromise between wife, children and mistress whilst a Mr X has reached no solution short of a cleavage from his family of six...'

Fragments of quotes from old Mags and underground documents sliced in with phrases from private letters. An old letter from Esterson and Laing advocating marihuana in place of alcohol.

A letter to Dr Layland of Napsbury, bearing Maurice Richardson's name at the bottom.

A forged letter to Criton from Alex: 'I was therefore impressed with your timely "event" at Kingsley Hall, in which though absent, I fully participated'—excluding Criton's 'Cage' project from the sigma collection.

Artaud's famous indictment of trivial form in art, attributed here to Anthony Caro. More cutup.

My letter opting out of the whole project printed in full. A cutup about castration.

A letter from Phil Cohen: 'Watch that lovely God Jeff when he speaks from the fools mouth he turns...a little naasty !'

Next a letter I have written to Criton trying to tell him of my adherence to the dream and my belief in art, only addressed to God and larded with sardonic Joyceanisms. It contains a pretty brutal condemnation of Criton's sexual revulsion. All this is increasingly mangled by Criton as the message of the original letter is driven home by me.

Then a scramble-up of Fainlight's 'Spider'.

A letter from Carl Weissner.

A forged letter from Cohen to me.

A letter from God to Alex Trocchi about me: 'I suggest the Laughing Cavalier of Nova breath throws some real vitriol into Sara's—Jeff's daughter—face. We could tie Jeff on a chair so that he could watch again with real eyes'. The point being that my own methods are used against me.

A forged letter from Dave Trace.

Finally a cut-up attributed to William Burroughs composed of every personal secret, our cowardices, pretensions and inadequacies stirred into a pungent curdle and thrown back in our faces. There are pictures, the noblest sculptures of Bacchus and

236

Apollo sliced down the middle and stuck onto burned figures—the atrocity photos from the sTigma. Old pages from the Mag and Amaranth. Bomb drawings.

The sun lurches about in my head from nausea and humiliation. I ring up Ronnie Laing.

'Did you get the latest *Moving Times*?'

'Yes.'

'I just wanted you to know I didn't have anything to do with it. It was Criton.'

'Well I guessed that.'

'I don't know what to do.'

'All you *can* do,' says Ronnie, 'is spread the word around that the guy's a nut case.'

IV

This book is primarily for squares, for the mums and dads who pretend the future is secure, for the politicians who can only stop the disintegration of their society by banning the bomb, for the Beatles fan who never listened to Elvis, for the aging ted who never listened to Muddy Waters, for the Ivy League hipster who never heard of Bird, for the flower child who never read Ginsberg and doesn't know she's disguised as Ginsberg's mother photographed at summer camp, for the anti-Vietnik who never thinks about the Bomb, for the micro-skirted art student who was never raped by Picasso, for the finger-popping ad-men and the colour-supplement intellectuals, for the pseudo-Leavisites in the Universities and the USAF folk-groups. At different points throughout, the first person plural refers to 'We, the human beings', 'We, of the post war generations', 'We, of the anti-bomb movement', and finally 'We, of the Underground'.

This last part is not addressed to squares. It's addressed to the Underground, the artists and alienated thinkers of four years ago whose ideas have run away from under their feet. That's who I mean by 'We' in the ensuing chapter.

To them I want to say that drugs are an excellent strategy against society but a poor alternative to it. The same can be said of the nihilist element in the philosophy and religion accompanying the drug culture.

Drugs and the subculture have been counter-enforcing one another increasingly over the post-Hiroshima years and since 1963 have accellerated the onslaught that artists had been levelling at the established culture since de Sade.

Four years ago the Underground was anxious to bring about the following developments on a large scale:

(a) The spread of an ego-dissolving delirium wherein a tribal telepathic understanding could grow up among men.

(b) To re-ignite an overwhelming sense of wonderment at the Universe, to cultivate aesthetic perception in the face of utilitarian perception, to re-instate the metalled road as a silken ribbon and the hydraulic waterfall as a galaxy of light.

(c) To expand the range of human consciousness outside the continuing and ultimately soul-destroying boundaries of the political/utilitarian frame of reference.

(d) To institute an international tribe or class outside the destructive system of the nations.

(e) To outflank police, educationists, moralists through whom the death machine was/is maintained.

(f) To release forces into the prevailing culture that would dislocate society, untie its stabilizing knots of morality, punctuality, servility, and property.

(g) To institute a sense of festivity into public life whereby people could fuck freely and guiltlessly, dance wildly and wear fancy dress all the time.

(h) To eradicate utterly and forever the Pauline lie implicit in Christian convention, that people neither shit, piss nor fuck. To set up a common public idea of what a human being is that retains no hypocrisy or falsehood, and indeed, to reinstate a sense of health and beauty pertaining to the genitals and the arsehole.

We thought that if we worked hard with our duplicators, our movie cameras, our poetry readings, our happenings, our jazz, our cutups, we might, in a decade or two, set some of these developments into motion, and we hoped desperately that that might be in time to stop the suicide.

I can remember realizing these ideas for myself in my corner of the threatened world, as Ginsberg, Sanders, Kupferberg, Burroughs, Leary must have done in theirs— that a religion must be instituted which each individual may enfuel and conduct from his own utterly unique sensibility, that the corny authoritarian God of the churches must be dissolved to allow a man's life to gain meaning as an ecstatic sacrifice to Being, a sacrifice richly prolonged through fourscore years. I remember waking in my National Service wanking pit, with Nasser and Eden flipping their idiot wigs on the radio networks and the Strontium 90 thickening in the atmosphere and seeing that we were fleeing from that human condition that we had already refused by our piddling fastidiousness, that, having made unmentionable those alimentary and sexual functions by grace, yes *grace*, of which we are on earth, having thus denied our existence, we further sought to destroy it, to escape by nuclear suicide our existence which we had come to regard with such lame distaste. I remember seeing clearly that if the doors could be torn off the lavatories, off the birth chambers, off the bridal chambers, off the death chambers, if those lost and desperate railway station embraces I'd seen so often during the war could be carried through to a healthy public consummation, if we could once again dance round the phallus and grow golden corn from our dung, then that would be a start.

In the Underground we groped towards that start. Pop culture, LSD and the birth pill, with us prodding, proclaiming and directing, and the squares displaying unprecedented obscenity in Vietnam, made all these aims *faits accomplis* in the four brisk years from 1963 to 1967. There's nothing cops nor Underground nor Mafia can do about it now, thank God. The floral office girls, the tripped out engineering students, the pot-gentle student-teachers, the prick-wise young labourers to whom amphetamine is an old familiar, have outdistanced the schools, the churches, the law and the intellectuals. The psychedelic in-groups are an irrelevancy. What is happening is large-scale and serious. There seems to be a chance.

In 1965 we stood around in the half-built sTigma and said, 'For Christ's sake let's make something *nice*', and not one of us, no solitary one, unless it be Keith Musgrove with his feathered nest, could think of anything with a degree of pleasantry that we could make seriously and with conviction. It's warming to think that out of that bleak sickness there grew a festival of flowers, that the word 'Love', to us an embarrassment, would shortly be bandied about as a popular slogan. Please don't suppose I hold the Beatles' 'Love (is all ya need)' to be the genuine soul-scraping article, but it does create an ambience in which the real emotion can flower warmly, instead of having to struggle against law, prude, schoolteacher, sexually embittered parent, and prevailing fashions in stoicism and 'toughness'.

The strategy then, has started to work but, being strategy, presents no solid achievement other than the erosion of the square society. Bill Burroughs' 'good policeman' does his work and goes away. It behoves us now to be something more than a preventive force. The drugs, whilst accelerating our strategy, could create a vacuum as desolate as any H-bomb crater. Two 'heads' have used the same phrase to me recently—Lyn, of Thomas Traherne: 'Well what was he on?' Tim, of Max Ernst: 'Well what was he on?' It's clearly necessary now to get firm hold of the fact that the nature of vision is human not chemical.

The scene, till now, has been accumulatively negative, necessarily so, the destruction of the destroyers. Hideously, that destruction has been brought about by the exemplary self-destruction of the young, many of whom now espouse that limp concern for pure spirit that is as life-destroying as square materialism. To dissolve the world, the self, the ego, into the general vibrancy of the cosmos is to refuse the unique function of being physical ('like a human'). That the Id, the energies, the fundamental self, is nothing more than a part of the sum of cosmic energy is, I believe, true. That the conscious, the self-conscious mind, the ego, the *identity*, is an obstruction to one's union with the cosmos is also true. What is missed by the mystics, however, is that there is a purpose, and a *divine* purpose, to the human alienation from the cosmos. The recognition, definition of Being, in wonderment and ecstasy can only be carried out by a conscious entity alienated from the eternal totality. You can't dig It if you *are* It. No man beholds his own face.

Self-consciousness is, then, the faculty which (a) divides human beings off from Being and thus (b) bestows upon humanity that sense of *otherness* from Being, that distancing from the cosmos whereby the worshipping, *identifying* reaction of wonderment becomes possible. *True wonderment is not a realization but a hopeless ecstasy of longing.* To satisfy the longing is to terminate wonderment and leave its cosmic function unfulfilled.

The proper functioning of wonderment is enfuelled by that continuous illumination from the cosmic self, the quick, the automatic spiritual self. In modern technological living the spiritual cosmic self has been so estranged that the wonderment faculty was near-completely numbed. You *can not* regard the world in terms of its utilitarian potential, in terms of how well you can harness it to still your petty fears, and, at the same time, maintain your proper function as the agent of wonderment. It was, then, necessary to re-establish that contact with the cosmic self, to revive one's faculty of wonder. It was necessary to turn to 'inner space', to bathe oneself in the virulent music streaming like sperm and light from the stratospheres of the mind. LSD has brought this awareness about.

It is now necessary to come back from inner space. Having revived the faculty of wonderment it is necessary to apply it, to channel one's cosmic self through one's unique identity, to illuminate and strengthen the currently despised ego and thus to *recognize* the same cosmic energy manifest in the splendours of the *outer material world*. If we cannot translate the spiritual into terms of constructive physical action, if spiritual vision cannot inform our physical ocular vision, then the spiritual is none of our damn business.

R. D. Laing has often referred to but never defined that point in history when man became estranged from his mind, that point to which, he claims, we must now return to undo the catastrophic errors of modern civilization. I would suggest that that point was not a point in history, that it was a point in evolution, that it was the point in evolution when the lumbering animal ape became aware of himself, became responsible for himself, became *alienated* from the cosmic energies which propelled his animal existence, became *alienated* from his cosmic self, became *alienated* from his mind. I would suggest that not only is this alienation from the cosmos the condition which we call human (to such an extent that 'alien' and 'human' are almost interchangable adjectives) but that such a separation is a vital element in the cosmic pattern, that man is naturally un-natural and that this is an absolute enrichment rather than a psychic tragedy. I would suggest that any wish to escape this fundamental function is a wish to escape life, is a *death wish*.

I am completing this in November, 1967. Before it reaches print it will be out of date and a lot of the questions I ask here will be answered, which is fine, because readers can then judge the accuracy of my assessments and the value of my word. At the time of writing it seems clear that as far as the Underground is concerned the Freakout is over. We can leave it to the kids with their longer breath and nimbler feet. The virus will spread and nobody can stop it. LSD is too easily manufactured. Marihuana is too easily grown. Everybody knows not to use heroin now. Shortly the birth pill will be available over the counter unless the government is completely besotted. The Beatles and the Stones are still young and increasingly aware of what they have to do. The kinky-booted pillheads who 'Twisted and Shouted' at 16 are voting age now: Says a California policeman, 'But now, goddamnit, it's different. You never know when some kid's going to swing on you, or pull a gun, or maybe just take off running. The badge doesn't mean a damn thing to them. They've lost all respect for it, all fear. Hell, I'd rather bust a dozen Hell's Angels every day of the week than have to break up one fight in a big high school beer party. With the motorcycle crowd you at least know what you're up against, but these kids are capable of anything. I mean it they give me the creeps. I used to understand them, but not any more.'[1]

Meanwhile it behoves the artists, the laboratory men, to turn away from the Nothingness. They are equipped now with a range of exaltation and despair in their sensibilities unknown since Shakespeare. They have been lower and higher than any group of men in the modern world. It is time they turned back to the engagement, to stress and struggle, will and ego. It's time to apply their supremely informed sensibilities to action, decisive, constructive action that leaves behind it a concrete achievement as testimony to its worth. It's time to come away from the mobile arts, poetry, jazz, theatre, dance, clothes. Too great a preoccupation with mobility constitutes a refusal

[1] Quoted by HUNTER S. THOMPSON in *Hell's Angels*, Penguin.

of existence. Movement, like drugs, is good tactics but a poor alternative to the established culture. It is the temporary denial of existence and existence must be our ultimate province. Sartre says, 'Motion is the upsurge of the exteriority of indifference at the very heart of the in-itself', which is to say that motion is that Nothingness which Sartre elsewhere says is 'curled like a worm at the very heart of Being'.

Every artist worth his salt knows by now that in order to produce anything of worth he must lean on the cosmos and let it carry him through at least some of the way. It is time that we gave power and body to the true music of the gods by cultivating the craftsman in us. It is surely time we turned away from the Americans, a nation of agoraphobic neurotics whose only native excellence lies in the skill and grace of their movement (the benefit of which the world has felt) who are, in any case, in an irrecoverable state of civic rot, and called upon the native European sense of classic form and rational serenity. It is time the hipsters learned how to count. It is time we asked ourselves what we are going to do with a future should we now, after the sickness and the vision, gain one. Can we devise a fine architecture of ecstatic muscle and musical light? Can we apply a quivering phallic strength to our civic organization and our economy? Can we build and think and organize with the passions of perpetual inner illumination?

Of course we can. We can begin now. Let us take down our improvisations so that they can be perfected by skilled interpreters. Let us grab what land we can and build with what we can afford as Epstein built his massive monuments on a pittance in an old shack in Epping Forest, as Simon Rodia built his Watts Towers. Let us build adventures, environments, mazes and gardens we can walk in and be reinformed continuously of our fine vitality. Let us turn away from the contemplators and listen to the architects, the activists, the engineers, the Archigram Group with their Plug-In City scheme, Cedric Price the Fun Palace designer, Geoffrey Shaw and his constructions in plastic, Keith Albarn and his furniture sculpture. And let's do it off our own bat, independently, like we did the movies and the mags, winning what we can on casual jobs and confidence tricks, and never waiting for the handout or the commission.

Let's not wait for those cripples in the administration to hand out money or land, and let's not wait for them to grant us the future that they owe us. They won't. They can't. Let's start thinking in terms of permanence now and build our own damn future.

INDEX OF SELECTED NAMES

Albarn, Keith, 244
Alberts, The, 117, 120, 124
Aldermaston March, 40, 44–8, 50, 183
Alpert, Richard, 187, 188, 197
Amis, Kingsley, 54
Ancients, The, 68
Andrews, George, 172
Antrobus, John, 118
Apollinaire, Guillaume, 71, 77–84, 86
Approches, 175
Archigram, 204, 244
Armstrong, Louis, 38
Arrowsmith, Pat, 44, 50–1
Artaud, Antonin, 92, 93, 95, 99, 154, 236
Arts Laboratory, 150, 201
Arts Together, 148–50
Aspinwall, Dave, 47
Auerhahn Press, 162, 173
Ayler, Albert, 10

Bacon, Francis, 75, 139, 212
Baez, Joan, 59, 165
Balch, Anthony, 145–7, 171
Baldwin, James, 62
Ball, Hugo, 85, 87, 119
Barber, Chris, 39
Barger, Sonny, 35
Baudelaire, Charles, 72–3
Bax, Martin, 150
Beach, Mary, 155, 173, 178
Beagle, Peter, 60
Beatles, The, 34, 122, 123–4, 186, 192, 193, 199, 200, 203, 205, 229, 238, 240, 243
Bechet, Sydney, 38, 39
Becket, Samuel, 75
Behan, Brendan, 55
Beiderbecke, Bix, 9
Benn, Gottfried, 54

Bentine, Michael, 116
Berge, Alban, 75
Berke, Joe, 134, 198, 209, 220, 224, 227, 233
Blake, Peter, 68, 120
Blake, William, 68, 168, 183, 229
Blazek, Douglas, 173, 178
Blesh, Rudi, 37
Bogart, Humphrey, 21
Bondhus, Barry, 64
Boulez, Pierre, 122
Bowles, Paul, 172
Boyle, Mark, 119, 199, 200, 204
Brady, Ian, 127–30
Braine, John, 44, 53
Brando, Marlon, 29, 31, 114
Brecht, Bertold, 53
Bremser, Ray, 101
Breton, André, 54, 85, 91, 92–5, 175
Brock, Edwin, 53, 108
Brown, Arthur, 10, 118, 199, 204
Brown, Kenneth H., 163
Brown, Pete, 114, 181, 182, 232
Bruce, Lenny, 107, 129, 219
Burleson, Bob, 173
Burroughs, William, 99, 107–8, 112, 118, 122, 136, 142–4, 145–7, 149, 154, 155, 159, 168, 171, 172, 178, 181, 187, 202, 204, 205, 212, 218, 219, 226, 236, 239, 241
Butler, Bill, 148, 177, 182, 224, 226

Cabaret Voltaire, 85, 87, 119
Cage, John, 119
Calder, John, 144, 150, 181, 229
Campaign for Nuclear Disarmament, 46–9, 205
Camus, Albert, 37
Cardew, Cornelius, 119, 204
Carmichael, Stokeley, 63

Caroline, Radio, 121
Carter, April, 44
Cassady, Neal, 100, 102
Cézanne, Paul, 73, 81
Chandler, Terry, 51
Chase, James Hadley, 21
Cheyney, Peter, 21–2
City Lights, 102, 161, 172
Clapton, Eric, 204
Clarke, George, 50, 51
Cobbing, Bob, 142, 148, 150, 161, 182, 210, 214–17
Cohn, Al, 102
Cohn-Bendit, Dany, 8
Coleman, Ornette, 10, 183
Collins, Canon, 43, 47, 48
Coltrane, John, 10
Colyer, Ken, 39
Committee of 100, 49–51, 53, 139, 206, 212
Concrete Poetry, 149
Conner, Bruce, 118, 171, 173
Conquest, Robert, 54
Cooper, David, 109, 211, 216–17, 224, 233
Corso, Gregory, 101, 102, 172, 182, 221, 229
Cousins, Frank, 49
Crane River Jazz Band, 39
Cream, The, 10, 204
Creeley, Robert, 221
Currel-Brown, Peter, 138, 140, 225

Davies, Cyril, 34
Davie, Donald, 54
Dean, James, 31, 42, 107
Debray, Regis, 9
Delaney, Shelagh, 55
Dewy, Ken, 119, 224
Diaghilev, Serge, 80
Diggers, The, 196–7
Dine, Jim, 119
Direct Action Committee, 44
Donnegan, Lonnie, 40
Dorn, Ed, 174
Driberg, Tom, 44
Duchamp, Marcel, 89, 118, 123
Duff, Peggy, 43, 48, 184, 201
Dutschke, Rudi, 8
Dylan, Bob, 59, 122, 165

Eden, Sir Anthony, 26, 43, 201, 240
Eliot, T. S., 74
Eluard, Paul, 92, 94
Esam, John, 182
Evans, Mike, 124
Exploding Galaxy, The, 200, 201, 203
Expressionism, 75

Fainlight, Harry, 168, 182, 199, 232, 236
Faithful, Mr and Mrs Glyn, 215–17
Faithful, Marianne, 186
Faulkner, William, 54
Fauves, The, 81
Fearing, Kenneth, 99, 100
Ferlinghetti, Lawrence, 102, 172, 182, 194
Fiedler, Leslie, 197, 202
Field, Marcus, 229, 232
Fishwick, Gertrude, 43
Fluxus, 119
Foley, Del, 182
Foot, Michael, 48
Francis, Sam, 100
Freitas, Michael de, 199
Froge, Gait, 171
Fugs, The, 204
Futurism, 75

Gaitskell, Hugh, 49
Galanskov, Yuri, 176
Genet, Jean, 29, 122
Georgakas, Dan, 177, 178, 220, 232
George, Stefan, 74
Gillespie, Dizzy, 24
Ginsberg, Allen, 35, 57, 82, 99, 100–2, 107, 112, 113, 114, 122, 123, 149, 164, 168, 172, 182, 183, 191, 192, 197, 204, 218, 228–9, 239
Girodias, Maurice, 171
Godwin, Anthony, 182, 224
Goon Show, The, 115–18
Gosling, Ray, 28, 30, 33, 114, 142, 177
Goya, Francesco, 68
Grable, Betty, 21
Grateful Dead, The, 122, 195
Greco, Juliette, 37
Griffiths, Malcolm 'Gas', 211, 227
Grogan, Emmet, 195–7
Grootveld, Robert Jasper, 179
Grosz, George, 91

Grove Press, 162
Gruber, F., 75
Guevara, Che, 9
Gunn, Thom, 31, 53, 114
Guston, Philip, 100
Gysin, Brion, 118, 172

Haight-Ashbury, 172, 193–5, 200
Haley, Bill, 28
Hand, Alex, 177, 178
Hansen, Al, 119
Hansford Johnson, Pamela, 127, 130
Happenings, 118–19
Harwood, Lee, 148, 181
Hausmann, Raoul, 92
Hawkins, Spike, 181, 182
Haynes, Jim, 182, 198, 201, 222
Hell's Angels, 35, 243
Helms, Chet, 195–6
Hendrix, Jimi, 10
Henri, Adrian, 119, 124, 222, 230
Hesse, Herman, 98
Herman, Woody, 24
Hernton, Calvin, 147
Hinde, Thomas, 53
Hindley, Moira, 127–30
Hiroshima, 20, 48, 50, 75
Hockney, David, 120
Hollo, Anselm, 142, 182
Holroyd, Stuart, 54
Hopkins, Bill, 54
Hopkins, John 'Hoppy', 199, 202, 204
Horovitz, Mike, 114, 181, 182, 232
Houédard, Dom Pierre Sylvester, 149, 177
Howlin' Wolf, 29
Huelsenbeck, Richard, 87, 88, 92
Hughes, Ted, 53
Huncke, Herbert, 102
Hungry Generation, The, 176
Hydrogen Bomb National Campaign, 43

Impressionism, 72
Incredible String Band, The, 199, 204
Institute of Direct Art, The, 119, 132
International Times, The, 186, 197, 203, 204, 232

Jacob, Max, 71, 80
Jagger, Mick, 186, 202

Janco, Marcel, 87, 119
Jarry, Alfred, 71, 80
Jefferson Airplane, The, 122, 195
Jodorowsky, Alexandro, 175, 177
Johns, Jasper, 118
Jones, Leroi, 191
Jordan, Louis, 16
Joyce, James, 54, 85, 97

Kafka, Franz, 75, 214
Kandinsky, Wassily, 96
Kaprow, Allan, 119
Kienholz, Edward, 118
Kerouac, Jack, 99, 100, 101, 112, 114, 172
Kesey, Ken, 35, 195
Keys, John, 147, 207, 219, 227, 234
Kinks, The, 34
Kline, Franz, 100
Korner, Alexis, 34, 39
Kupferberg, Tuli, 168, 239
Kustow, Mike, 52, 228

Lacey, Bruce, 117, 144, 149, 162, 182, 207, 222, 224
Ladd, Alan, 21
Laforgue, Jules, 74
Laine, Frankie, 25
Laing, R. D., 81, 108, 109–12, 128, 149, 187, 197, 207, 211, 216–17, 218, 221, 233, 237, 242
Lake, Veronica, 21
Lamantia, Philip, 155
Larkin, Philip, 53
Lasslet, Gordon, 176–7
Lasslet, Rhaunie, 199
Latham, John, 119, 144, 149, 181, 202, 215–16, 222, 224, 229
Lautréamont, Comte de, 71, 73, 80, 109, 128
Lavrin, Beba, 211
Lea, Klaus, 183
Leadbelly, 38, 40
Leary, Timothy, 183, 187, 188, 190, 197, 201, 203, 205, 210, 239
Lebel, Jean-Jacques, 119, 175, 230
Legman, Gershon, 135
Lenin, Vladimir Ilyich, 85
Lennon, John, 124, 162, 229
Leonni, Paolo, 230
Lessing, Doris, 41, 53

Lewis, George, 39
Littlewood, Joan, 55, 150
Living Theatre, The, 162–4, 179, 183, 196
Lomax, Alan, 38
Lorca, Garcia, 54, 174
Lucie-Smith, Edward, 53, 162
Luter, Claude, 38
Lyttleton, Humphrey, 38

MacBeth, George, 53, 108, 182, 222, 226
McCartney, Paul, 186, 197, 229
McClure, Michael, 102, 173
MacColl, Ewan, 39
McGough, Roger, 124, 230
McGrath, Tom, 128, 181, 182, 198, 203, 204, 214–17, 232
Mailer, Norman, 15, 17, 62, 65, 82, 168
Malcolm X, 63
Marcuse, Herbert, 9, 57
Marowitz, Charles, 224
Marzalek Bernard, 63
Masson, André, 92, 118
Mayakovsky, Vladimir, 53, 75–6
Mayall, John, 10
Medalla, David, 134, 200
Melly, George, 44
Metzger, Gustav, 119, 132
Metzner, Ralph, 187, 188
Mezzrow, Mezz, 12, 14, 16
Michel, John, 9
Miles, 150, 181, 186, 198
Miller, Henry, 99
Milligan, Spike, 44, 80, 116–18, 124, 182
Mingus, Charlie, 10
Mitchell, Adrian, 108, 130, 227
Moody Blues, The, 10
Moore, Jack, 199, 222
Moore, John, 148, 226, 228, 232
Morrison, Norman, 60
Morton, Jelly Roll, 11, 13, 38
Mothers of Invention, The, 122, 204
Motherwell, Robert, 100
Mottram, Eric, 182
Move, The, 119, 199
Mulligan, Gerry, 102
Musgrove, Keith and Heather, 129, 144, 148, 156, 161, 209, 218, 219, 220, 222, 224, 225, 240

Mustill, Norman Ogue, 173

Nadaism, 178
National Liberation Front, 177
New Directions, 162
Nietzsche, Friedrich, 71, 73, 75
Norse, Harold, 155, 172, 174

Ohnesorg, Benno, 7
Oldenburg, Claes, 119
Oliver, King, 38
Olson, Charles, 100
Ono, Yoko, 119, 171, 202
Operation Gandhi, 44
Ortiz, Ralph, 119, 132
Osborne, John, 42, 44, 53, 54
Osborne, Mike, 204, 226, 227

Panassié, Hughes, 37
PANic Movement, The, 177–8
Parker, Charlie, 'Bird', 17, 20, 25, 53, 98, 107, 178, 238
Patchen, Kenneth, 99
Patten, Brian, 124, 230, 232
Pauling, Linus, 44
Peace News, 43, 184, 197
Peace Pledge Union, 43
Peanuts Club, 182
Pélieu, Claude, 155, 159, 172, 178
Pelz, Werner, 44
People Show, The, 200, 201, 204
Philadelphia Association, The, 198, 211, 218, 222, 224, 232, 233
Picabia, Francis, 90
Picasso, Pablo, 54, 58, 71, 80–3, 142, 176
Pink Floyd, The, 10, 199
Plymell, Charlie, 173, 178
Pollock, Jackson, 100, 107
Porter, Peter, 53, 108
Portman, Michael, 172
Pottle, Pat, 51
Pound, Ezra, 54, 75
Presley, Elvis, 28–30, 31, 35, 42, 238
Pretty Things, The, 34, 120
Prévert, Jacques, 89
Price, Cedric, 244
Propper, Dan, 122
Provos, The, 179, 180

Quant, Mary, 121

Randle, Mike, 44, 50, 51
Rauschenberg, Robert, 170
Ray, Johnny, 25, 31
Reich, Wilhelm, 164
Renshaw, Uncle John, 39
Richter, Dan and Jill, 155, 172, 182, 232
Rilke, Rainer Maria, 74
Rimbaud, Arthur, 71, 72, 73, 81, 151
Robertson, Bryan, 141
Rogers, Shorty, 102
Rolling Stones, The, 34, 120, 243
Rosenquist, James, 118, 120
Rosenthaal, Irvin, 102, 172
Rothko, Mark, 100, 149
Rousseau, Henri, 83, 84
Rowan, John, 144, 149, 161
Russell, Bertrand, 44, 49–52
Russian Underground, 176
Rustin, Bayard, 44, 59, 227

Sade, The Marquis de, 70–1, 72, 75, 77, 85, 98, 109, 127, 238
Sanders, Ed, 59, 60, 167, 202, 239
Sandys, Duncan, 26
Sartre, Jean-Paul, 37, 75, 142, 218
Satie, Eric, 80
Scaffold, The, 124
Schoenberg, Arnold, 74, 96
Schoenman, Ralph, 50, 51
Schwitters, Karl, 89
Scott, Rev. Michael, 44
Scragg, Sebastian, 177
Secombe, Harry, 116
Seeger, Pete, 39, 59
Sellers, Peter, 116
Shaw, Geoffrey, 180, 244
Shepp, Archie, 10
Sigal, Clancy, 214–17
sigma, 156–9, 180, 182, 187
Sillitoe, Alan, 53, 114, 127
Situationists, The International, 119, 174
Smith, Jack, 145, 171, 172
Snyder, Gary, 102, 168, 191, 197
Social Deviants, The, 199
Soft Machine, The, 199
Sommerville, Ian, 172, 221
Soper, Donald, 43
Spock, Dr Benjamin, 7, 65
Steele, Harold and Sheila, 44

Steele, Tommy, 40
Stein, Gertrude, 81, 84
Still, Clifford, 100
Stockhausen, Karlheinz, 119
Stravinsky, Igor, 58, 80
Sutch, Screaming Lord, 117, 204

Tamla Motown, 124
Temperance Seven, The, 117, 120
Tennessee Ernie, 25
Teufel, Fritz, 179
Tomazos, Criton, 137–42, 144–5, 147–8, 149, 150–2, 184, 207–10, 217–21, 222, 223–8, 232–7
Tomlin, Dave, 199, 228
Tonk, 124, 223
Trace, Dave, 137, 218, 220, 222, 224, 236
Trocchi, Alexander, 102, 128, 133, 144, 150, 156, 159, 171, 175, 179, 181–2, 187, 204, 213–17, 219, 221–3, 226, 229, 232, 235, 236
Turner, J. M. W., 70
Tynan, Kenneth, 54–5
Tzara, Tristan, 85–7, 91, 93, 95, 98, 149

UFO, 150, 199, 203
Underground Press Syndicate, 197, 206

Valéry, Paul, 73
Valoch, Jiri, 177
Van Gogh, Vincent, 72, 75, 109
Van Tijen, Tjeb, 180
Verlaine, Paul, 74
Vinkenoog, Simon, 171, 178, 180
Vorticism, 75
Vostel, Wolf, 119, 179

Wain, John, 54
Waller, Fats, 16
Warhol, Andy, 169–71
Warren, Dave, 149
Waters, Muddy, 13, 29, 238
Watkins, Islwyn 'Nick', 144, 149, 150, 156, 222, 224
Watson, Leo, 16

Watters, Lu, 38
Webern, Anton, 54
Weissner, Carl, 155, 159, 178, 236
Wesker, Arnold, 53, 55, 58, 150, 200, 212
Westbrook, Mike, 204, 227
Whalen, Philip, 102, 167, 168
Who, The, 119
Wilcock, John, 186, 198
Wilcocks, Dick, 144, 148, 178, 182, 209, 226
Williams, Tennessee, 29, 115

Wilson, Colin, 54
Wilson, Steve, 32
Wright, Barbara, 149
Wright, Mick, 47

Young, Lester, 32, 171

Zappa, Frank, 197
Zero Dimension Group, 119, 176

Playpower

'This gaudy mosaic of anecdote, quotation, prophecy and wild unsupported assertion is by far the most comprehensive survey yet attempted of international underground culture ... enormously sane and healthily challenging ...'
Kenneth Tynan OBSERVER

'Coarse, shallow and nasty ...' *Merwyn Jones* NEW STATESMAN

'A deeply felt and honourable book ...'
Mordecai Richler GUARDIAN

'It's witty, packed with information, crimson with the de-gutted entrails of other underground books, and racily written by one of the few writers on the inside really able to look out.' PUNCH

'Almost totally devoid of intellectual content.'
SYDNEY MORNING HERALD

'Fantastically brilliant.' *Abbie Hoffman*

'The first international book on the underground – not written with the phoney detachment of an academic, but written by someone who is an excellent journalist and is also someone totally involved in what he has written ... McLuhan is dead – long live Neville.' INTERNATIONAL TIMES

'A switched on mole's eye view of the sixties.' SPECTATOR

'(Neville's) happy, innocent book contains the germs of a new fascism.' SUNDAY TIMES

'The best work yet on what in pleasanter days used to be called the Love Generation.' ROLLING STONE

'*Play Power* is the *Mein Kampf* of an international conspiracy to overthrow the Anglo-Saxon way of life.'
Commander Rees Millington on '24 *Hours*'

'Should be read in every school, office, army hut or other institution ...' *John Peel*

'The human story of a young Australian who comes to London and finds happiness by bringing out the worst magazine in the history of the world.' PRIVATE EYE

Complete list of Paladin titles

MACHIAVELLI: A DISSECTION Sydney Anglo
THE QUEST FOR ARTHUR'S BRITAIN ed. Geoffrey
  Ashe
THE INFORMED HEART Bruno Bettelheim
THE CHILDREN OF THE DREAM Bruno Bettelheim
THE PARABLE OF THE BEAST John Bleibtreu
THE TRIAL OF JESUS OF NAZARETH
  S. G. F. Brandon
ASPECTS OF THE FRENCH REVOLUTION Alfred
  Cobban
DRUGS OF HALLUCINATION Sidney Cohen
THE PURSUIT OF THE MILLENNIUM Norman Cohn
AWOPBOPALOOBOP ALOPBAMBOOM Nik Cohn
PSYCHIATRY AND ANTI-PSYCHIATRY David
  Cooper
THE FALL OF THE BRITISH EMPIRE Colin Cross
THE STRANGE DEATH OF LIBERAL ENGLAND
  George Dangerfield
THE HIDDEN ORDER OF ART Anton Ehrenzweig
THE EVER-CHANGING SEA David B. Ericson &
  Goesta Wollin
CRIME AND PERSONALITY H. J. Eysenck
BLACK SKIN WHITE MASKS Frantz Fanon
MAN'S RISE TO CIVILISATION Peter Farb
LOVE AND DEATH IN THE AMERICAN NOVEL
  Leslie A. Fiedler
THE RETURN OF THE VANISHING AMERICAN
  Leslie A. Fiedler
A DICTIONARY OF DRUGS Richard B. Fisher & George
  A. Christie
MAN MODIFIED David Fishlock
MAN AND ANIMAL ed. Heinz Friedrich
DECISIVE BATTLES OF THE WESTERN WORLD
  Maj.-Gen. J. F. C. Fuller, ed. John Terraine
THE BOG PEOPLE P. V. Glob

A DICTIONARY OF SYMPTOMS Dr Joan Gomez
THE FEMALE EUNUCH Germaine Greer
SEX AND RACISM Calvin C. Hernton
ON THE TRACK OF UNKNOWN ANIMALS Bernard
   Heuvelmans
JOURNEY THROUGH BRITAIN John Hillaby
THE DECLINE OF WORKING-CLASS POLITICS
   Barry Hindess
HOMO LUDENS Johan Huizinga
EXPLOITATION Robin Jenkins
OSCAR WILDE Philippe Jullian
RUSSIA IN REVOLUTION Lionel Kochan
MARXISM AND BEYOND Leszek Kolakowski
ANATOMY OF THE SS STATE Helmut Krausnick &
   Martin Broszat
THE POLITICS OF ECSTASY Timothy Leary
THE PSYCHOLOGY OF ANXIETY Eugene E. Levitt
THE BRITISH SEAMAN Christopher Lloyd
THE END OF ATLANTIS J. V. Luce
THE BORGIAS Michael Mallett
A NEW HISTORY OF THE UNITED STATES William
   Miller
PLAYPOWER Richard Neville
BOMB CULTURE Jeff Nuttall
RENAISSANCE AND RENASCENCES IN
   WESTERN ART Erwin Panofsky
CLASS INEQUALITY AND POLITICAL ORDER
   Frank Parkin
THE MYSTERY OF ANIMAL MIGRATION Matthieu
   Ricard
THE SEXUAL RADICALS Paul A. Robinson
PREHISTORY Derek Roe
THE TRADITION OF THE NEW Harold Rosenberg
THE WAR OF THE FLEA Robert Taber
THE WAR BUSINESS George Thayer
BEFORE THE DELUGE Herbert Wendt
THE TRUMPET SHALL SOUND Peter Worsley
THE DRUGTAKERS Jock Young